The Itty-Bitty Knitty Committee

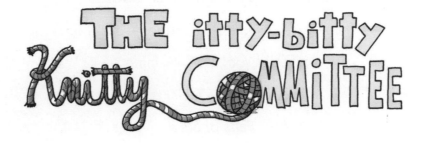

Other *Argyle Sweater* Books

The Argyle Sweater: A Cartoon Collection

50% Wool, 50% Asinine

Tastes Like Chicken

Puns of Steel

The itty-bitty Knitty Committee

An Argyle Sweater Collection by Scott Hilburn

Andrews McMeel
Publishing, LLC
Kansas City • Sydney • London

The Argyle Sweater is distributed internationally by Universal Uclick.

The Itty-Bitty Knitty Committee copyright © 2012 by Scott Hilburn. All rights reserved.
Printed in China. No part of this book may be used or reproduced in any manner whatsoever
without written permission except in the case of reprints in the context of reviews.

Andrews McMeel Publishing, LLC
an Andrews McMeel Universal company
1130 Walnut Street, Kansas City, Missouri 64106

www.andrewsmcmeel.com

www.theargylesweater.com

12 13 14 15 16 SHO 10 9 8 7 6 5 4 3 2 1

ISBN: 978-1-4494-1021-6

Library of Congress Control Number: 2011937837

Foreword

Here's the first sign that Scott Hilburn and his *Argyle Sweater* don't need any help from somebody like me: I tried to look up *argyle sweater* on Wikipedia—thinking that I possibly could start off with some argyle sweater fun facts, like that they were originally made from recycled tea towels, or that the design actually was first discovered in middle America inscribed by angels onto golden plates, or that somebody famous (and fun) was shot while wearing one—but this Wiki entry now is devoted solely and completely to Scott's comic.

People always say to me, "Hey, Paul, you're a cartoonist, and you like to wear argyle socks, and your hair looks great. . . . Why does Scott call his comic strip *The Argyle Sweater*?" And I say, "Why thanks, but look, just because I'm someone who's successful enough to afford his own computer *and* Internet connection and can use them to find out things such as what Scott really thinks is most important in a greeting card (that it's funny), or what Kim Kardashian thinks about peas (she hates them), doesn't mean the answer to that question is readily available." One would either have to ask Scott, or make something up.

If you break it down, a sweater also can be referred to as a top, a pullover, or a jumper. And argyle is a diamond pattern in a diagonal checkerboard arrangement. And the word *the* is *la* or *le* in French, which Scott is not. Therefore, another name for the comic could be *Checkerboard Jumper*. What jumps most industriously on a checkerboard? A king, of course. Scott's message is that he wants to be the king of comics.

Argyle sweaters also are itchy. They need to be paired with a collared shirt, otherwise they're unbearable. Clearly they were introduced by the giant-collared-shirt emporiums of the sixteenth century, in much the same way dentists popularized Halloween, or Camay popularized coal mining. And we're the suckers who bought into it.

But Scott, you don't need such trickery to win the public's adulation. You can do that just by being yourself, and continuing to produce one of the most consistently hilarious outside-the-box comics in operation. Yes, your characters have no eyes and therefore look untrustworthy, and they have no waists and therefore render belts superfluous, but that's just part of their charm. I urge you not to concern yourself with advertising gimmicks or angry Oprah Winfrey fans, and just to continue pushing the envelope with your freakish wit, pretzelized puns, hilarious drawing, and home run–hitting punch lines.

In Isaac Asimov's *Foundation* series, set thirty thousand years in the future, a character is described sitting on a park bench reading comics. Coming from a speculative genius such as Asimov, it's comforting to know that at such a distant time in the future the human race's asses still will fit on park benches, and it's also comforting to know that *Blondie* and *Marmaduke* won't have to bear the load of being the only comics still running in thirty thousand years. *The Argyle Sweater* is a classic garment, and it's here to stay.

Long live the king!

—Paul Gilligan, AD 2011

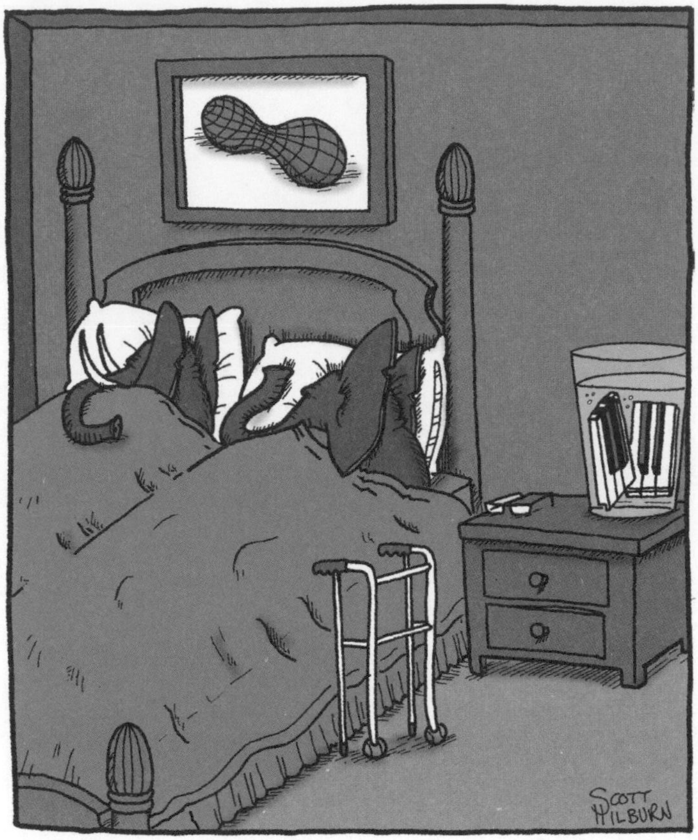
SCOTT
HILBURN

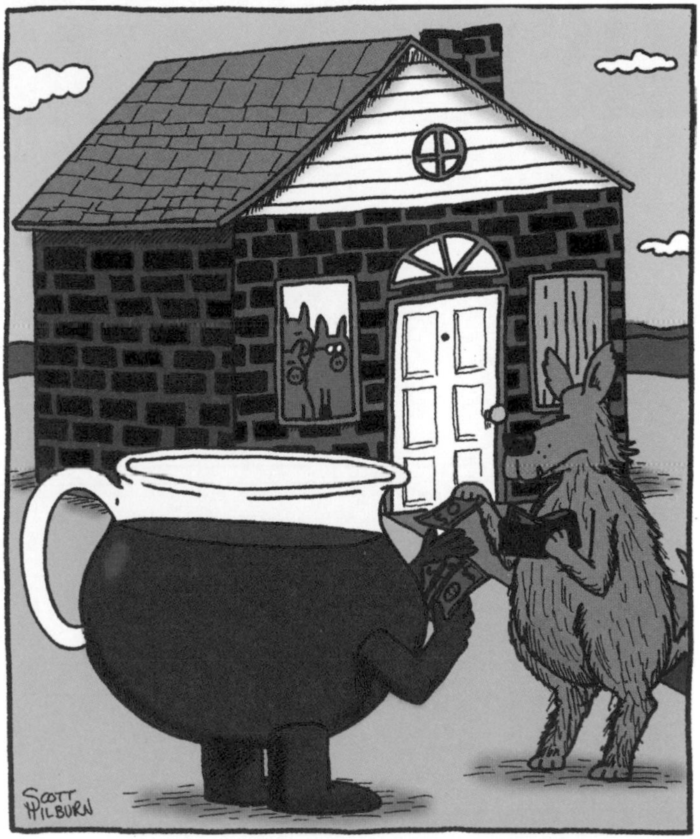
SCOTT
HILBURN

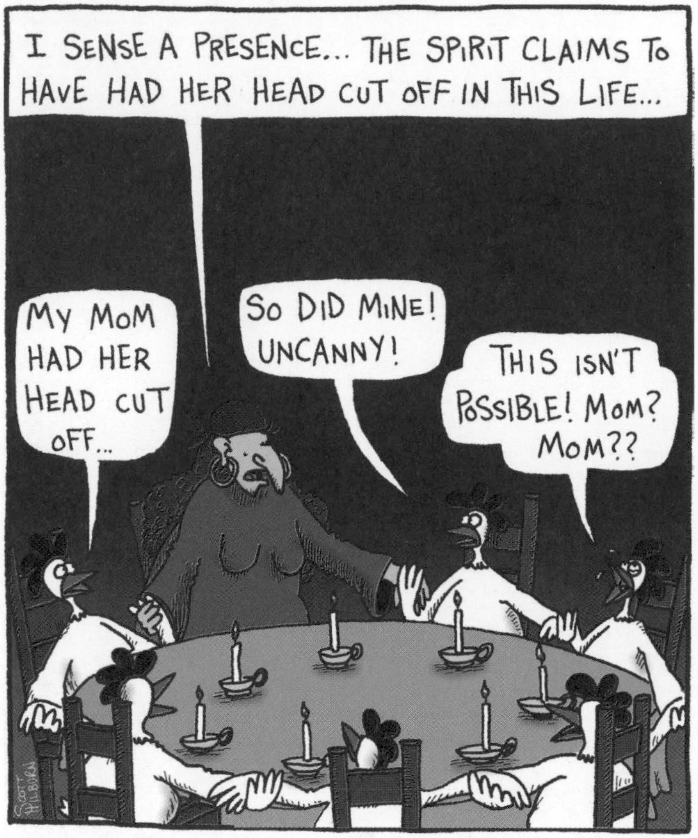
I SENSE A PRESENCE... THE SPIRIT CLAIMS TO HAVE HAD HER HEAD CUT OFF IN THIS LIFE...
MY MOM HAD HER HEAD CUT OFF...
SO DID MINE! UNCANNY!
THIS ISN'T POSSIBLE! MOM? MOM??
SCOTT HILBURN

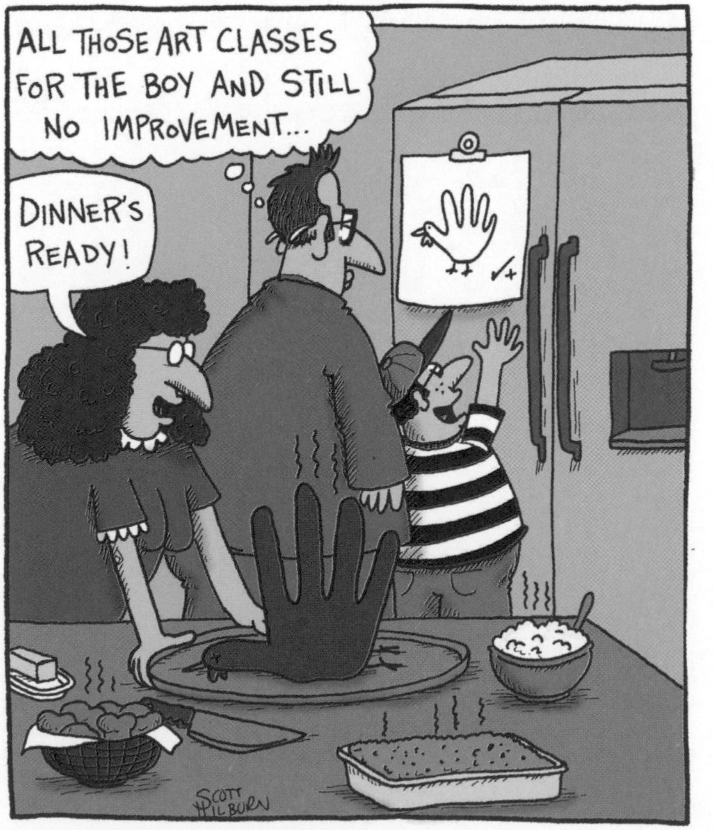
ALL THOSE ART CLASSES FOR THE BOY AND STILL NO IMPROVEMENT...
DINNER'S READY!
SCOTT HILBURN

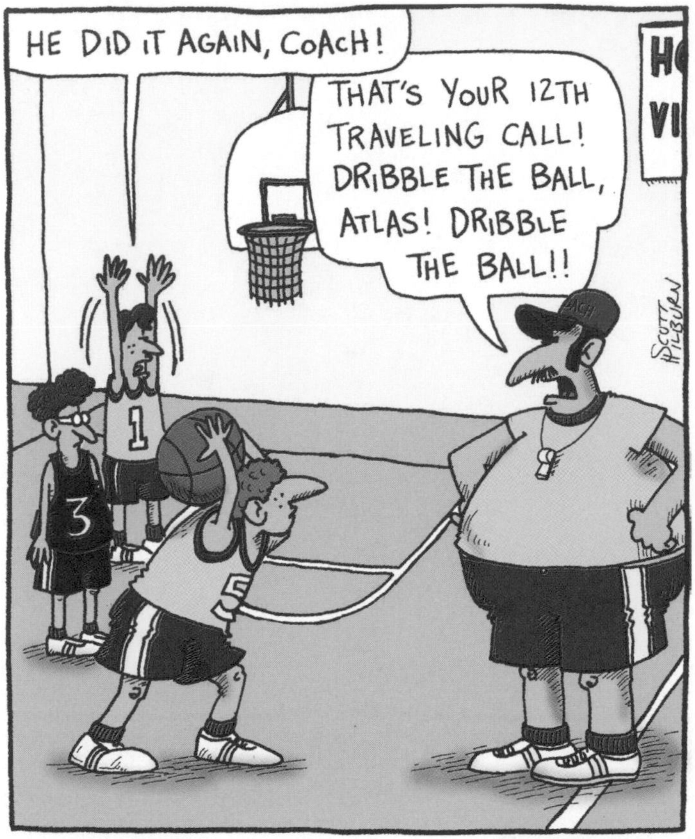
HE DID IT AGAIN, COACH!
THAT'S YOUR 12TH TRAVELING CALL! DRIBBLE THE BALL, ATLAS! DRIBBLE THE BALL!!
SCOTT HILBURN

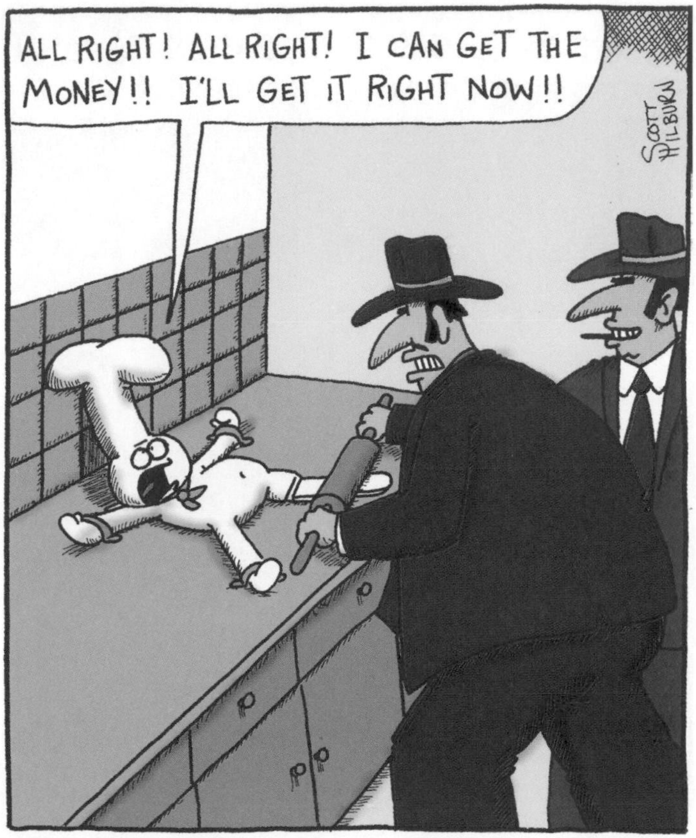
ALL RIGHT! ALL RIGHT! I CAN GET THE MONEY!! I'LL GET IT RIGHT NOW!!
SCOTT HILBURN

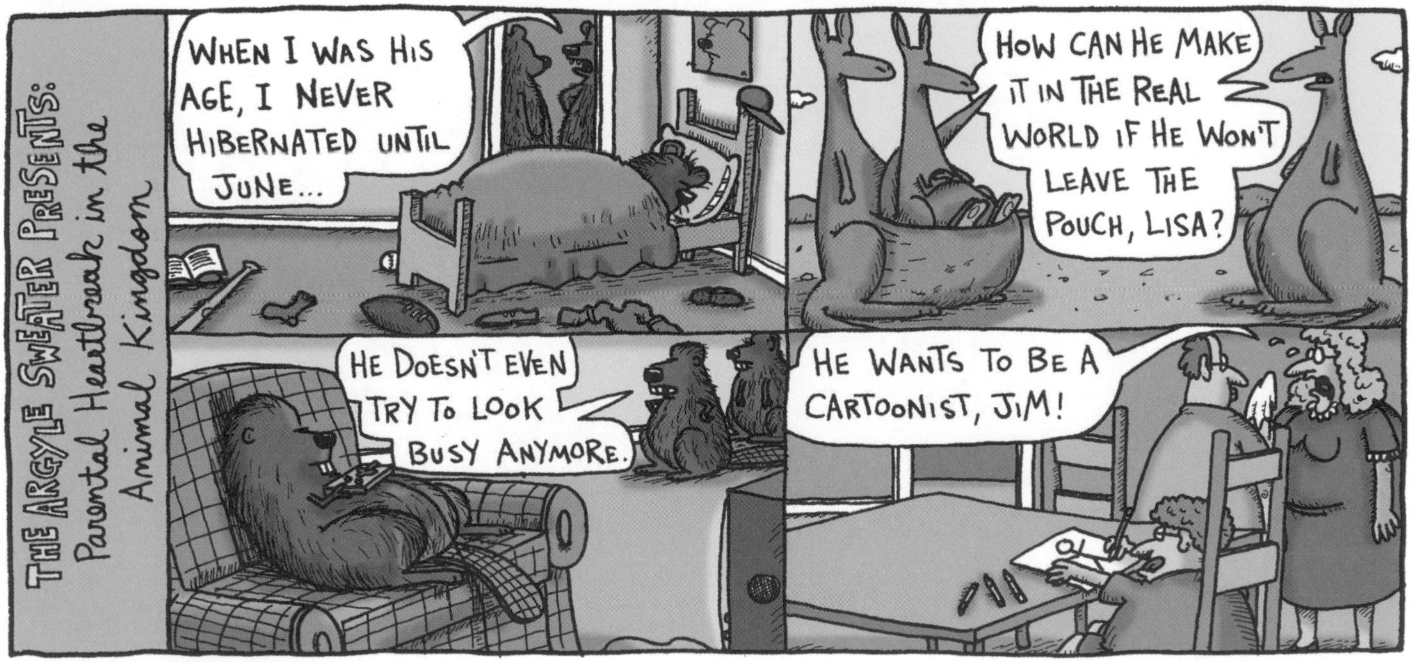
THE ARGYLE SWEATER PRESENTS:
Parental Heartbreak in the Animal Kingdom
WHEN I WAS HIS AGE, I NEVER HIBERNATED UNTIL JUNE...
HOW CAN HE MAKE IT IN THE REAL WORLD IF HE WON'T LEAVE THE POUCH, LISA?
HE DOESN'T EVEN TRY TO LOOK BUSY ANYMORE.
HE WANTS TO BE A CARTOONIST, JIM!

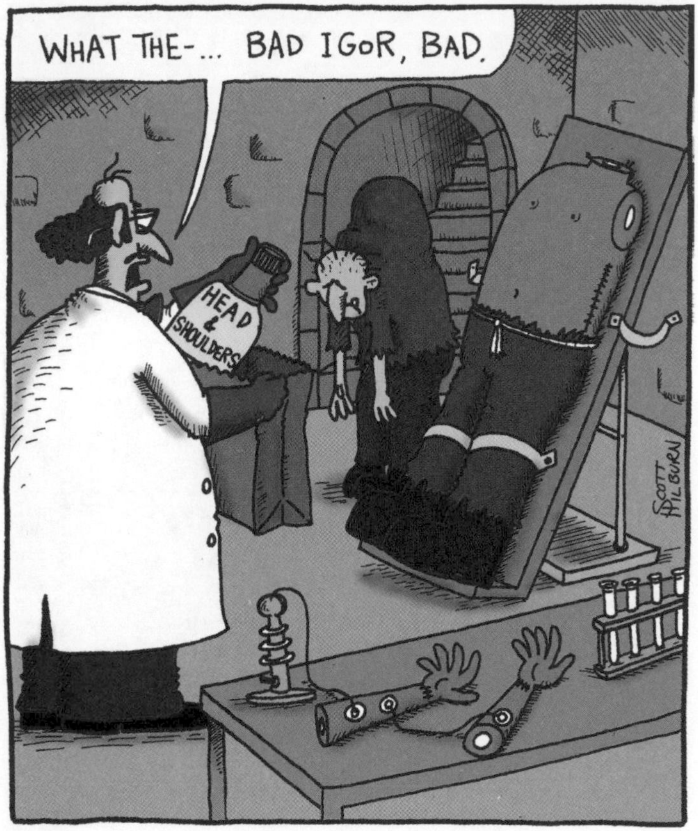
WHAT THE-... BAD IGOR, BAD.
HEAD & SHOULDERS
SCOTT HILBURN

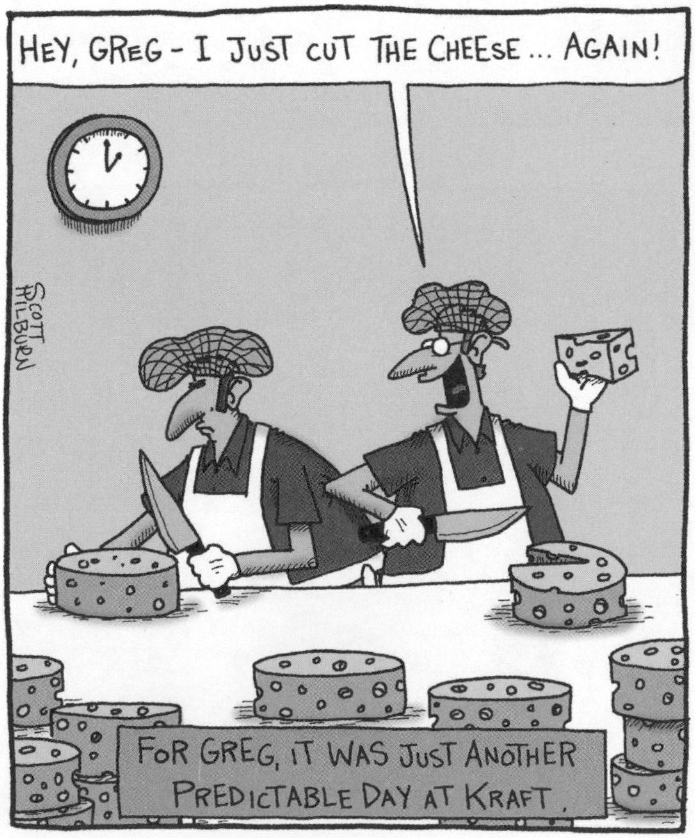
HEY, GREG - I JUST CUT THE CHEESE ... AGAIN!
SCOTT HILBURN
FOR GREG, IT WAS JUST ANOTHER PREDICTABLE DAY AT KRAFT.

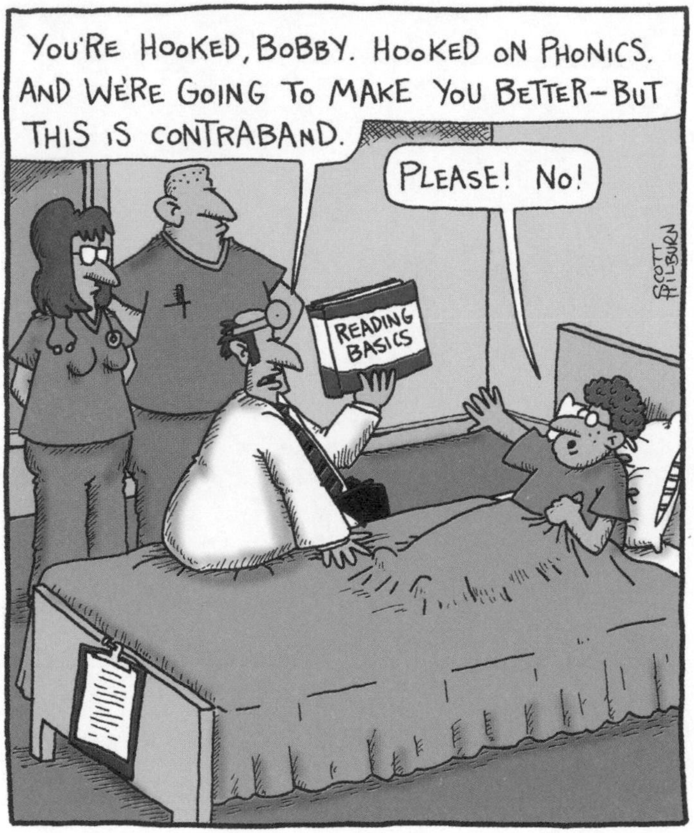
YOU'RE HOOKED, BOBBY. HOOKED ON PHONICS. AND WE'RE GOING TO MAKE YOU BETTER—BUT THIS IS CONTRABAND.
PLEASE! NO!
READING BASICS
SCOTT HILBURN

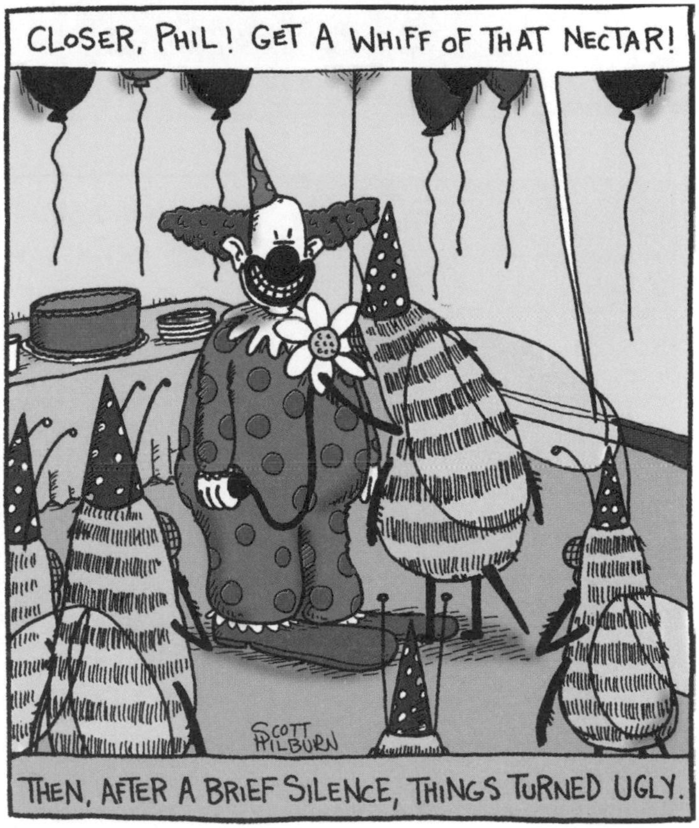
CLOSER, PHIL! GET A WHIFF OF THAT NECTAR!
SCOTT HILBURN
THEN, AFTER A BRIEF SILENCE, THINGS TURNED UGLY.

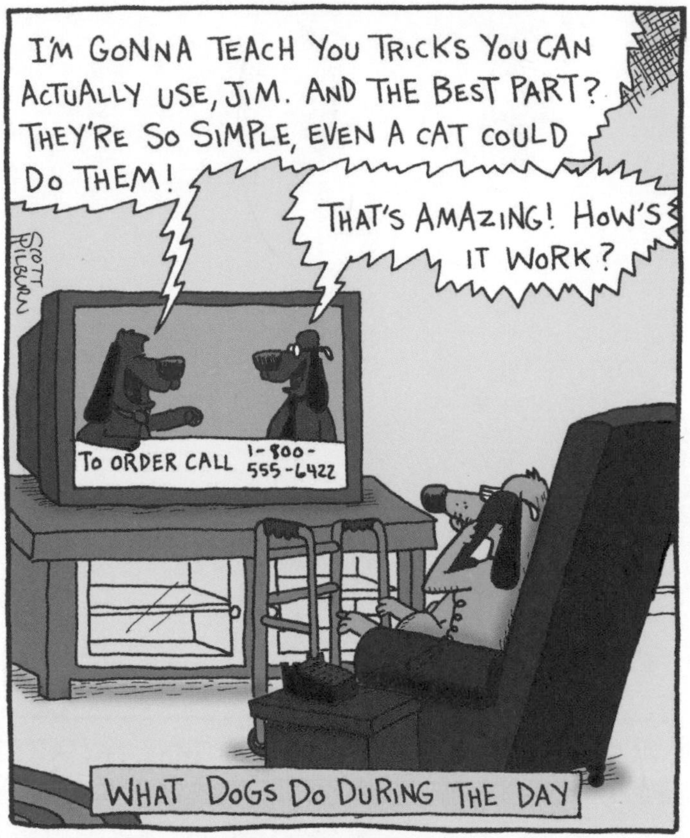
I'M GONNA TEACH YOU TRICKS YOU CAN ACTUALLY USE, JIM. AND THE BEST PART? THEY'RE SO SIMPLE, EVEN A CAT COULD DO THEM!
THAT'S AMAZING! HOW'S IT WORK?
TO ORDER CALL 1-800-555-6422
SCOTT HILBURN

WHAT DOGS DO DURING THE DAY

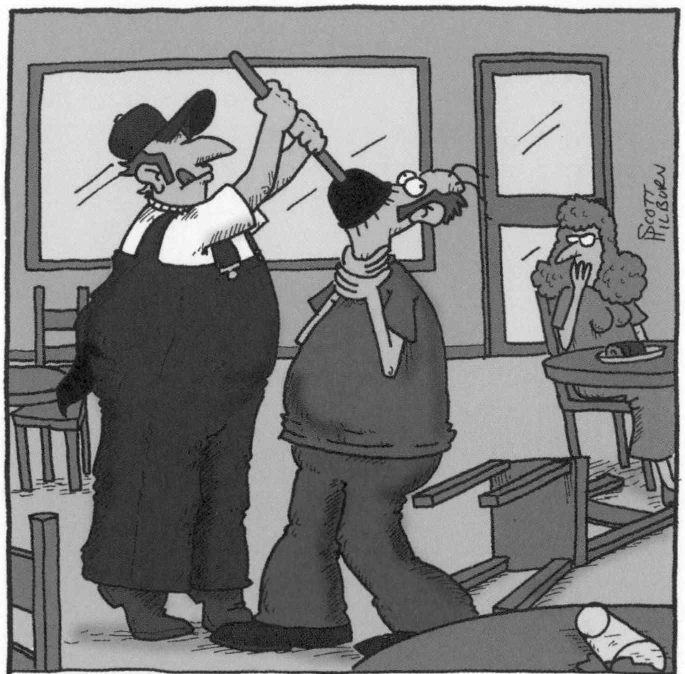
SCOTT HILBURN

FOR A SHORT PERIOD BEFORE THE HEIMLICH, JAKE'S PLUMBING TECHNIQUE WAS WIDELY ACCEPTED AS THE WAY TO CLEAR SOMEONE'S AIRWAY.

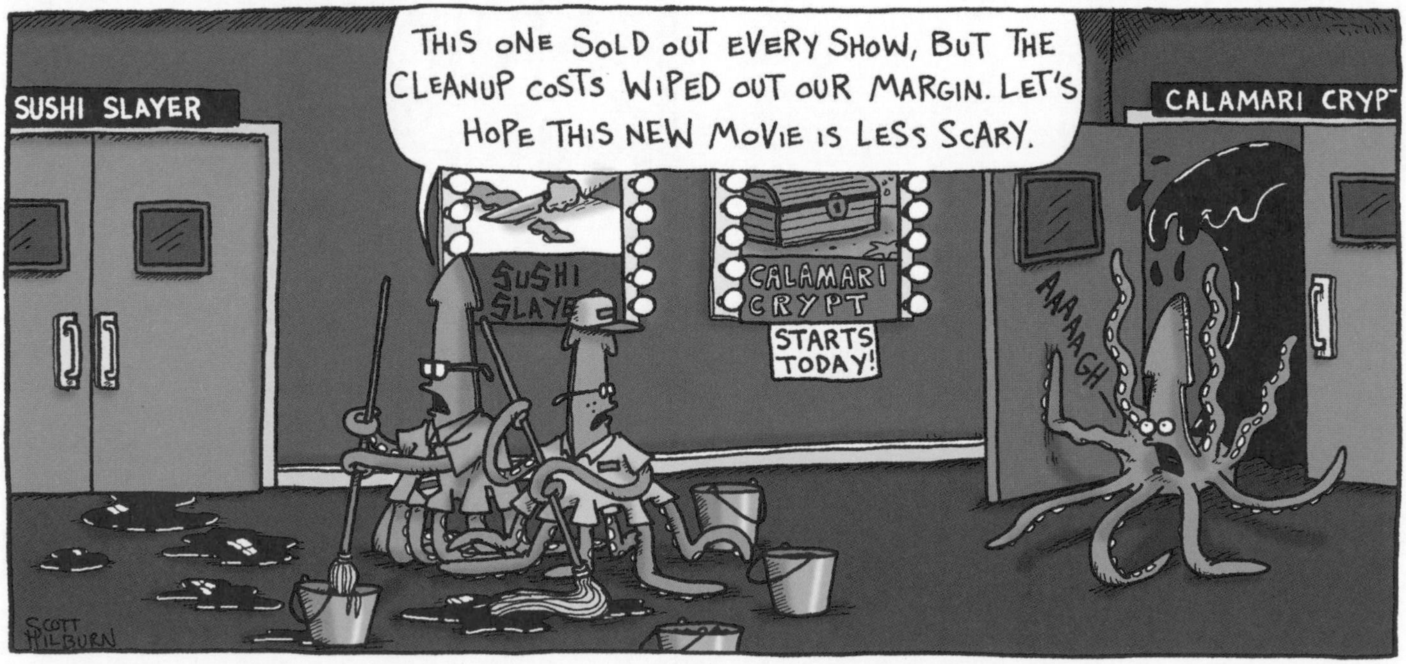
THIS ONE SOLD OUT EVERY SHOW, BUT THE CLEANUP COSTS WIPED OUT OUR MARGIN. LET'S HOPE THIS NEW MOVIE IS LESS SCARY.
SUSHI SLAYER
CALAMARI CRYP
CALAMARI CRYPT
STARTS TODAY!
AAAAAGH!
SCOTT HILBURN

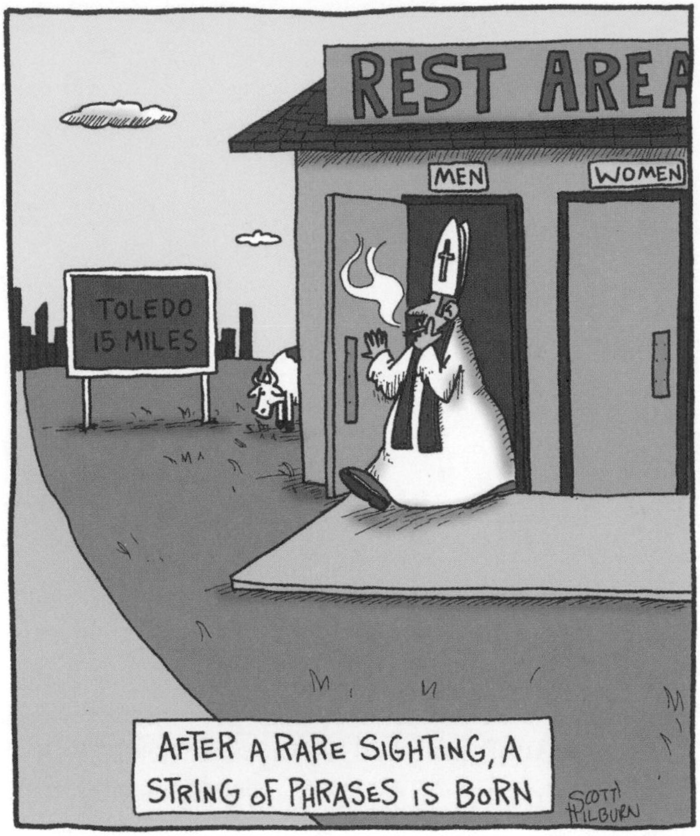
REST AREA
MEN
WOMEN
TOLEDO
15 MILES
SCOTT HILBURN

AFTER A RARE SIGHTING, A STRING OF PHRASES IS BORN

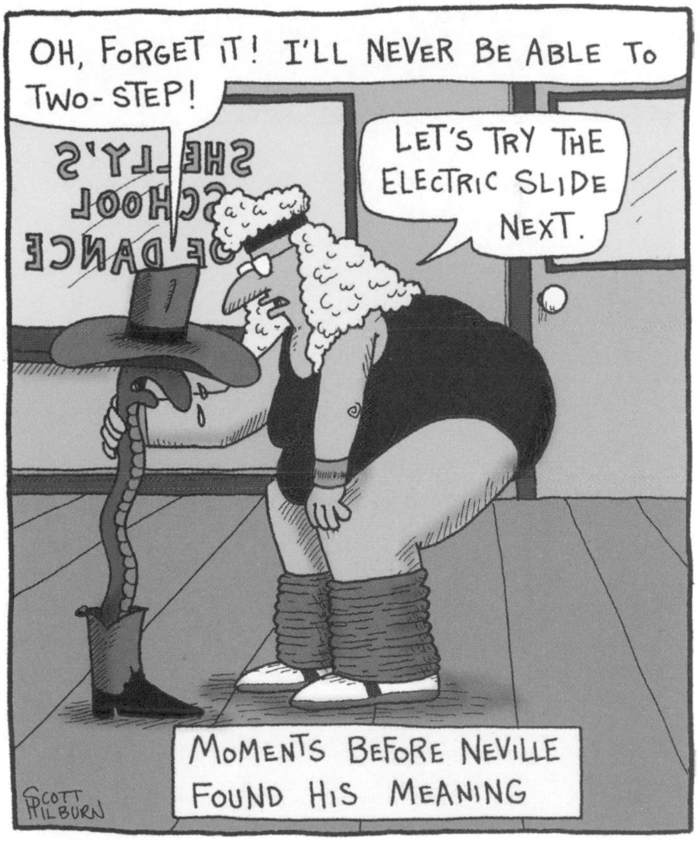
OH, FORGET IT! I'LL NEVER BE ABLE TO TWO-STEP!
LET'S TRY THE ELECTRIC SLIDE NEXT.
SCOTT HILBURN

MOMENTS BEFORE NEVILLE FOUND HIS MEANING

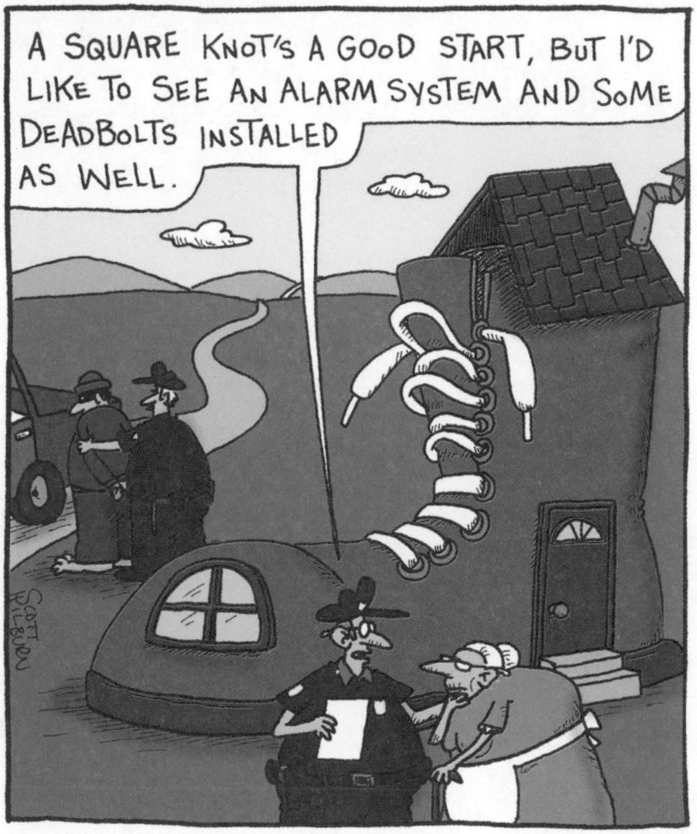
A SQUARE KNOT'S A GOOD START, BUT I'D LIKE TO SEE AN ALARM SYSTEM AND SOME DEADBOLTS INSTALLED AS WELL.

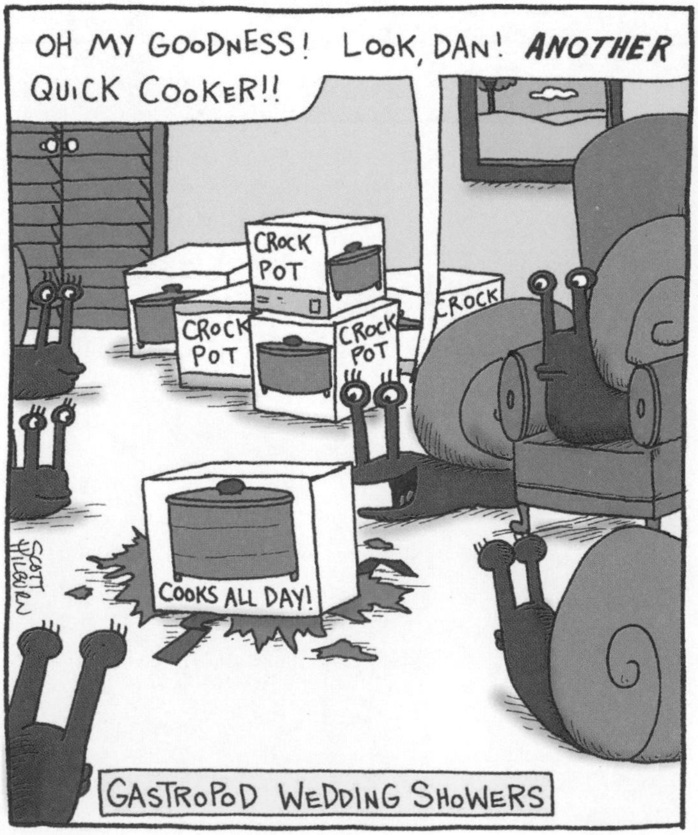
OH MY GOODNESS! LOOK, DAN! **ANOTHER** QUICK COOKER!!
CROCK POT
CROCK POT
CROCK POT
CROCK
COOKS ALL DAY!
GASTROPOD WEDDING SHOWERS

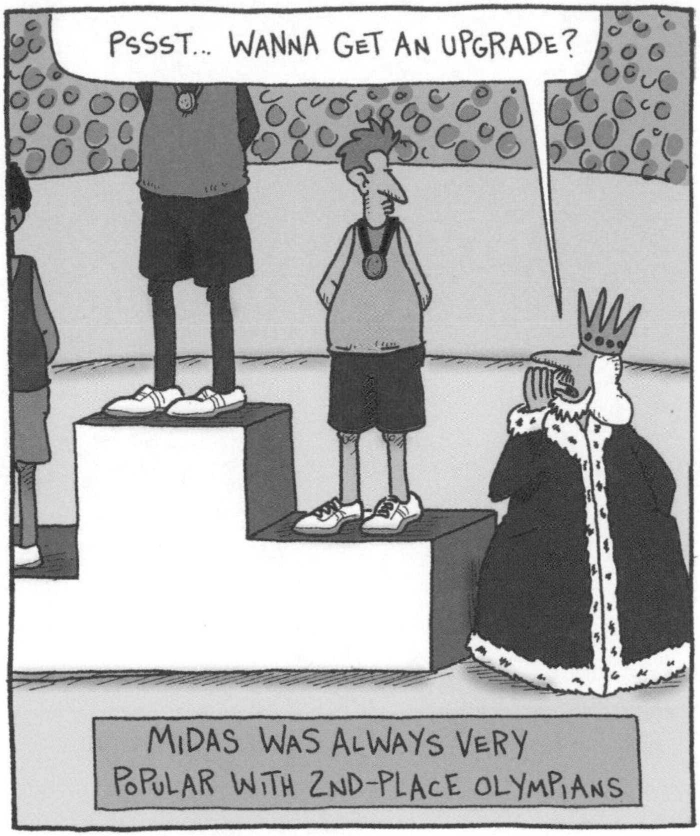
PSSST... WANNA GET AN UPGRADE?
MIDAS WAS ALWAYS VERY POPULAR WITH 2ND-PLACE OLYMPIANS

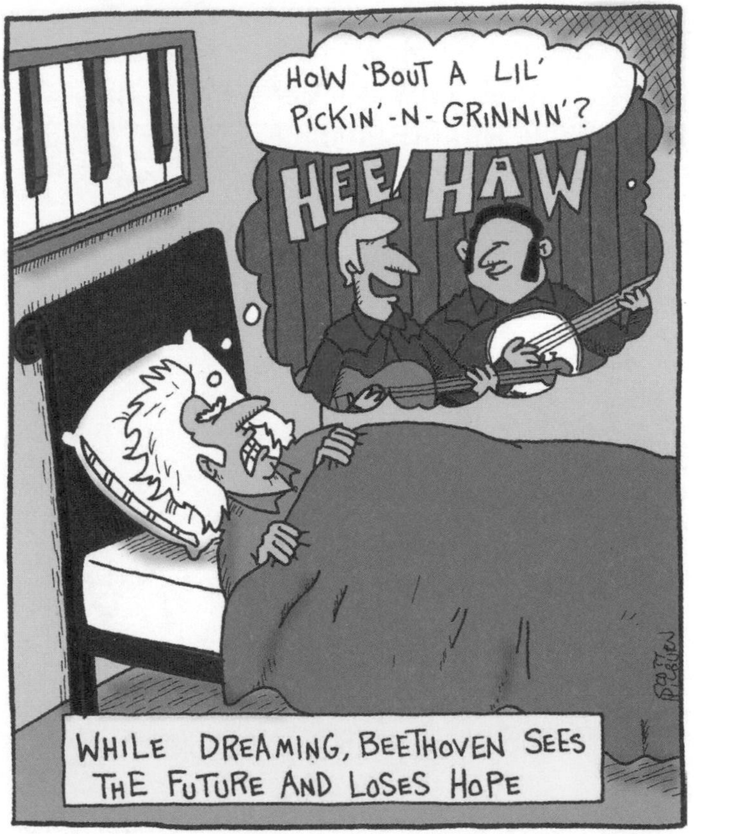
HOW 'BOUT A LIL' PICKIN'-N-GRINNIN'?
HEE HAW
WHILE DREAMING, BEETHOVEN SEES THE FUTURE AND LOSES HOPE

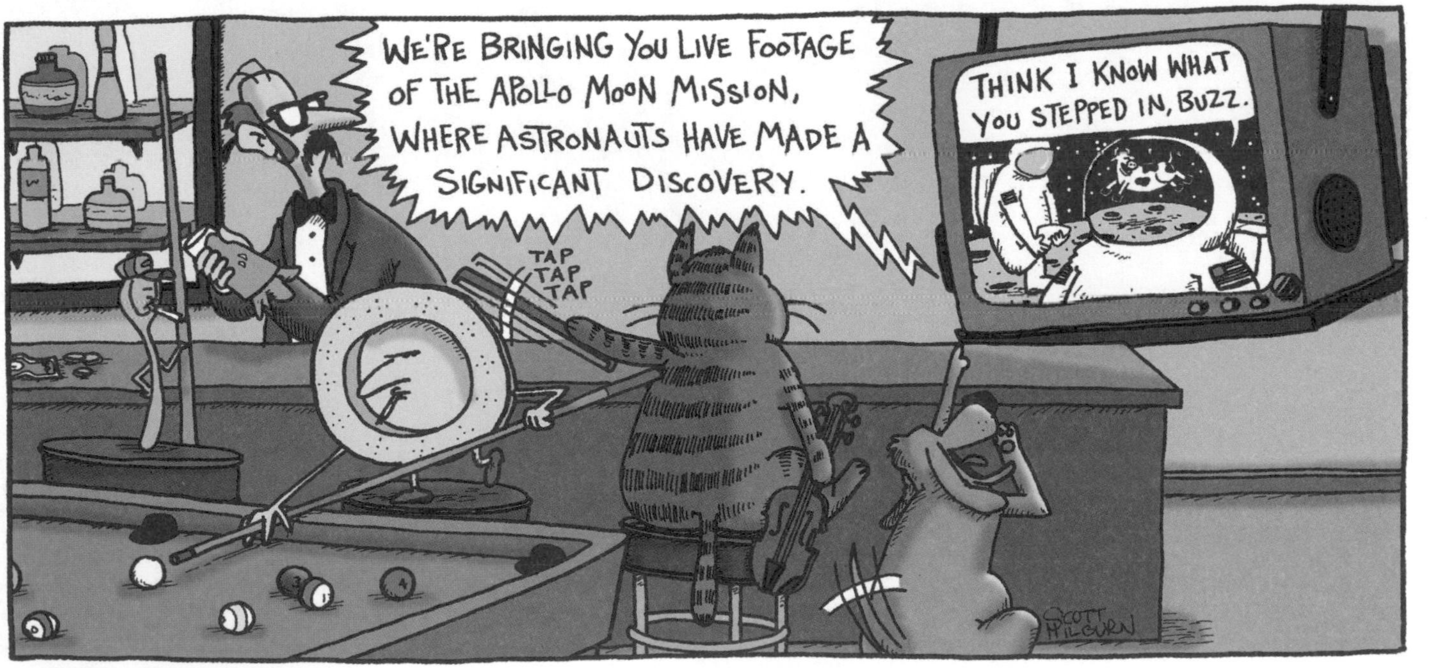
WE'RE BRINGING YOU LIVE FOOTAGE OF THE APOLLO MOON MISSION, WHERE ASTRONAUTS HAVE MADE A SIGNIFICANT DISCOVERY.
TAP TAP TAP
THINK I KNOW WHAT YOU STEPPED IN, BUZZ.
SCOTT HILBURN

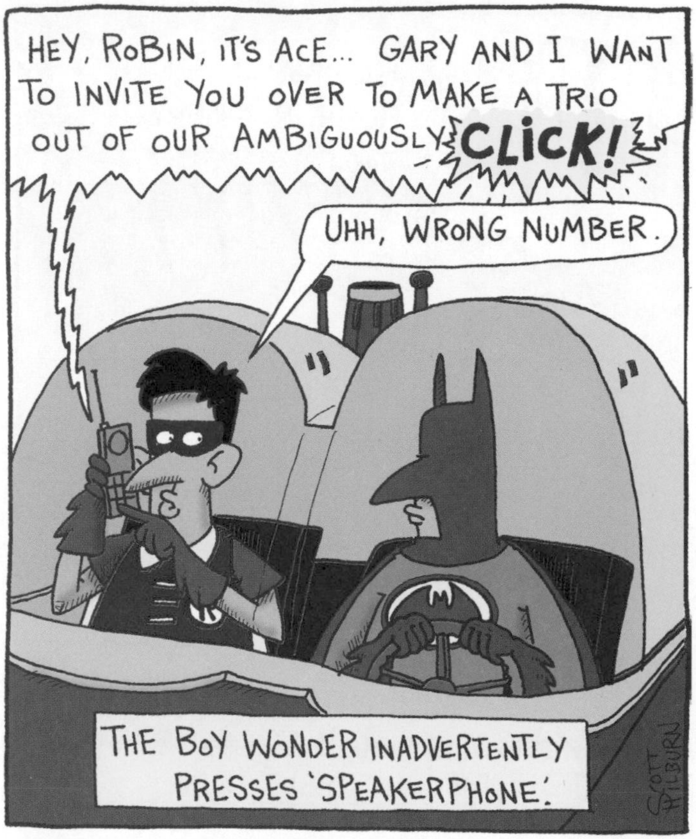
HEY, ROBIN, IT'S ACE... GARY AND I WANT TO INVITE YOU OVER TO MAKE A TRIO OUT OF OUR AMBIGUOUSLY
CLICK!
UHH, WRONG NUMBER.
THE BOY WONDER INADVERTENTLY PRESSES 'SPEAKERPHONE.'
SCOTT HILBURN

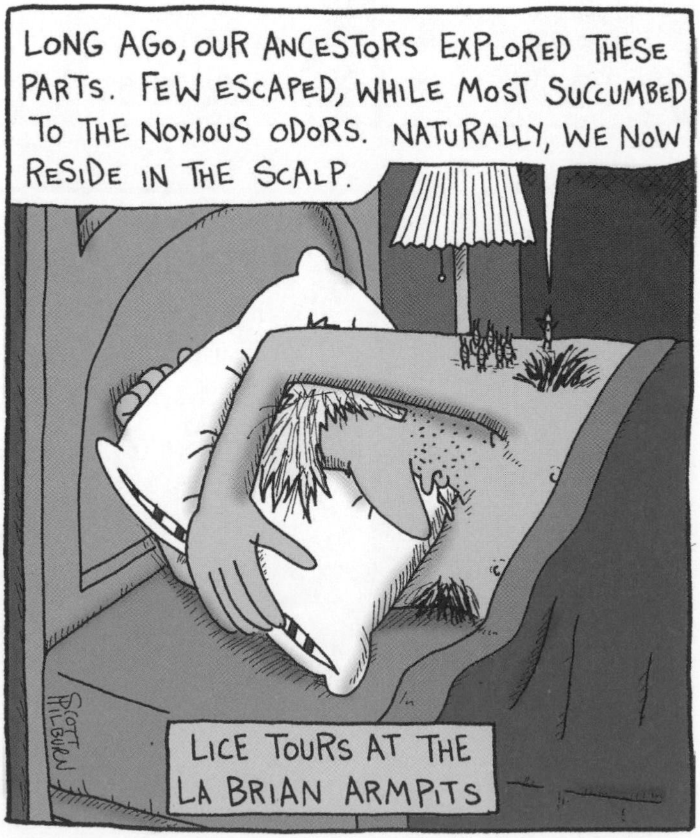
LONG AGO, OUR ANCESTORS EXPLORED THESE PARTS. FEW ESCAPED, WHILE MOST SUCCUMBED TO THE NOXIOUS ODORS. NATURALLY, WE NOW RESIDE IN THE SCALP.
LICE TOURS AT THE LA BRIAN ARMPITS
SCOTT HILBURN

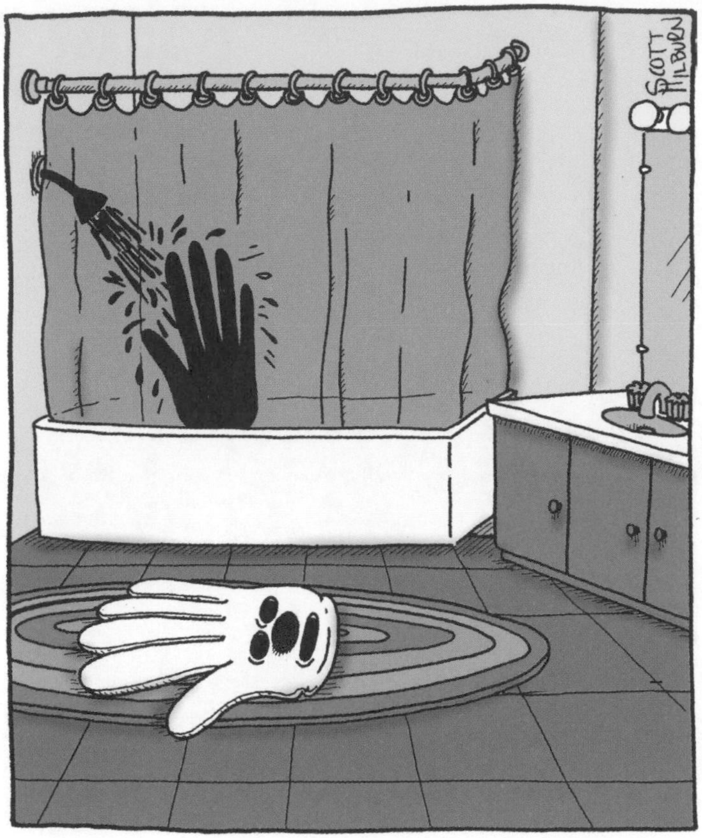

SCOTT HILBURN

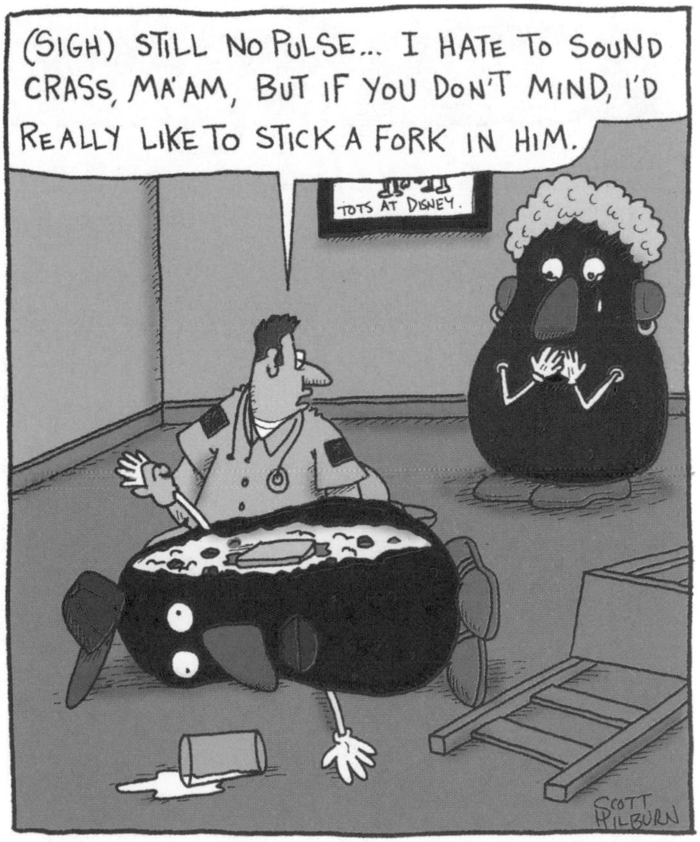

(SIGH) STILL NO PULSE... I HATE TO SOUND CRASS, MA'AM, BUT IF YOU DON'T MIND, I'D REALLY LIKE TO STICK A FORK IN HIM.
TOTS AT DISNEY.
SCOTT HILBURN

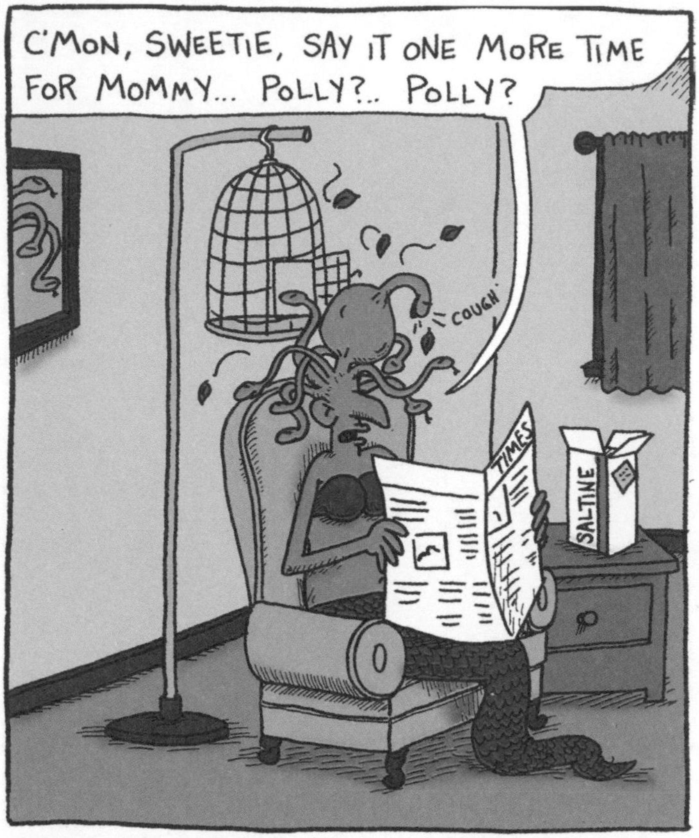
C'MON, SWEETIE, SAY IT ONE MORE TIME FOR MOMMY... POLLY?.. POLLY?
COUGH
TIMES
SALTINE

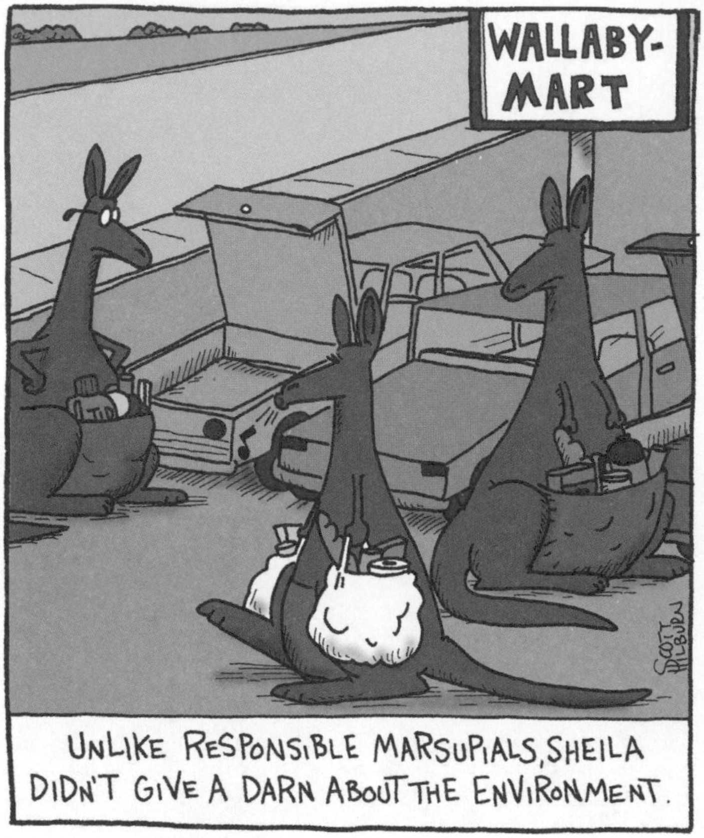
WALLABY-MART
SCOTT HILBURN
UNLIKE RESPONSIBLE MARSUPIALS, SHEILA DIDN'T GIVE A DARN ABOUT THE ENVIRONMENT.

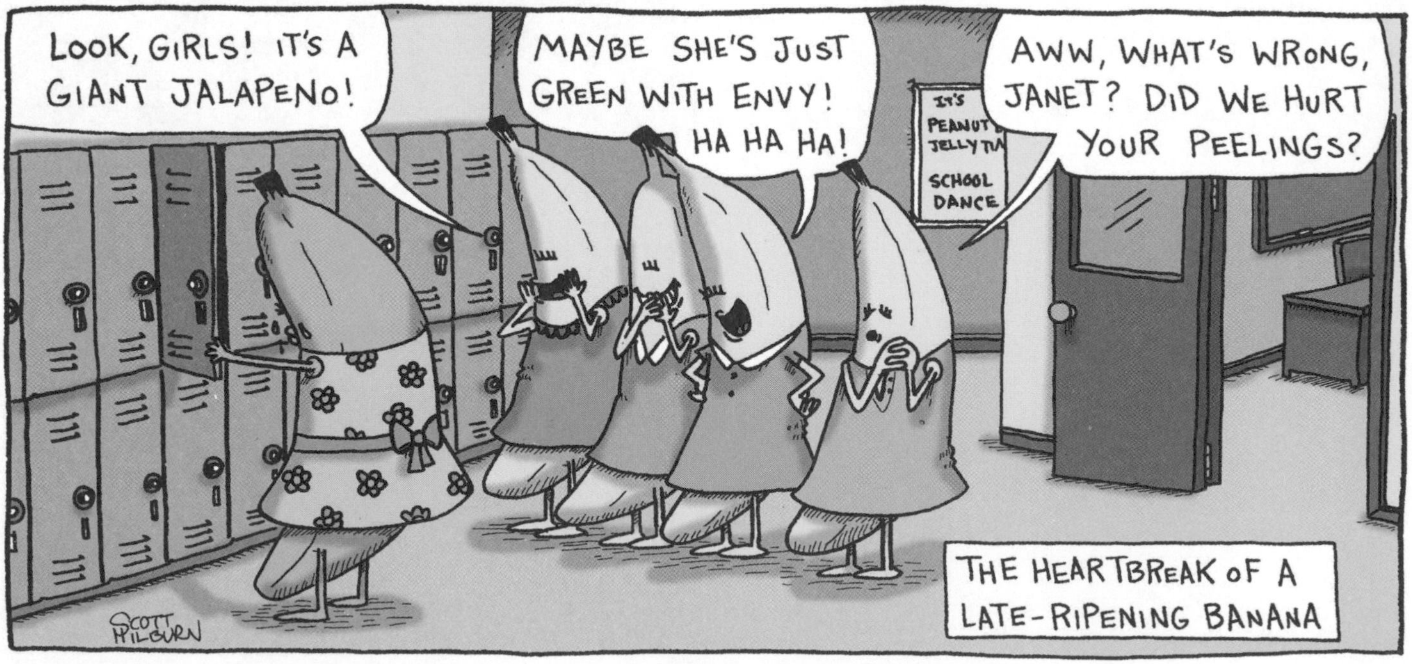
LOOK, GIRLS! IT'S A GIANT JALAPENO!
MAYBE SHE'S JUST GREEN WITH ENVY!
HA HA HA!
AWW, WHAT'S WRONG, JANET? DID WE HURT YOUR PEELINGS?
IT'S
SCHOOL DANCE
SCOTT HILBURN
THE HEARTBREAK OF A LATE-RIPENING BANANA

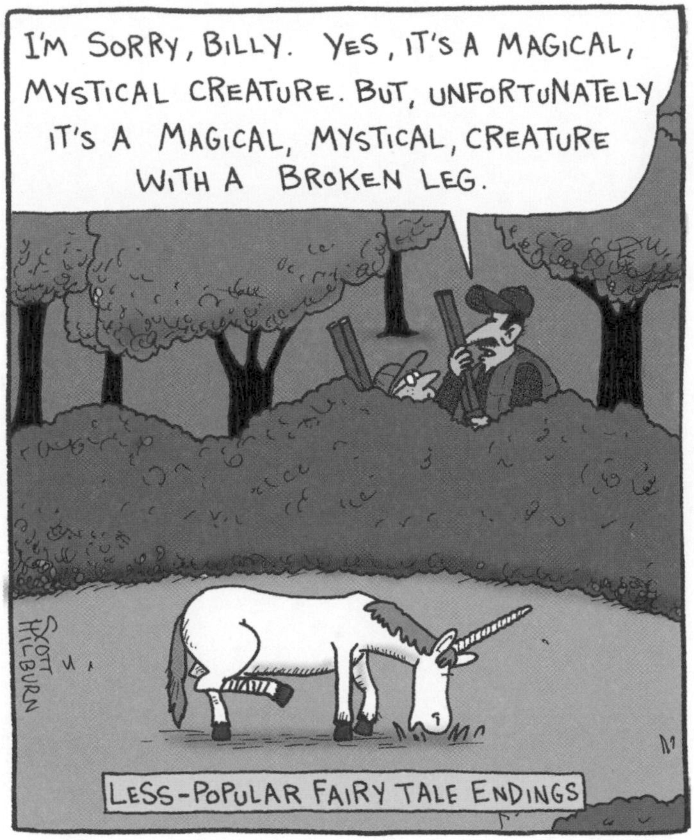
I'M SORRY, BILLY. YES, IT'S A MAGICAL, MYSTICAL CREATURE. BUT, UNFORTUNATELY IT'S A MAGICAL, MYSTICAL, CREATURE WITH A BROKEN LEG.
SCOTT HILBURN
LESS-POPULAR FAIRY TALE ENDINGS

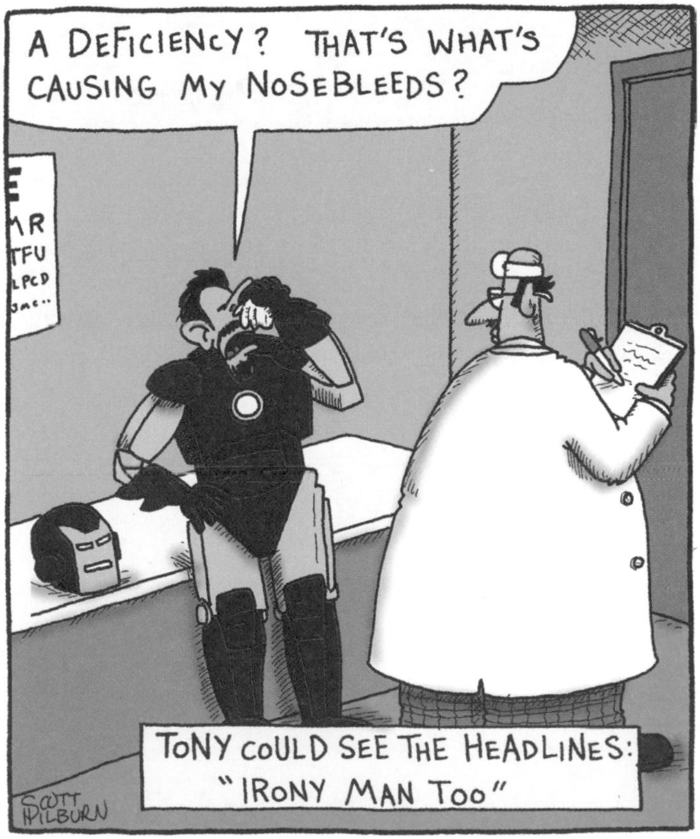
A DEFICIENCY? THAT'S WHAT'S CAUSING MY NOSEBLEEDS?
TONY COULD SEE THE HEADLINES: "IRONY MAN TOO"
SCOTT HILBURN

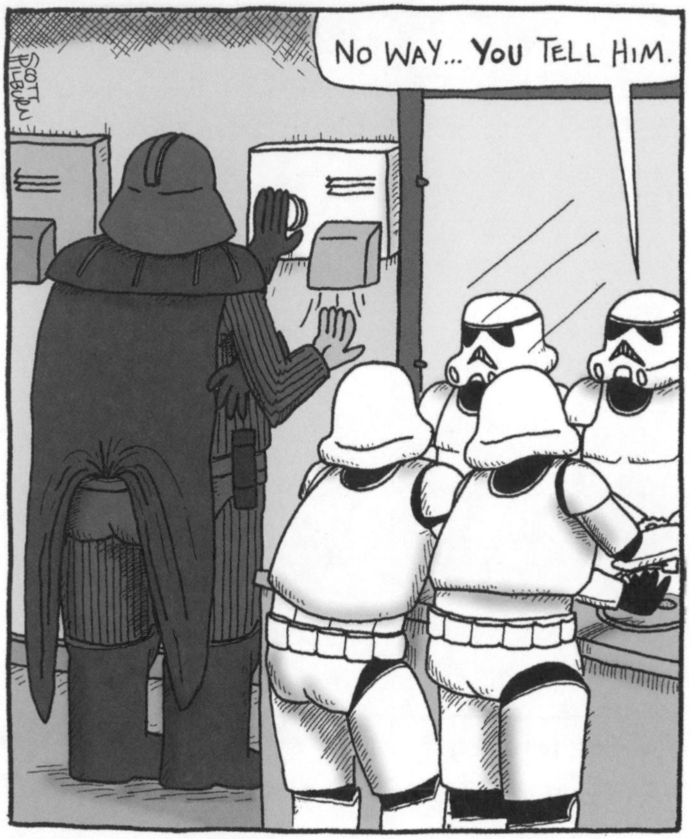
NO WAY... YOU TELL HIM.
SCOTT HILBURN

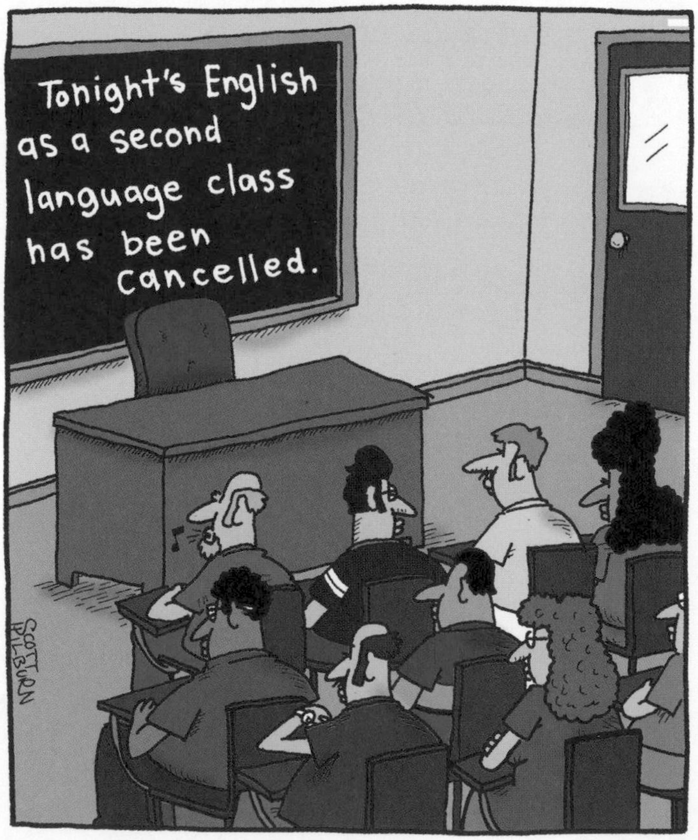
Tonight's English as a second language class has been cancelled.
SCOTT HILBURN

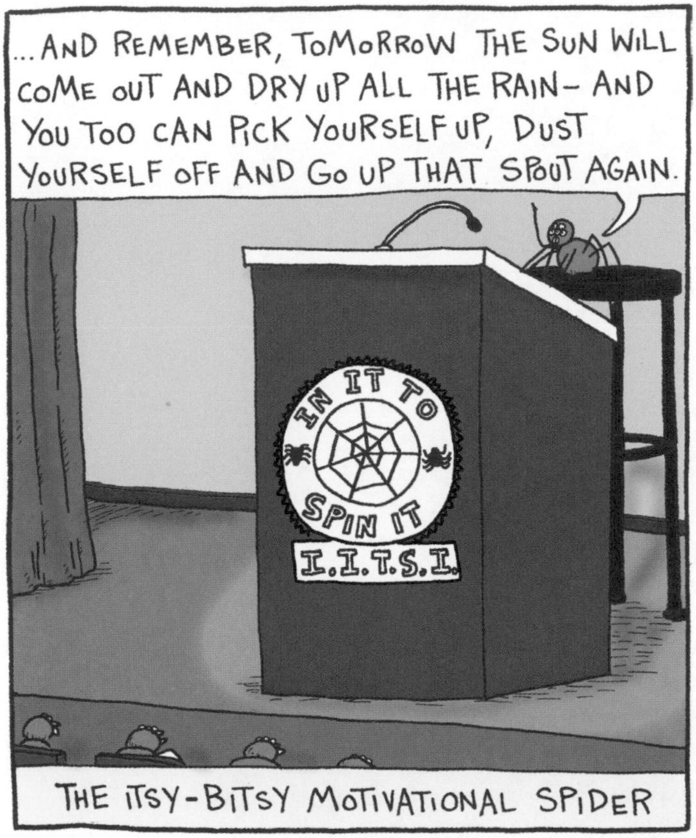
...AND REMEMBER, TOMORROW THE SUN WILL COME OUT AND DRY UP ALL THE RAIN– AND YOU TOO CAN PICK YOURSELF UP, DUST YOURSELF OFF AND GO UP THAT SPOUT AGAIN.
IN IT TO SPIN IT
I.I.T.S.I.
THE ITSY-BITSY MOTIVATIONAL SPIDER

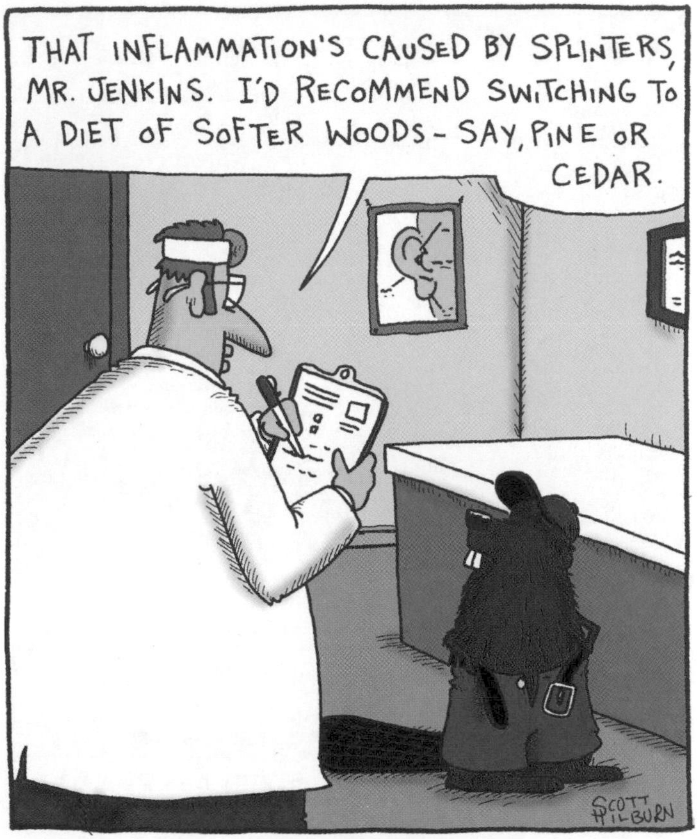
THAT INFLAMMATION'S CAUSED BY SPLINTERS, MR. JENKINS. I'D RECOMMEND SWITCHING TO A DIET OF SOFTER WOODS– SAY, PINE OR CEDAR.
SCOTT HILBURN

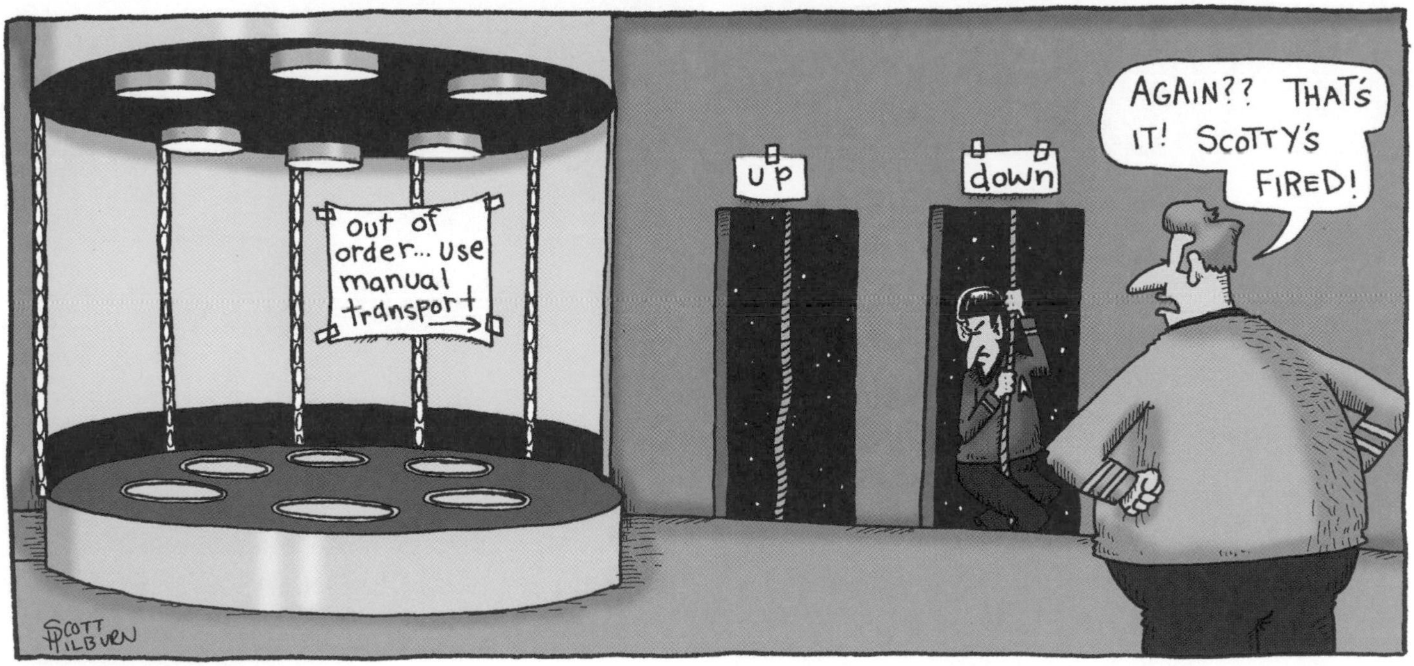
out of order... use manual transport
up
down
AGAIN?? THAT'S IT! SCOTTY'S FIRED!
SCOTT HILBURN

THE TRUE CAUSE OF THE FOREST FIRE, REVEALED

I'LL HAVE THE CHEESE FRIES, EXTRA RANCH, TWO HOT DOGS, A BACON CHEESEBURGER AN EXTRA LARGE MILKSHAKE WITH SPRINKLES AND... BOY, YOU'RE UGLY.

THE TIN WOODSMAN DISCOVERS THE ADVANTAGES OF HAVING NO HEART.

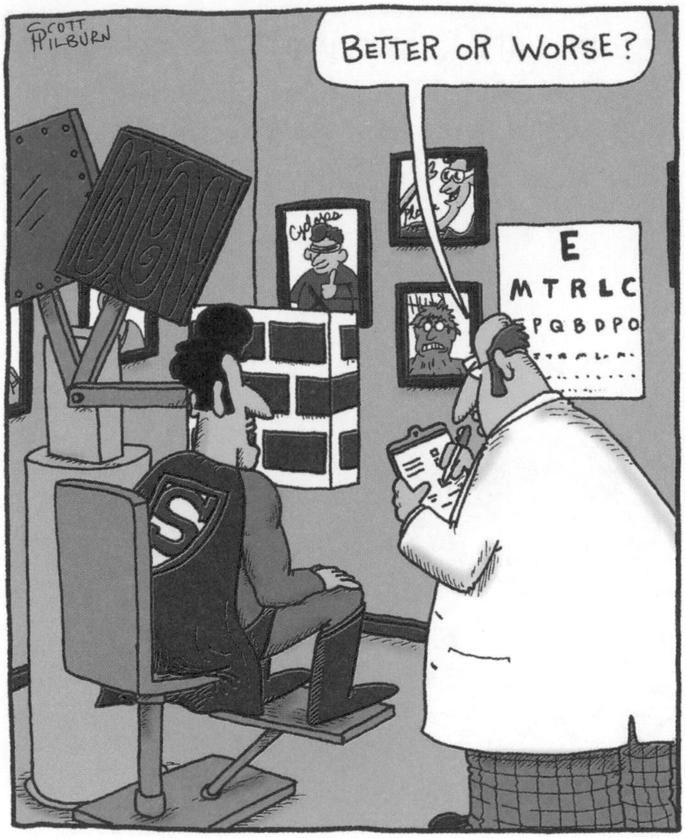
SCOTT HILBURN
BETTER OR WORSE?
E
M T R L C
P Q B D P O

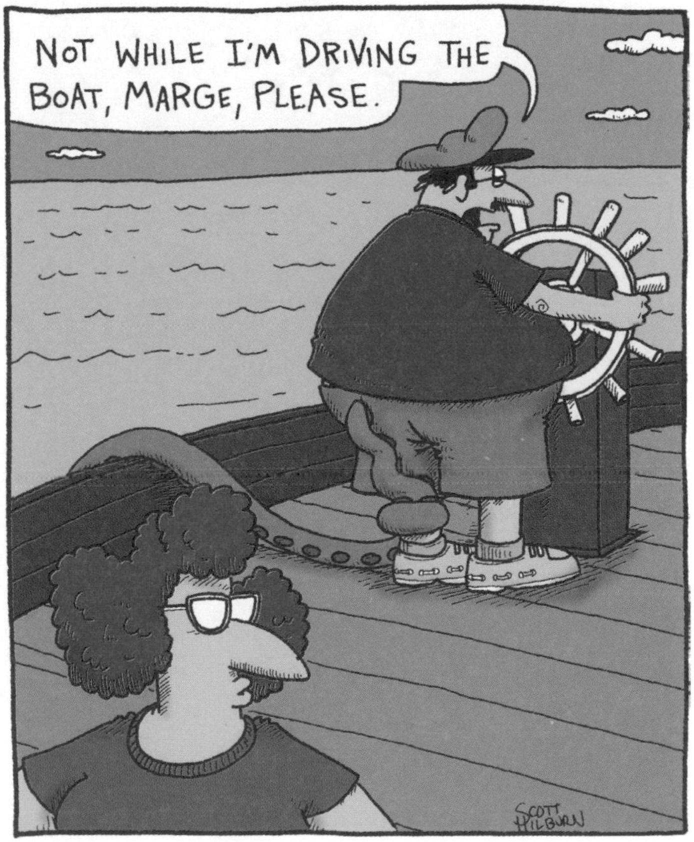
NOT WHILE I'M DRIVING THE BOAT, MARGE, PLEASE.
SCOTT HILBURN

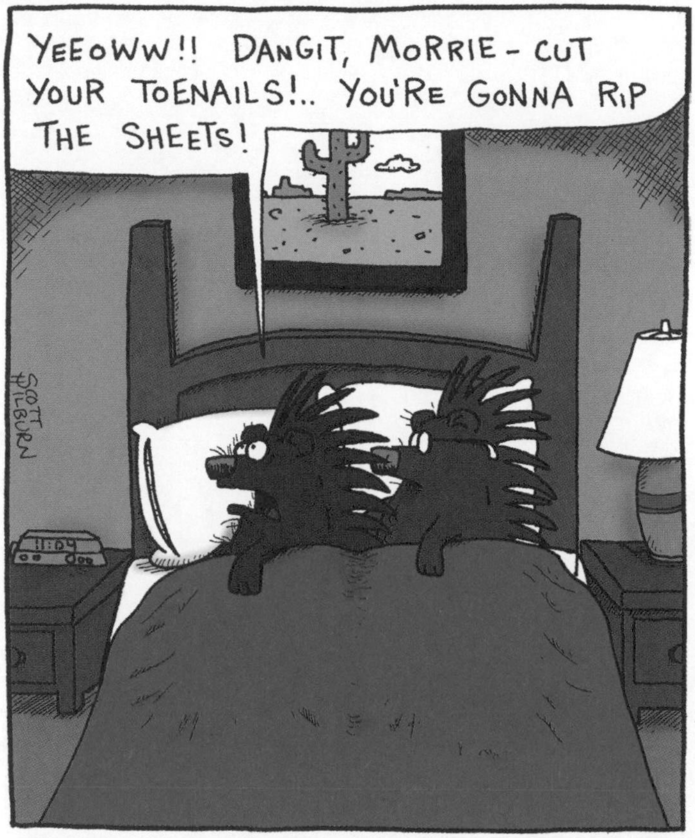
YEEOWW!! DANGIT, MORRIE - CUT YOUR TOENAILS!.. YOU'RE GONNA RIP THE SHEETS!
SCOTT HILBURN

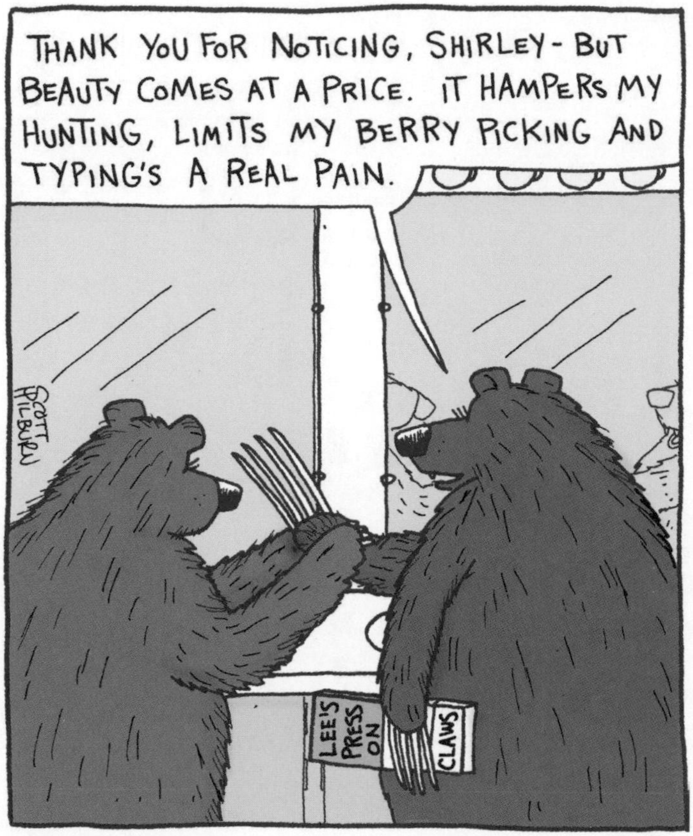
THANK YOU FOR NOTICING, SHIRLEY - BUT BEAUTY COMES AT A PRICE. IT HAMPERS MY HUNTING, LIMITS MY BERRY PICKING AND TYPING'S A REAL PAIN.
SCOTT HILBURN
LEE'S PRESS ON
CLAWS

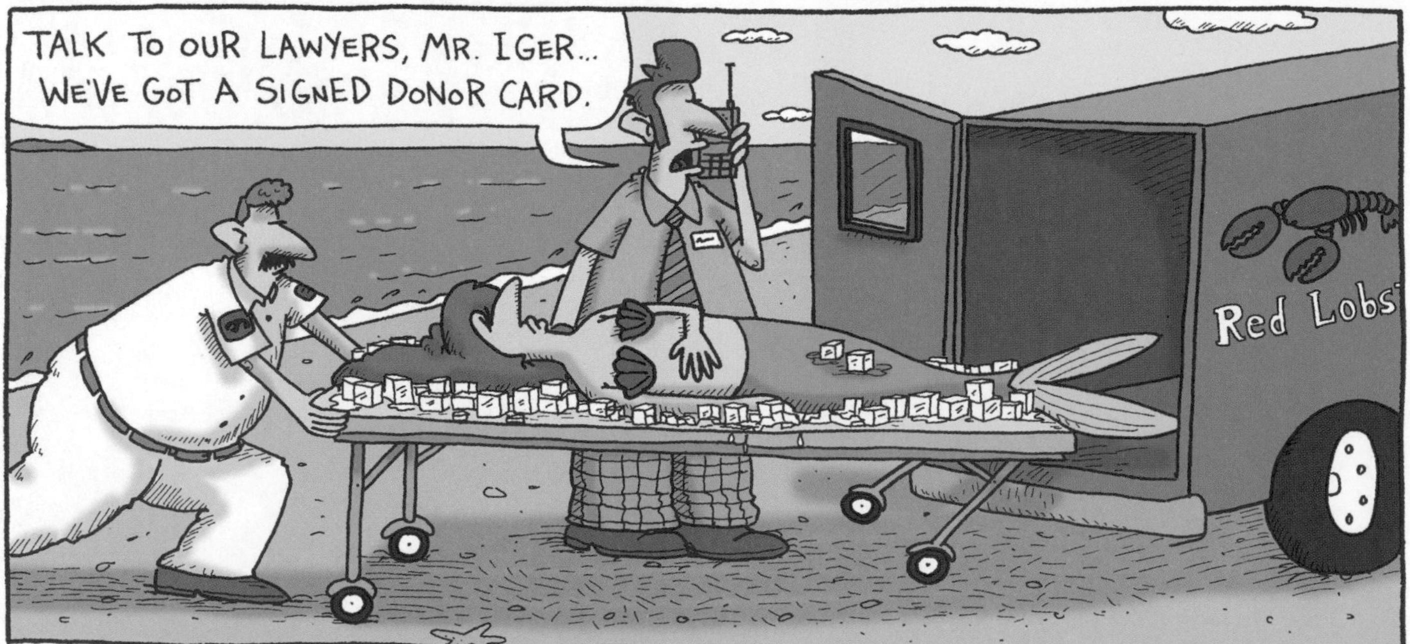
TALK TO OUR LAWYERS, MR. IGER... WE'VE GOT A SIGNED DONOR CARD.
Red Lobs

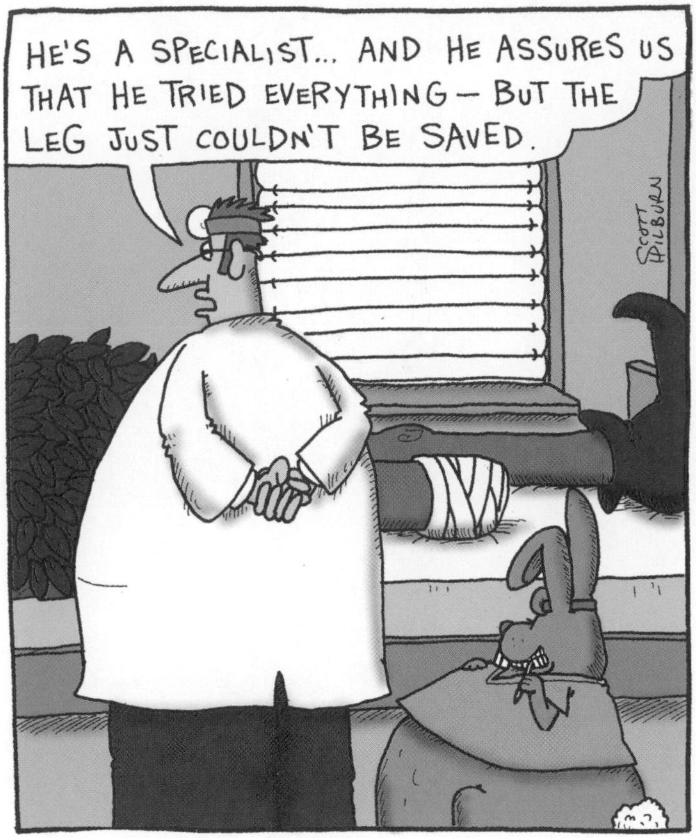
HE'S A SPECIALIST... AND HE ASSURES US THAT HE TRIED EVERYTHING — BUT THE LEG JUST COULDN'T BE SAVED.
SCOTT HILBURN

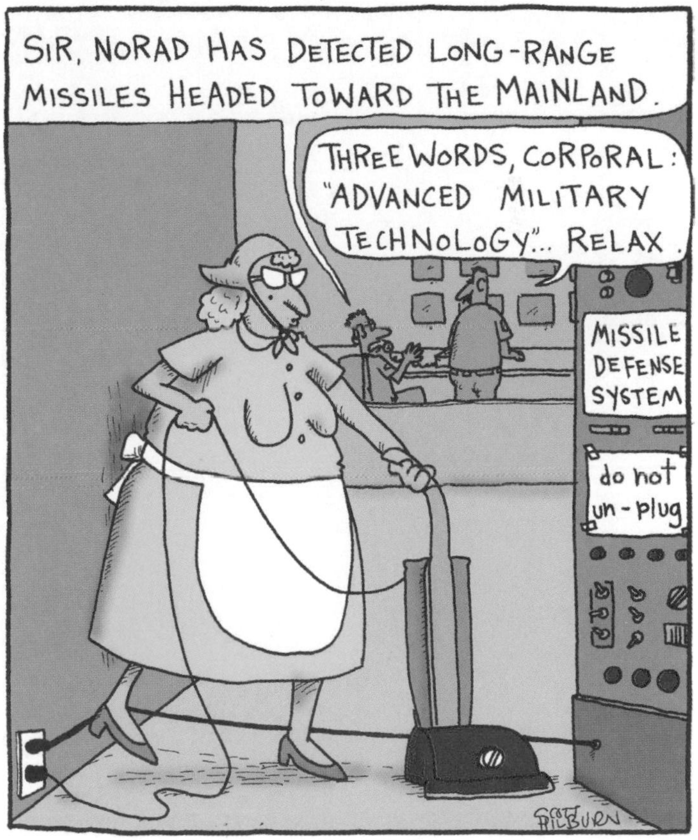
SIR, NORAD HAS DETECTED LONG-RANGE MISSILES HEADED TOWARD THE MAINLAND.
THREE WORDS, CORPORAL: "ADVANCED MILITARY TECHNOLOGY"... RELAX.
MISSILE DEFENSE SYSTEM
do not un-plug
SCOTT HILBURN

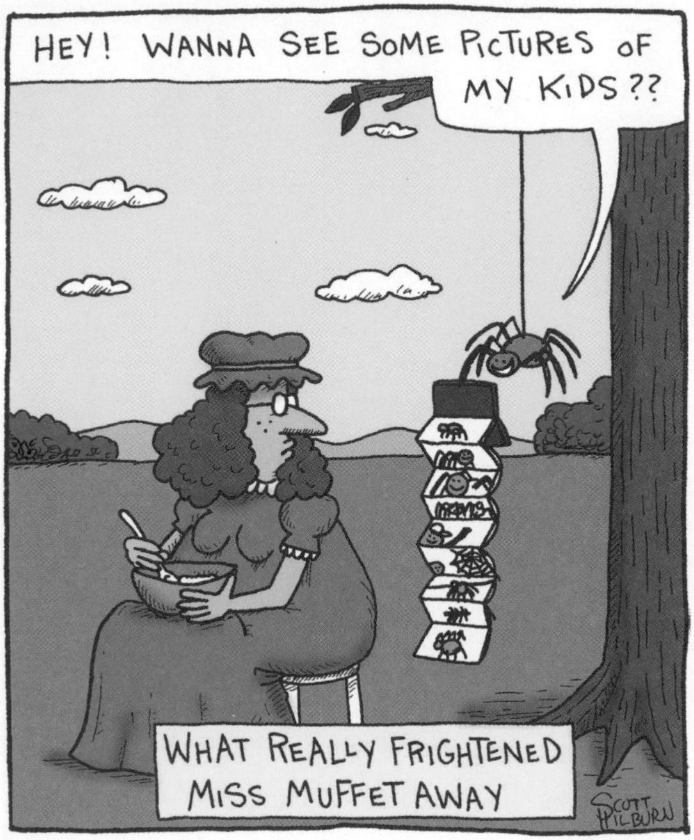
HEY! WANNA SEE SOME PICTURES OF MY KIDS??
WHAT REALLY FRIGHTENED MISS MUFFET AWAY
SCOTT HILBURN

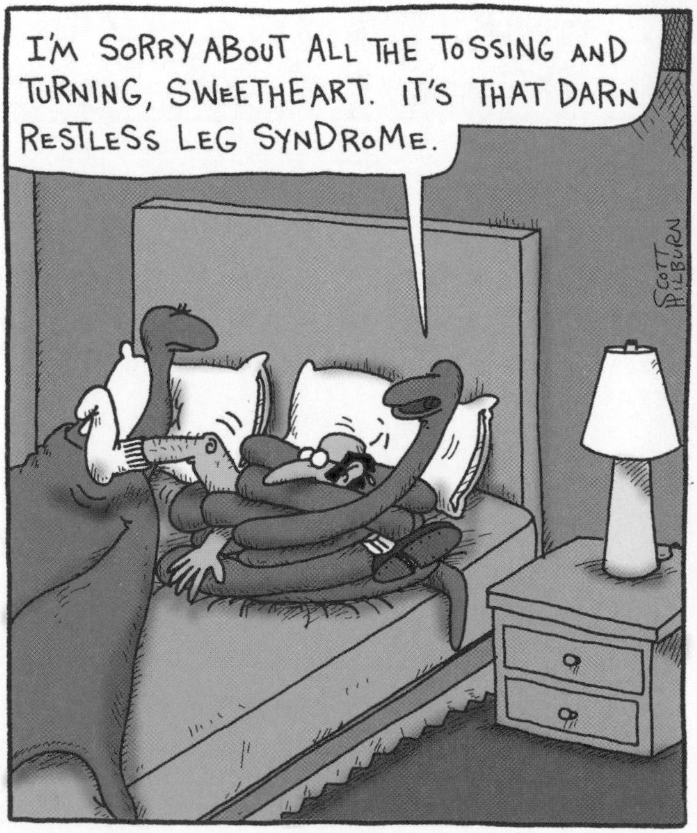
I'M SORRY ABOUT ALL THE TOSSING AND TURNING, SWEETHEART. IT'S THAT DARN RESTLESS LEG SYNDROME.
SCOTT HILBURN

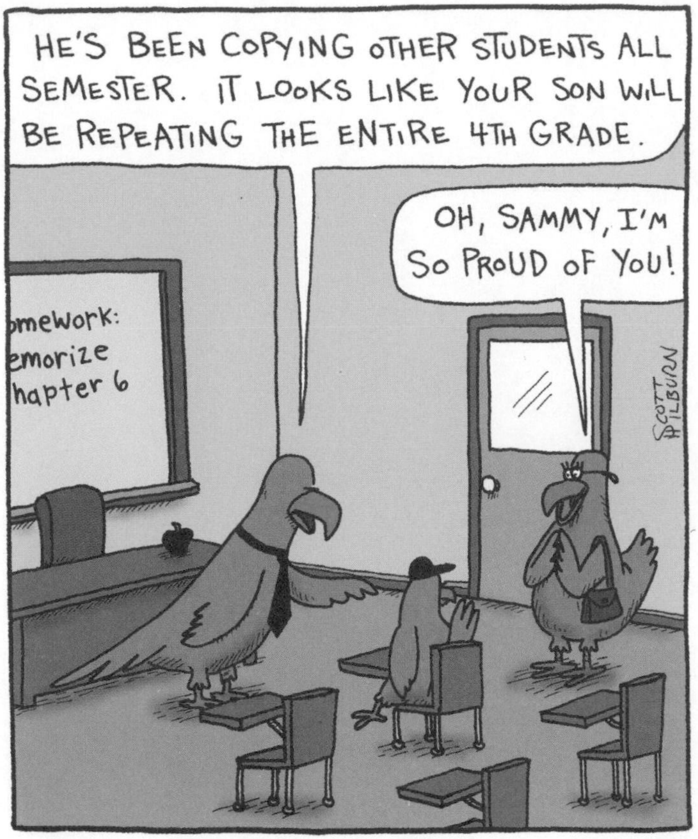
HE'S BEEN COPYING OTHER STUDENTS ALL SEMESTER. IT LOOKS LIKE YOUR SON WILL BE REPEATING THE ENTIRE 4TH GRADE.
OH, SAMMY, I'M SO PROUD OF YOU!
omework:
emorize
hapter 6
SCOTT HILBURN

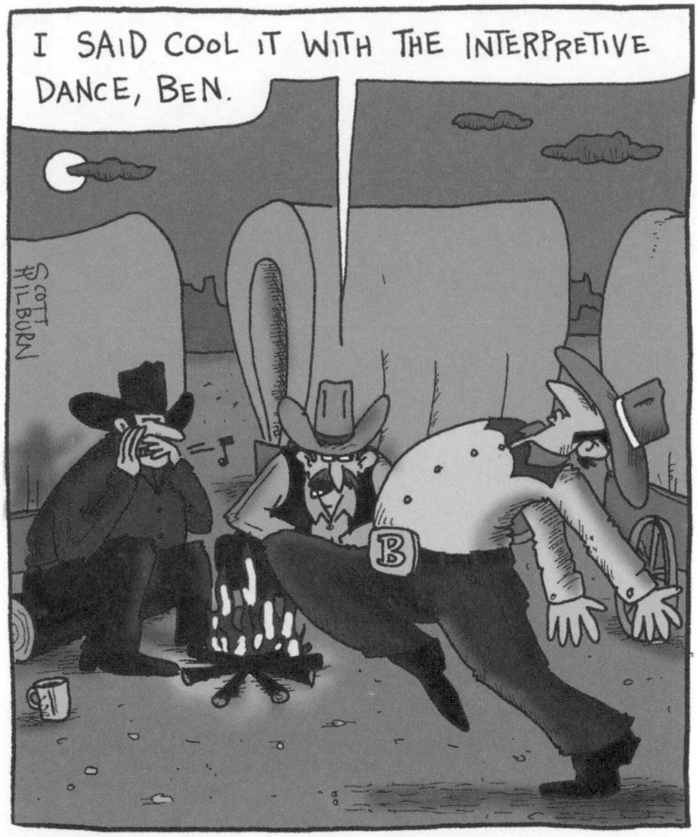
I SAID COOL IT WITH THE INTERPRETIVE DANCE, BEN.
SCOTT HILBURN
B

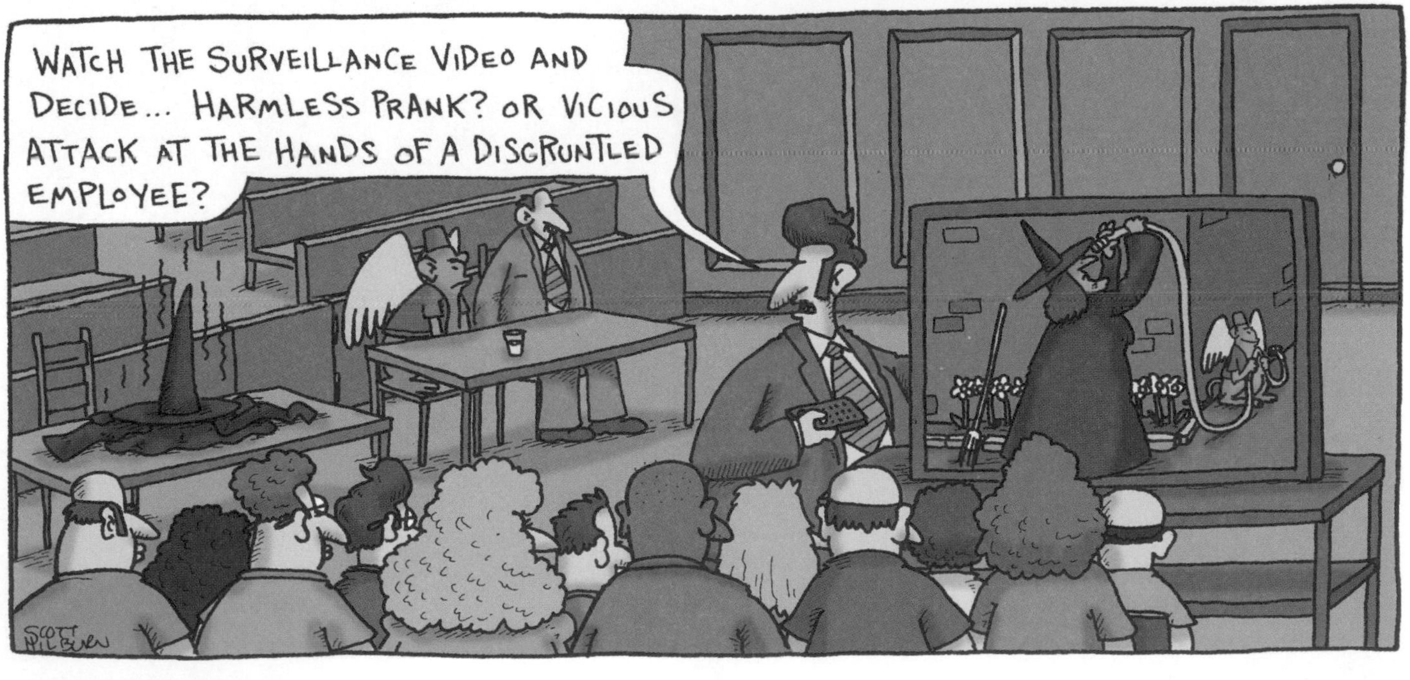
WATCH THE SURVEILLANCE VIDEO AND DECIDE... HARMLESS PRANK? OR VICIOUS ATTACK AT THE HANDS OF A DISGRUNTLED EMPLOYEE?
SCOTT HILBURN

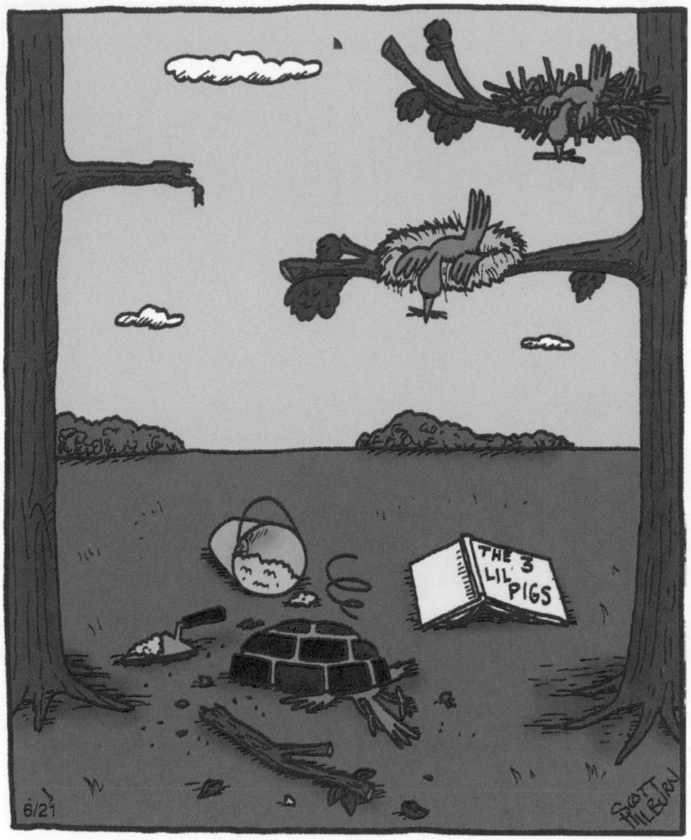
THE 3 LIL' PIGS
6/21
SCOTT HILBURN

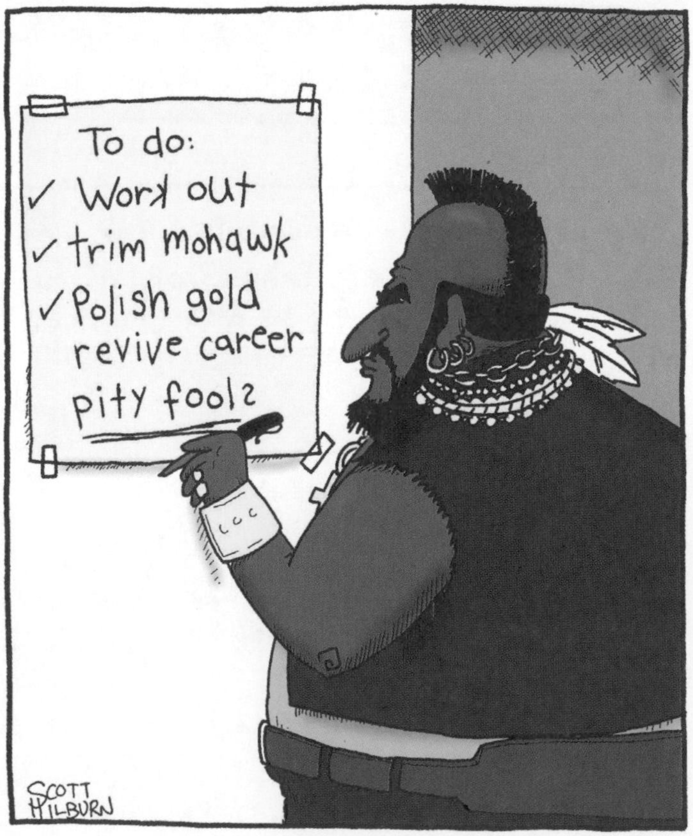
To do:
✓ Work out
✓ trim mohawk
✓ Polish gold
revive career
pity fools
SCOTT HILBURN

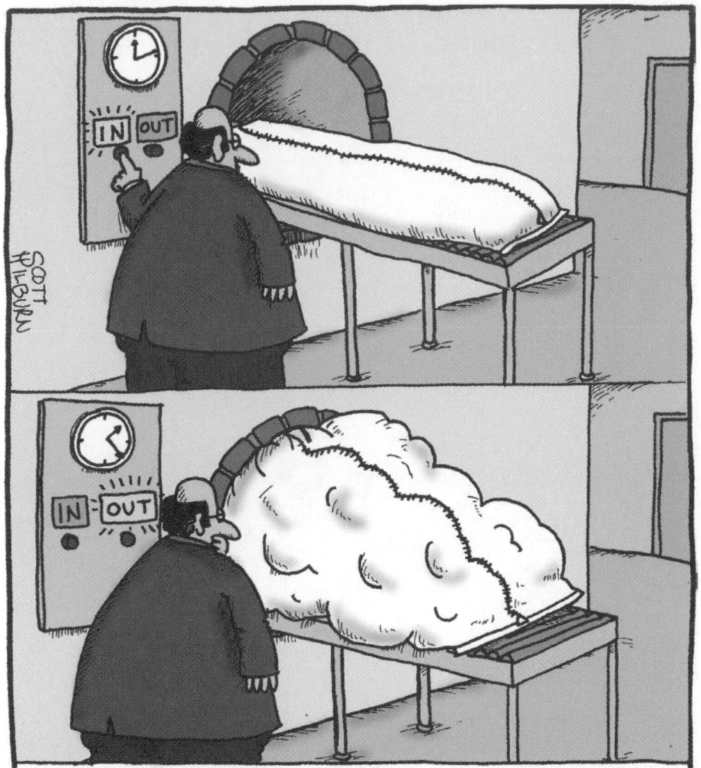
IN
OUT
SCOTT HILBURN

THE CREMATION OF ORVILLE REDENBACHER

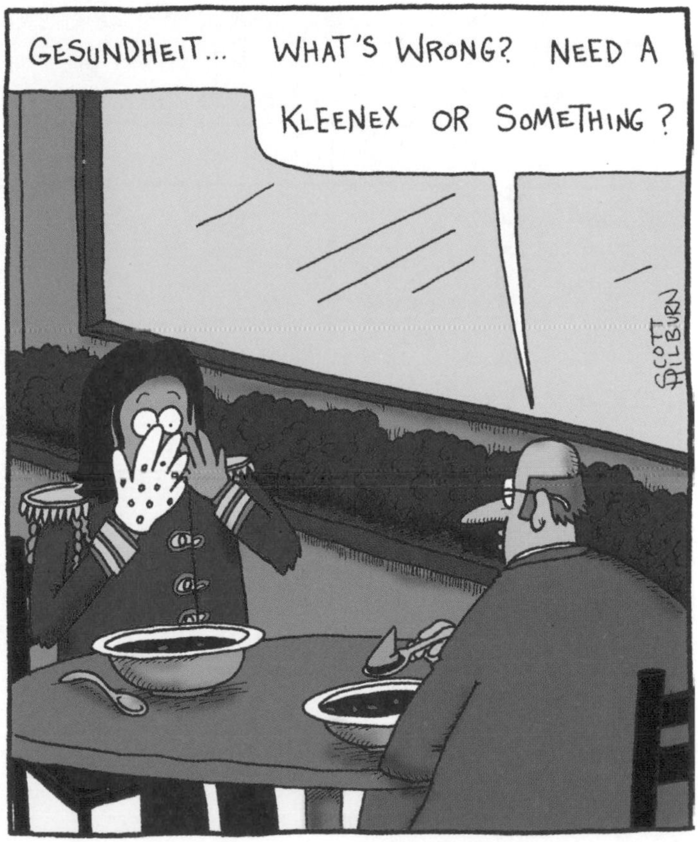
GESUNDHEIT... WHAT'S WRONG? NEED A KLEENEX OR SOMETHING?
SCOTT HILBURN

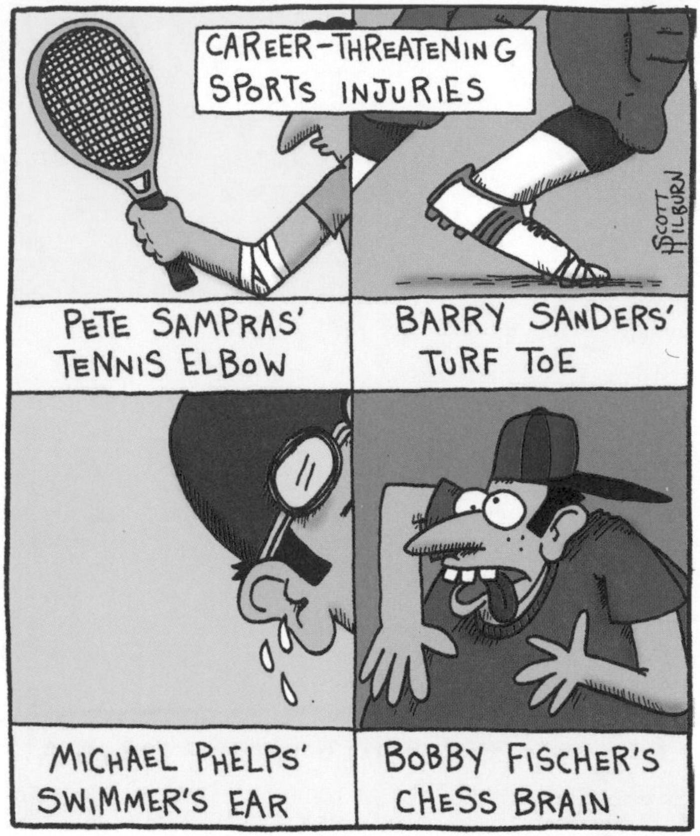
CAREER-THREATENING SPORTS INJURIES
PETE SAMPRAS' TENNIS ELBOW
BARRY SANDERS' TURF TOE
MICHAEL PHELPS' SWIMMER'S EAR
BOBBY FISCHER'S CHESS BRAIN
SCOTT HILBURN

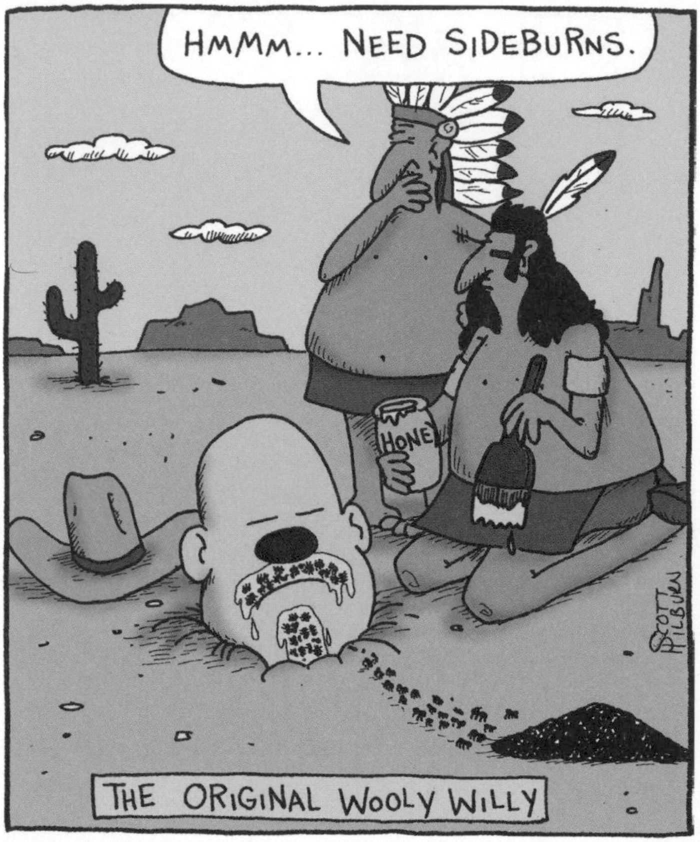
HMMM... NEED SIDEBURNS.
HONEY
THE ORIGINAL WOOLY WILLY
SCOTT HILBURN

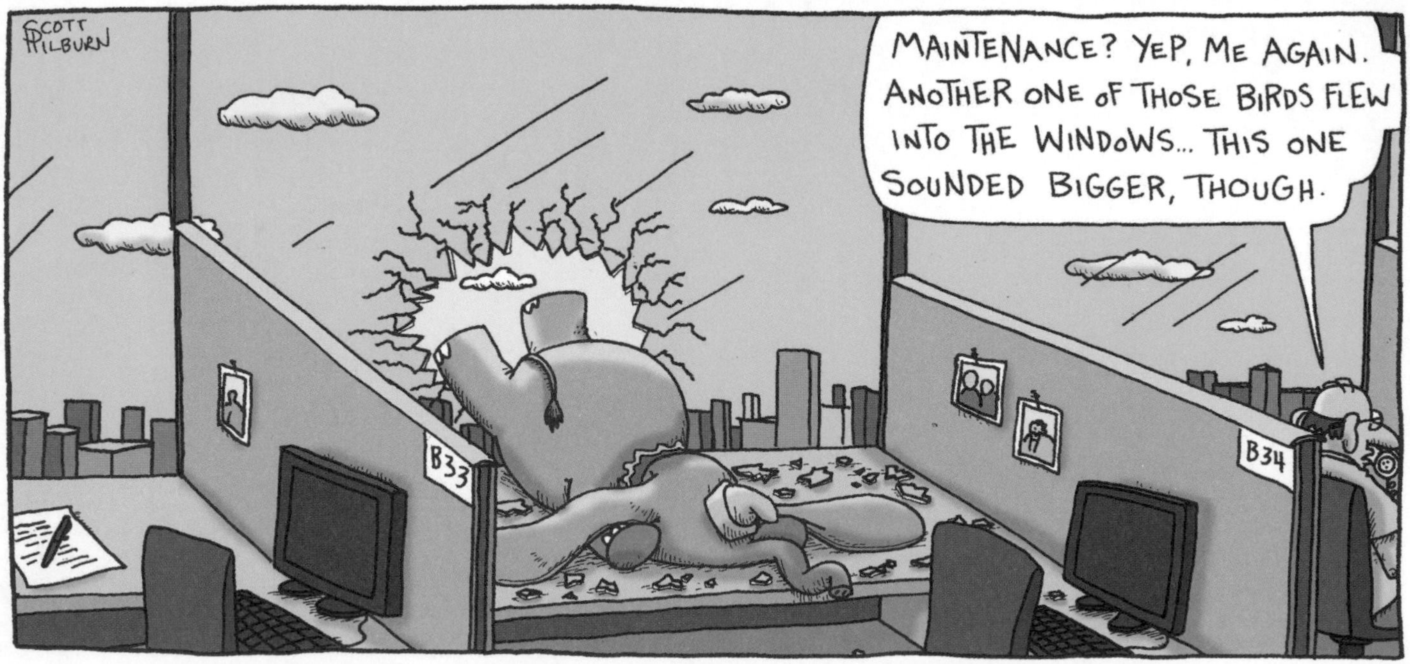
SCOTT HILBURN
MAINTENANCE? YEP, ME AGAIN. ANOTHER ONE OF THOSE BIRDS FLEW INTO THE WINDOWS... THIS ONE SOUNDED BIGGER, THOUGH.
B33
B34

UNLUCKY?
TONIGHT'S SEMINAR WILL CHANGE YOUR LIFE - 7:00
HORSESHOE
RANCH SUPPLY

WHAT? I JUST HAD MY TEETH WHITENED.

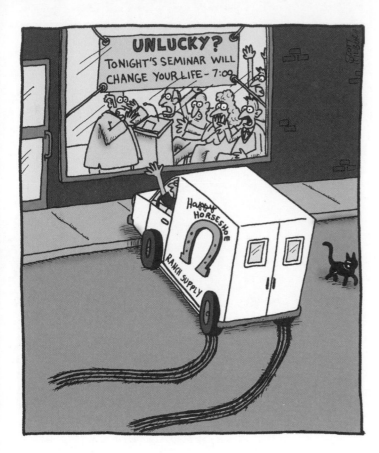

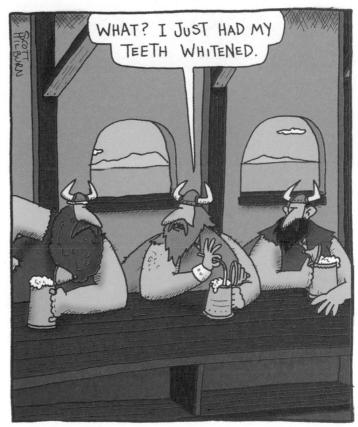

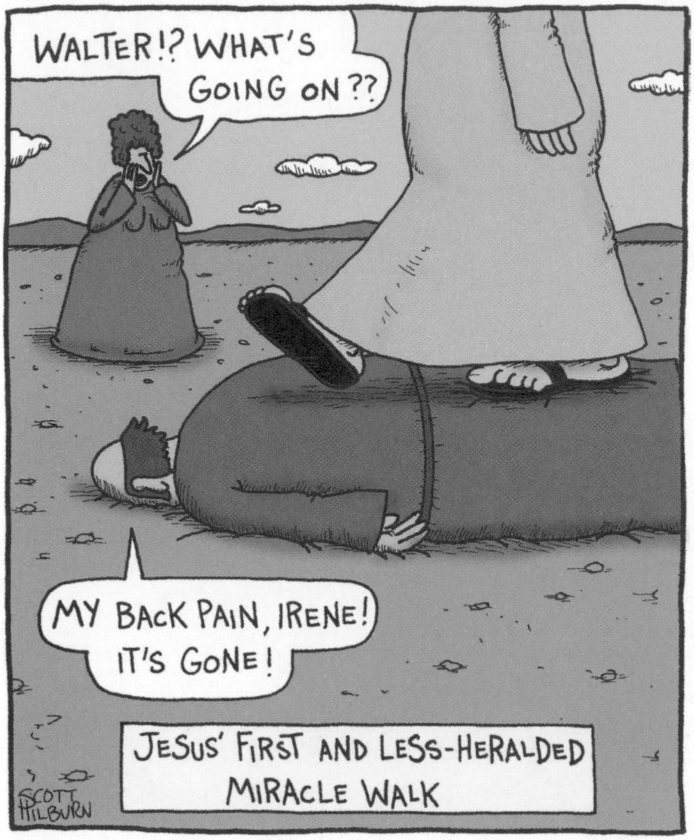
WALTER!? WHAT'S GOING ON??
MY BACK PAIN, IRENE! IT'S GONE!
SCOTT HILBURN
JESUS' FIRST AND LESS-HERALDED MIRACLE WALK

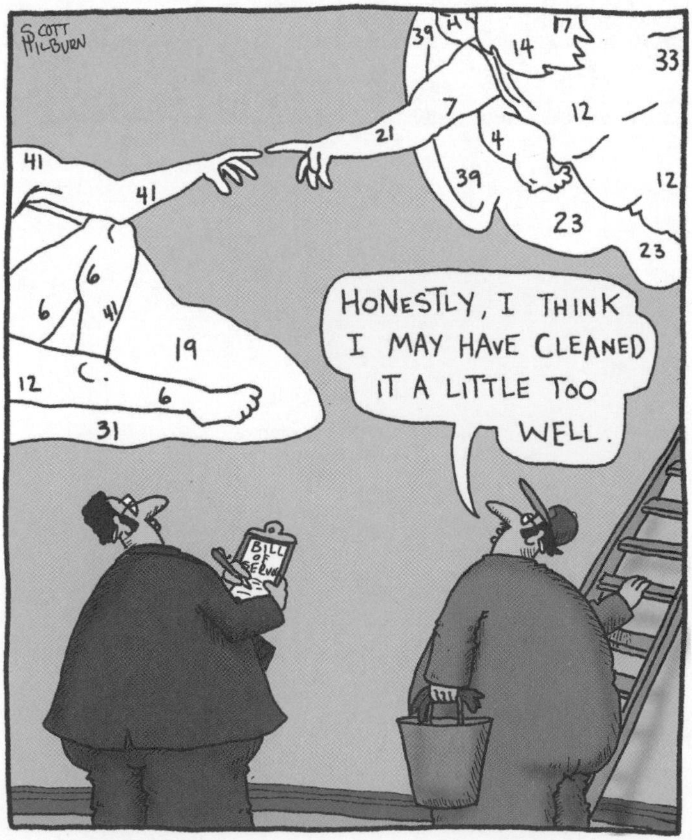
SCOTT HILBURN
HONESTLY, I THINK I MAY HAVE CLEANED IT A LITTLE TOO WELL.

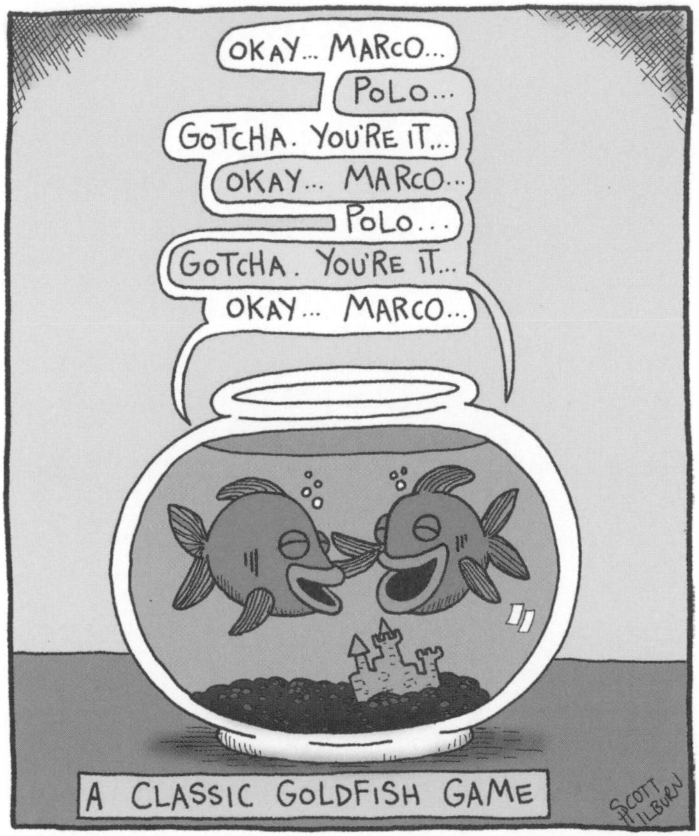
OKAY... MARCO...
POLO...
GOTCHA. YOU'RE IT...
OKAY... MARCO...
POLO...
GOTCHA. YOU'RE IT...
OKAY... MARCO...
A CLASSIC GOLDFISH GAME
SCOTT HILBURN

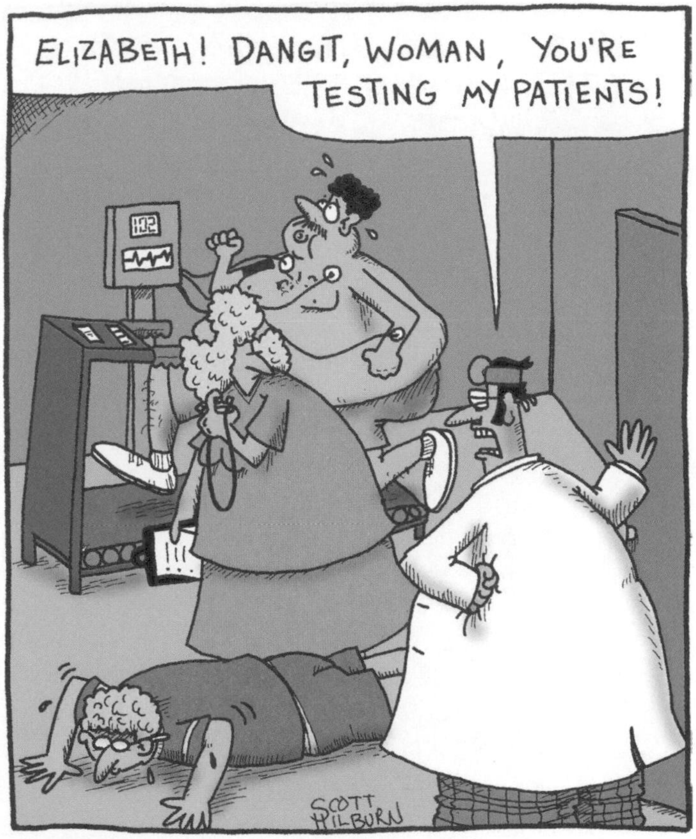
ELIZABETH! DANGIT, WOMAN, YOU'RE TESTING MY PATIENTS!
SCOTT HILBURN

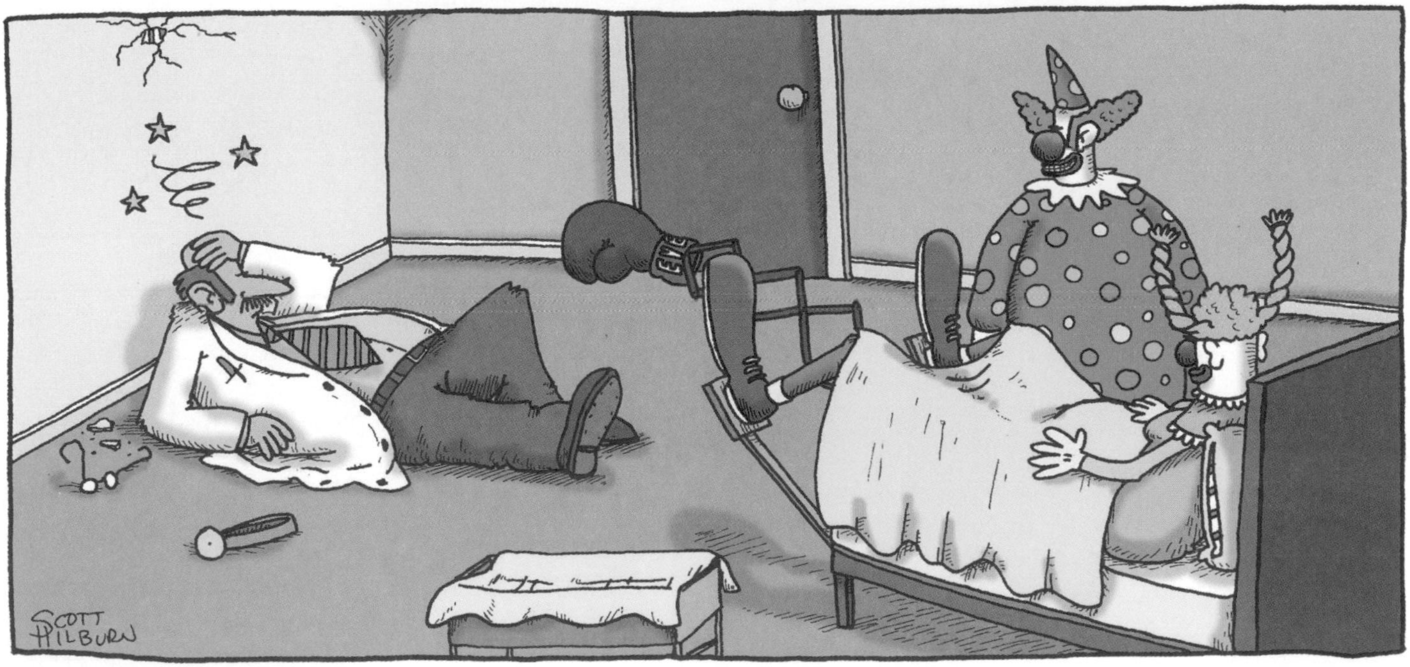
SCOTT HILBURN

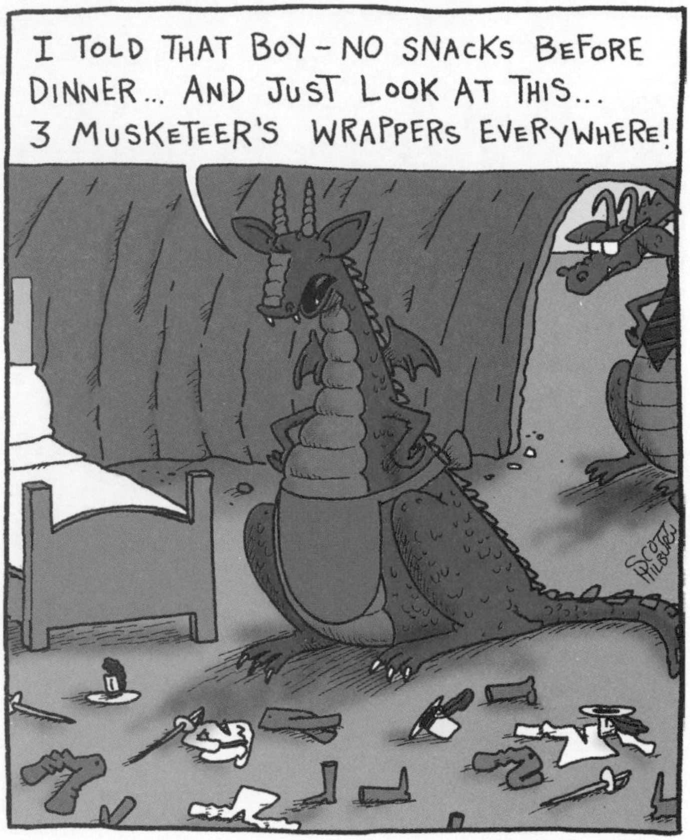
I TOLD THAT BOY - NO SNACKS BEFORE DINNER... AND JUST LOOK AT THIS... 3 MUSKETEER'S WRAPPERS EVERYWHERE!

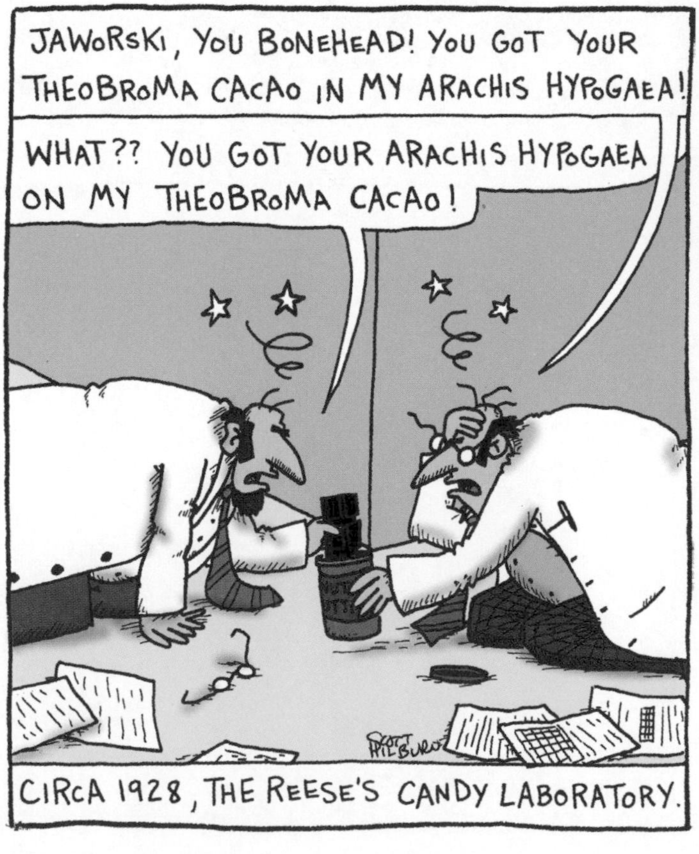
JAWORSKI, YOU BONEHEAD! YOU GOT YOUR THEOBROMA CACAO IN MY ARACHIS HYPOGAEA!
WHAT?? YOU GOT YOUR ARACHIS HYPOGAEA ON MY THEOBROMA CACAO!

CIRCA 1928, THE REESE'S CANDY LABORATORY.

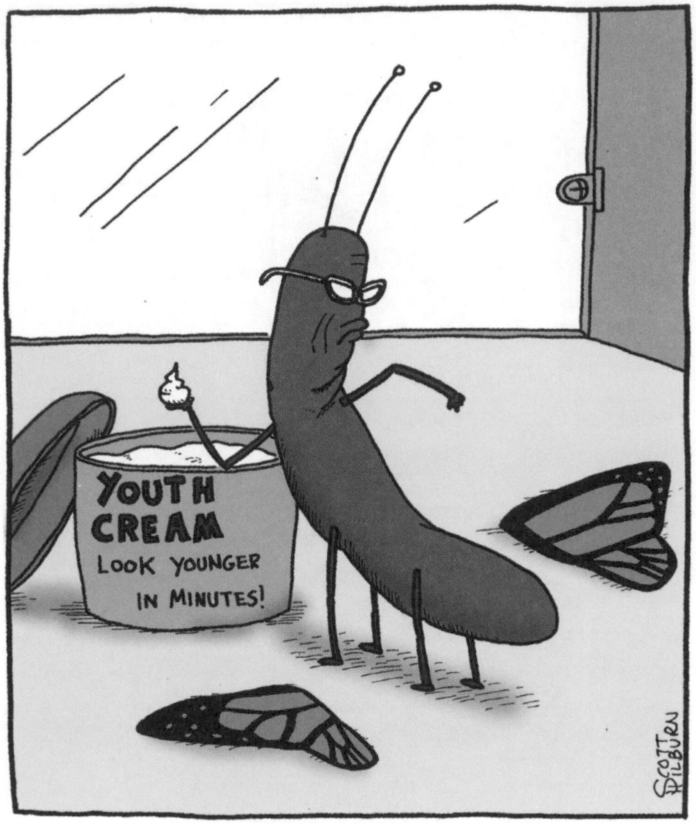
YOUTH CREAM
LOOK YOUNGER IN MINUTES!
SCOTT HILBURN

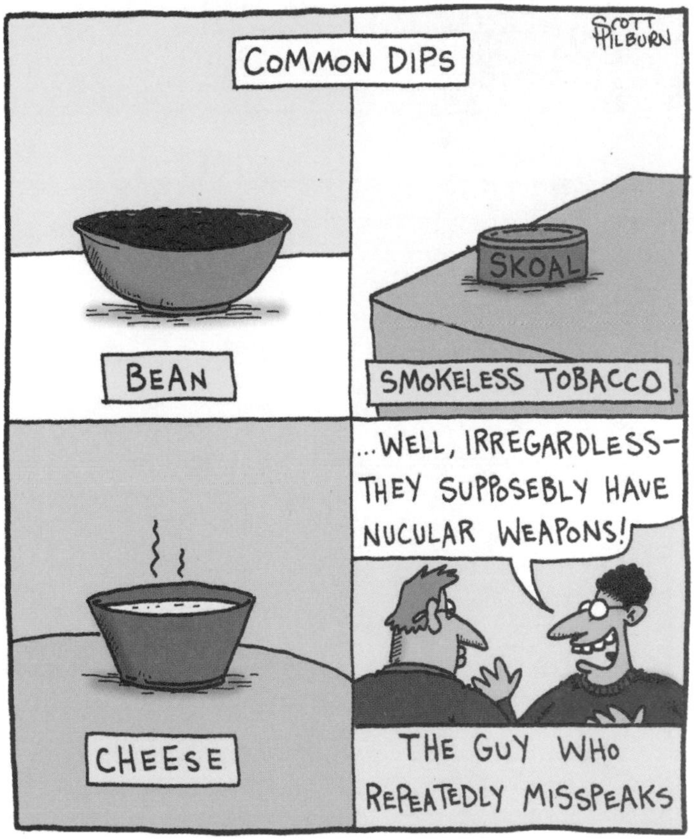
SCOTT HILBURN
COMMON DIPS
BEAN
SKOAL
SMOKELESS TOBACCO
CHEESE
...WELL, IRREGARDLESS— THEY SUPPOSEBLY HAVE NUCULAR WEAPONS!
THE GUY WHO REPEATEDLY MISSPEAKS

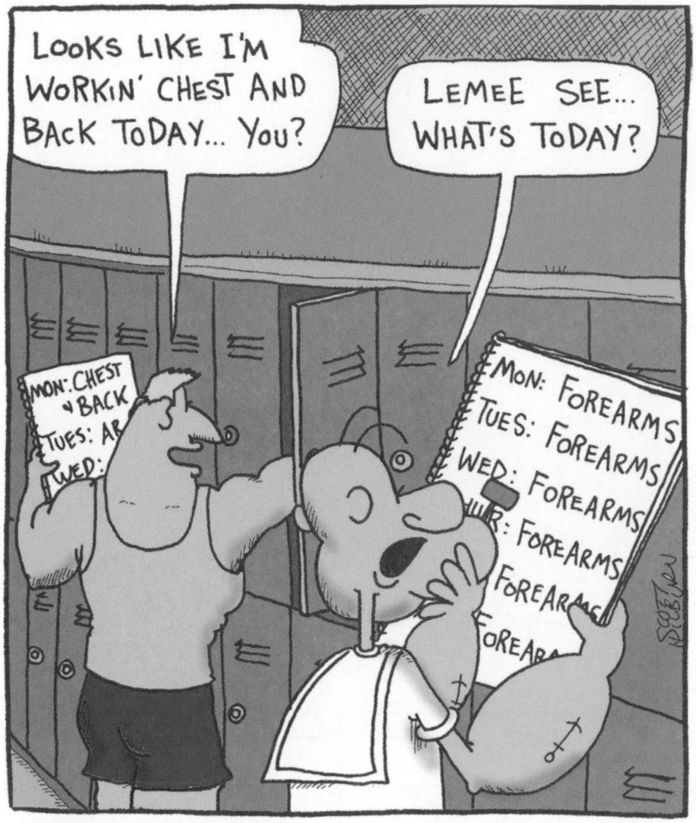
LOOKS LIKE I'M WORKIN' CHEST AND BACK TODAY... YOU?
LEMEE SEE... WHAT'S TODAY?
MON: CHEST & BACK
TUES: AR
WED:
MON: FOREARMS
TUES: FOREARMS
WED: FOREARMS
R: FOREARMS
FOREARMS
FOREA
SCOTT HILBURN

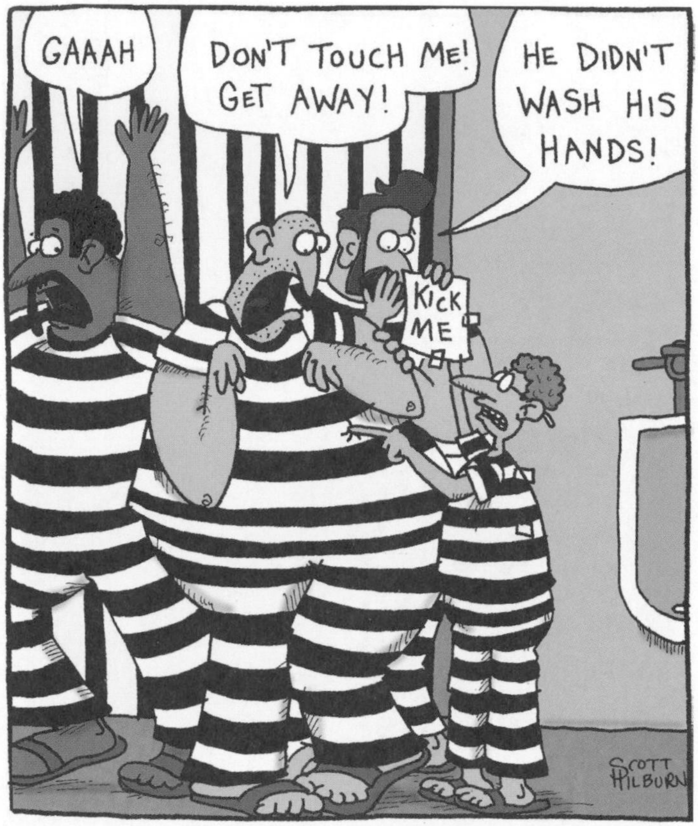
GAAAH
DON'T TOUCH ME! GET AWAY!
HE DIDN'T WASH HIS HANDS!
KICK ME
SCOTT HILBURN

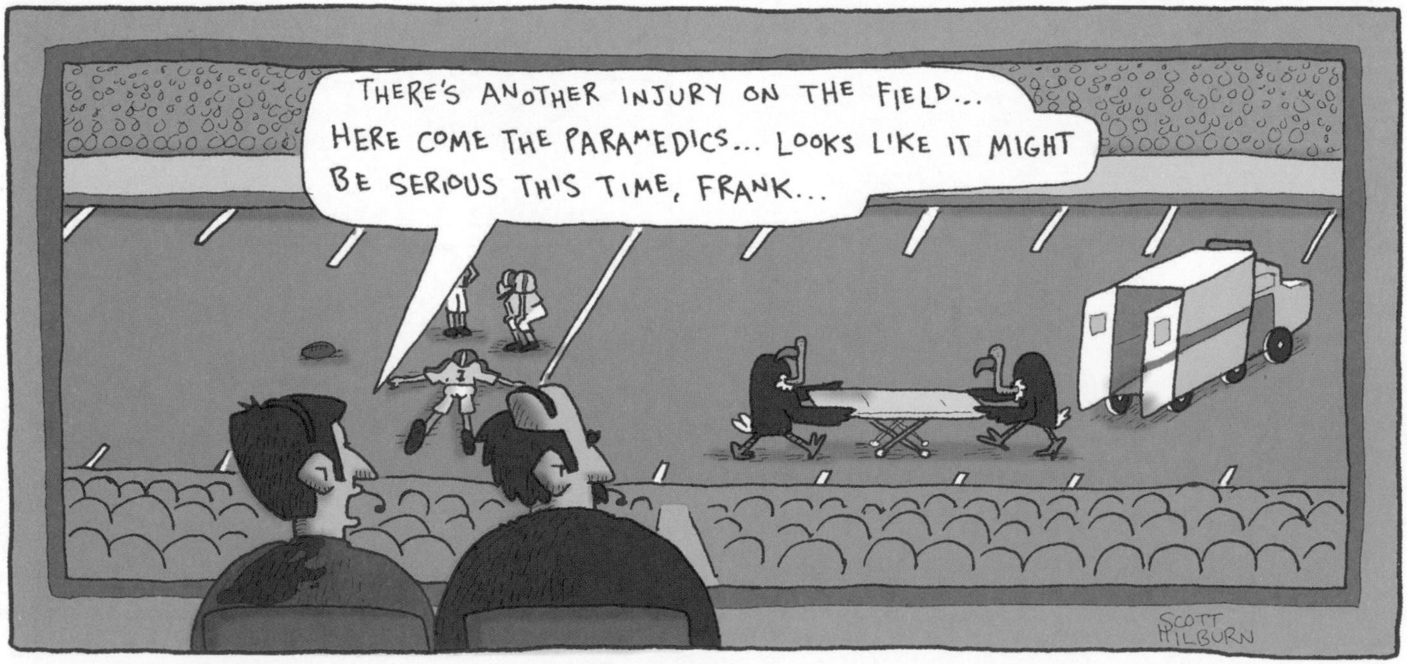
THERE'S ANOTHER INJURY ON THE FIELD... HERE COME THE PARAMEDICS... LOOKS LIKE IT MIGHT BE SERIOUS THIS TIME, FRANK...
SCOTT HILBURN

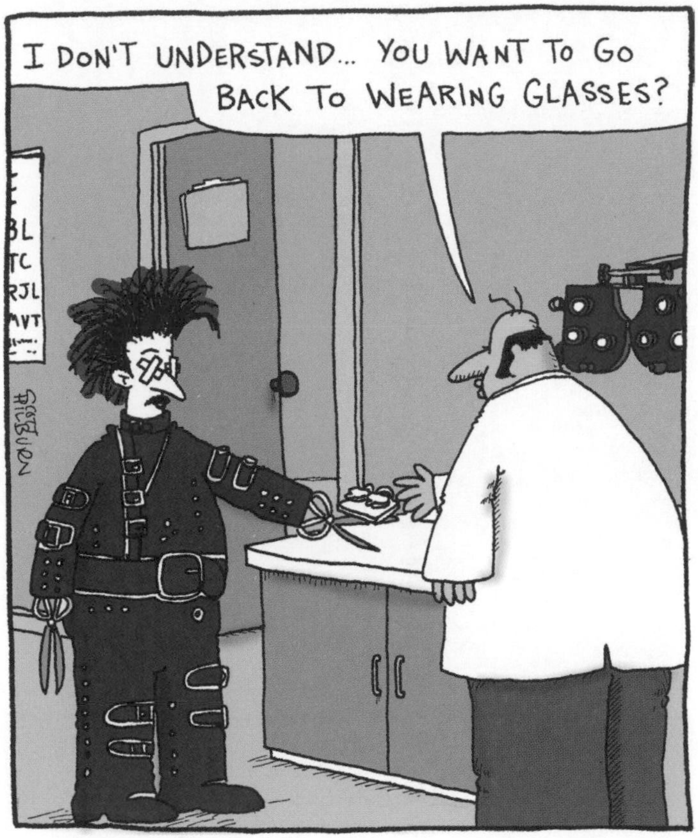
I DON'T UNDERSTAND... YOU WANT TO GO BACK TO WEARING GLASSES?

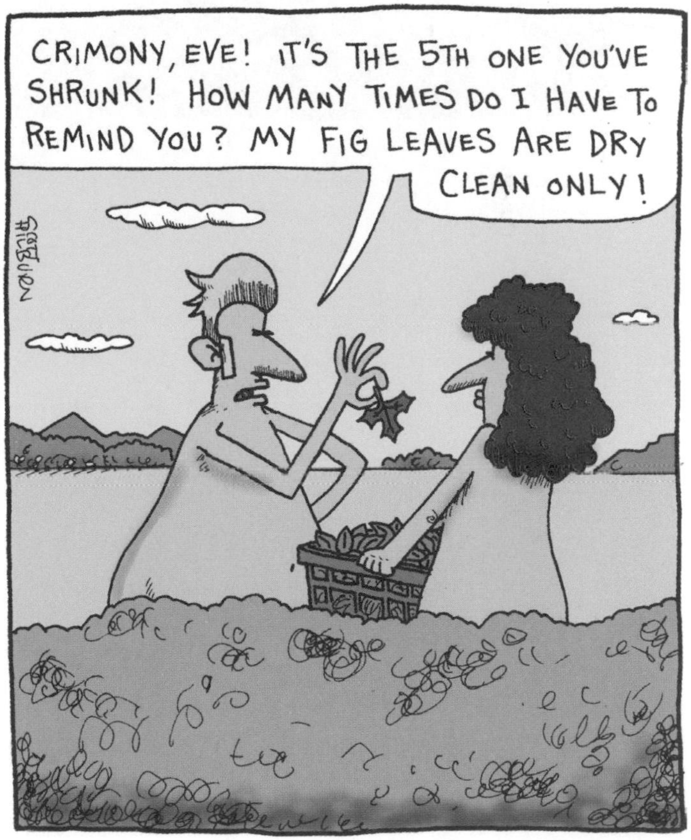
CRIMONY, EVE! IT'S THE 5TH ONE YOU'VE SHRUNK! HOW MANY TIMES DO I HAVE TO REMIND YOU? MY FIG LEAVES ARE DRY CLEAN ONLY!

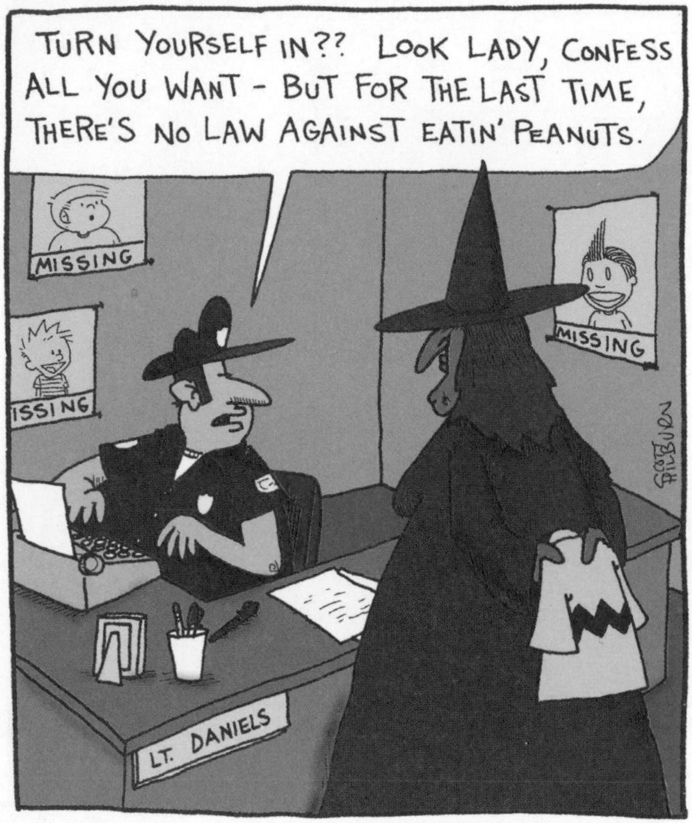
TURN YOURSELF IN?? LOOK LADY, CONFESS ALL YOU WANT - BUT FOR THE LAST TIME, THERE'S NO LAW AGAINST EATIN' PEANUTS.
MISSING
MISSING
ISSING
LT. DANIELS

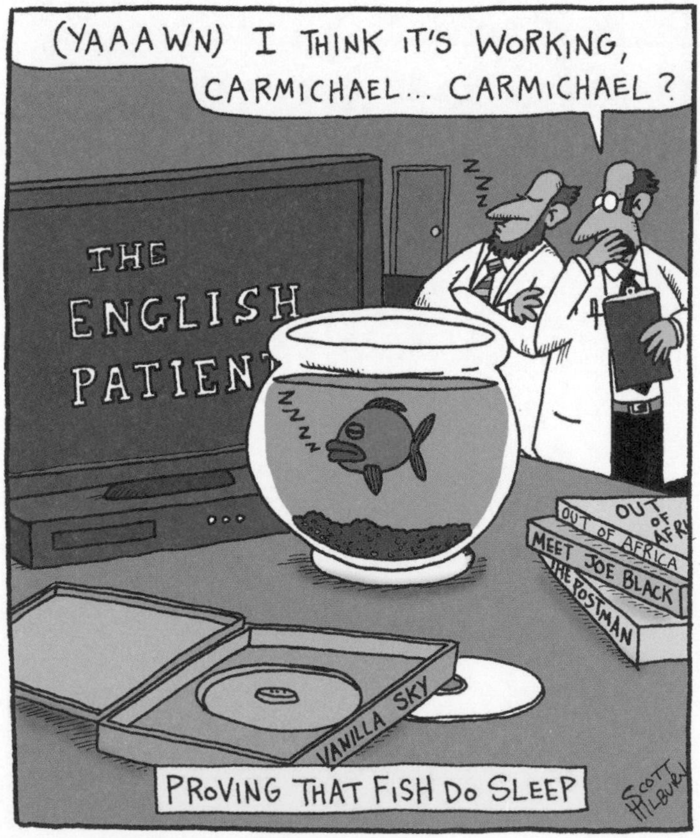
(YAAAWN) I THINK IT'S WORKING, CARMICHAEL... CARMICHAEL?
THE ENGLISH PATIEN
OUT OF AFRICA
MEET JOE BLACK
THE POSTMAN
VANILLA SKY

PROVING THAT FISH DO SLEEP

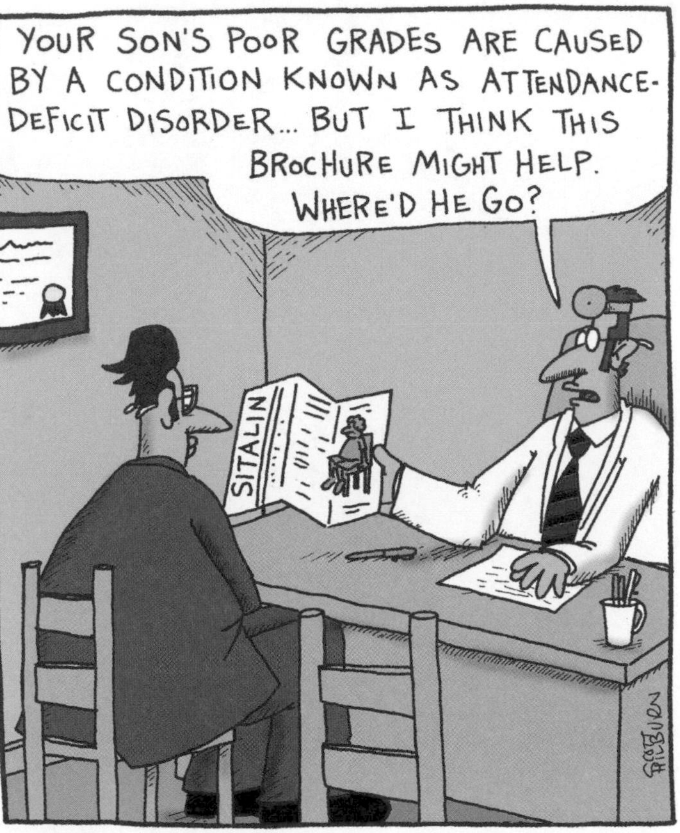
YOUR SON'S POOR GRADES ARE CAUSED BY A CONDITION KNOWN AS ATTENDANCE-DEFICIT DISORDER... BUT I THINK THIS BROCHURE MIGHT HELP. WHERE'D HE GO?
SITALIN

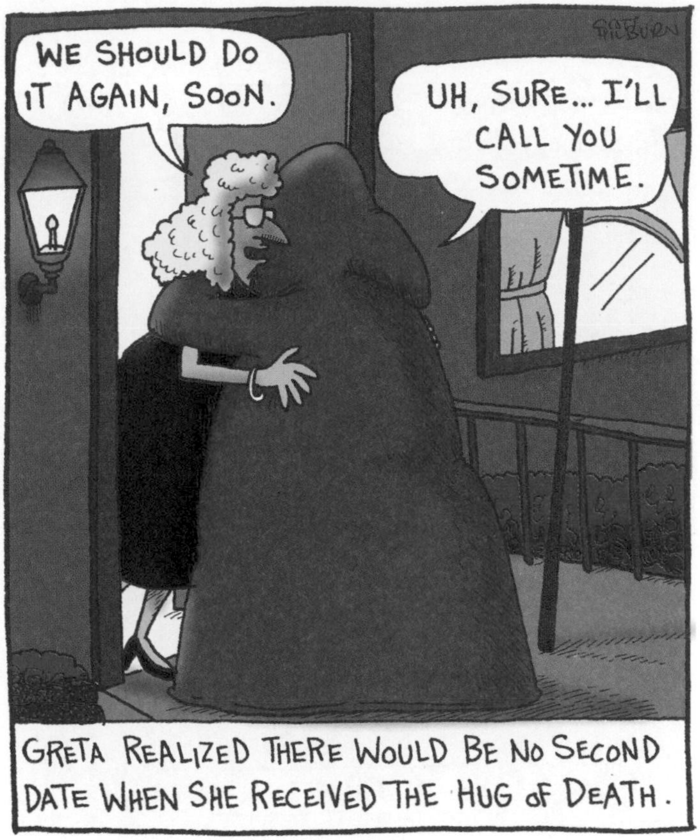
WE SHOULD DO IT AGAIN, SOON.
UH, SURE... I'LL CALL YOU SOMETIME.
GRETA REALIZED THERE WOULD BE NO SECOND DATE WHEN SHE RECEIVED THE HUG OF DEATH.

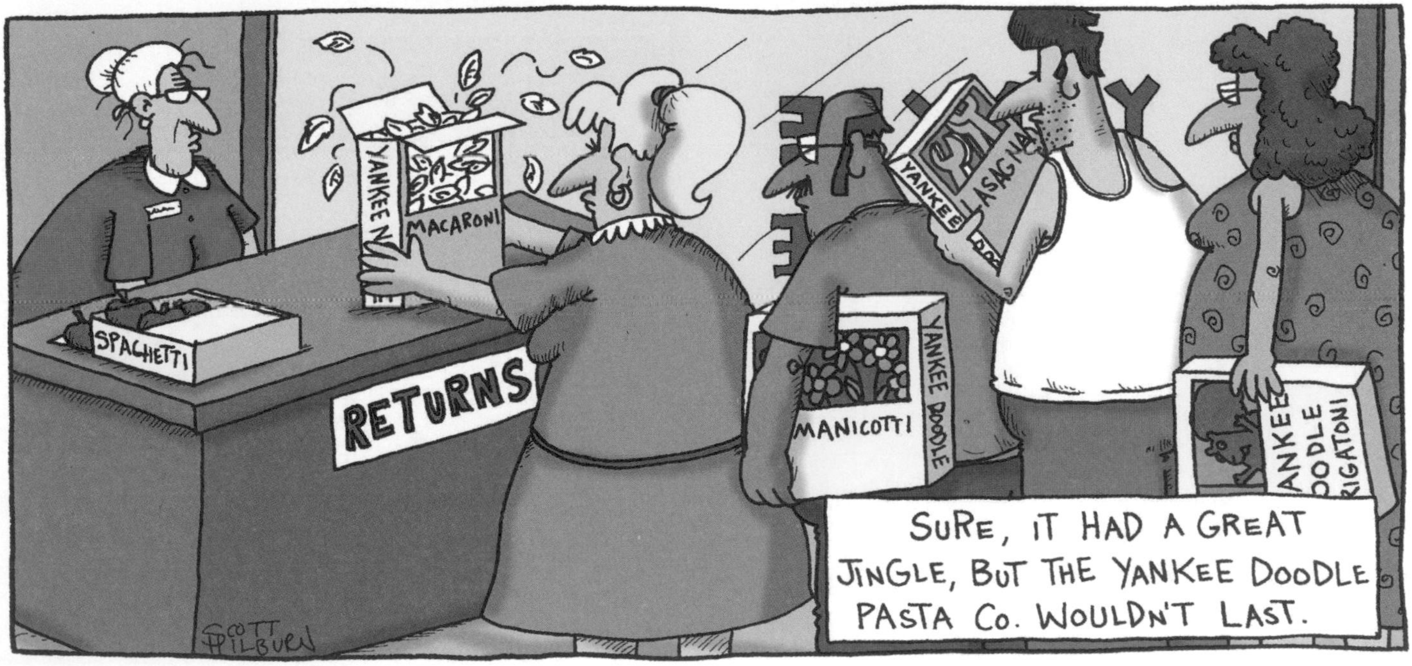
YANKEE N
MACARONI
SPAGHETTI
RETURNS
YANKEE
LASAGNA
MANICOTTI
YANKEE DOODLE
SURE, IT HAD A GREAT JINGLE, BUT THE YANKEE DOODLE PASTA CO. WOULDN'T LAST.

OH, GREAT... IT'S A SUBSTITUTE.
Poultry History- Ms. Eggbeaters
Chpt. 1:
Who came first?
SCOTT HILBURN
LIFE IN GRADE A

SCOTT HILBURN

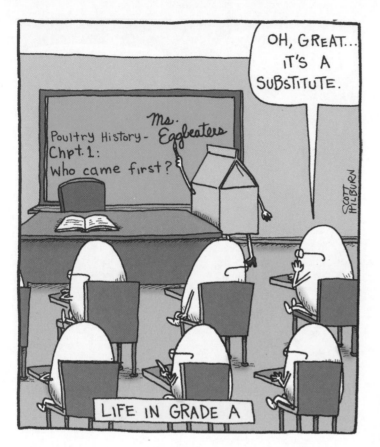

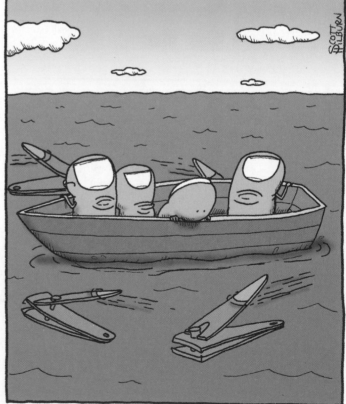

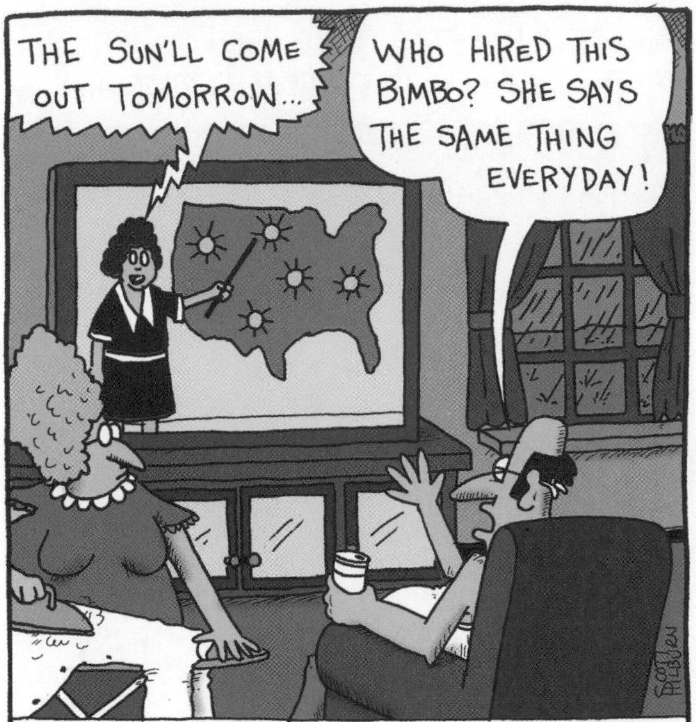
THE SUN'LL COME OUT TOMORROW...
WHO HIRED THIS BIMBO? SHE SAYS THE SAME THING EVERYDAY!
SCOTT HILBURN

PROSPEROUS IN OTHER MEDIA, ANNIE'S WEATHER CAREER PROVED LESS SUCCESSFUL.

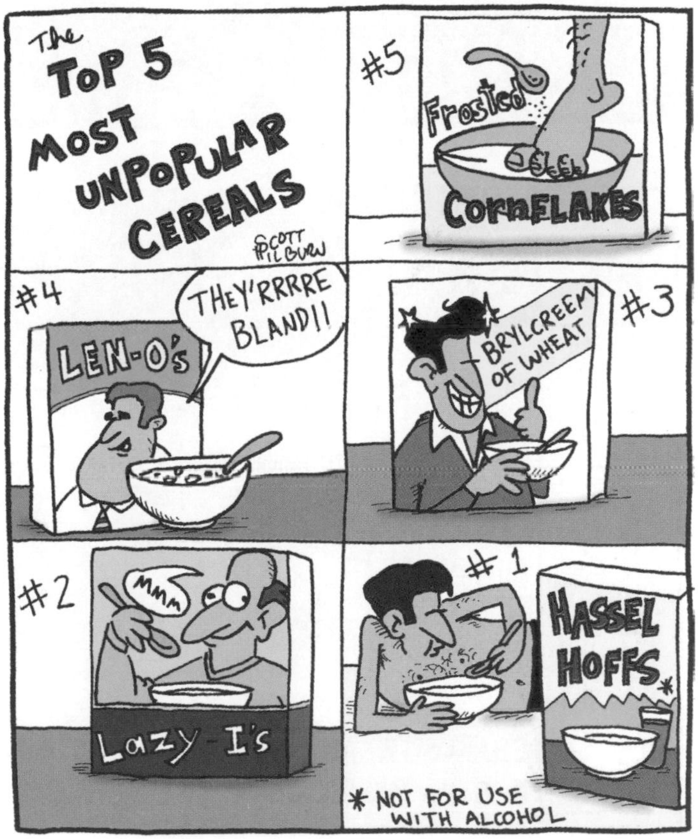
The TOP 5 MOST UNPOPULAR CEREALS
SCOTT HILBURN
#5
Frosted CornFLAKES
#4
LEN-O's
THEY'RRRRE BLAND!!
#3
BRYLCREEM OF WHEAT
#2
MMM
Lazy-I's
#1
HASSEL HOFFS*
* NOT FOR USE WITH ALCOHOL

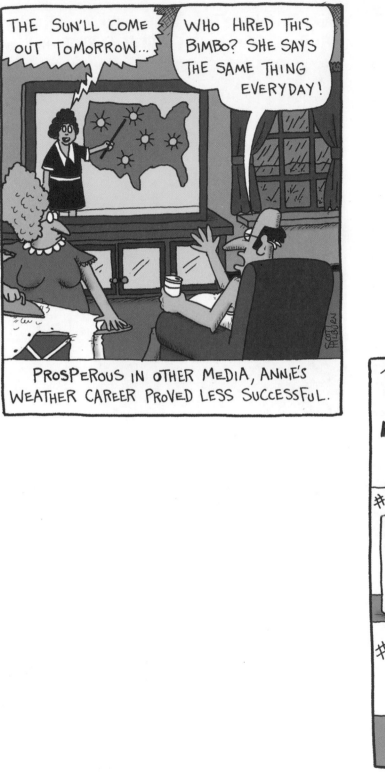

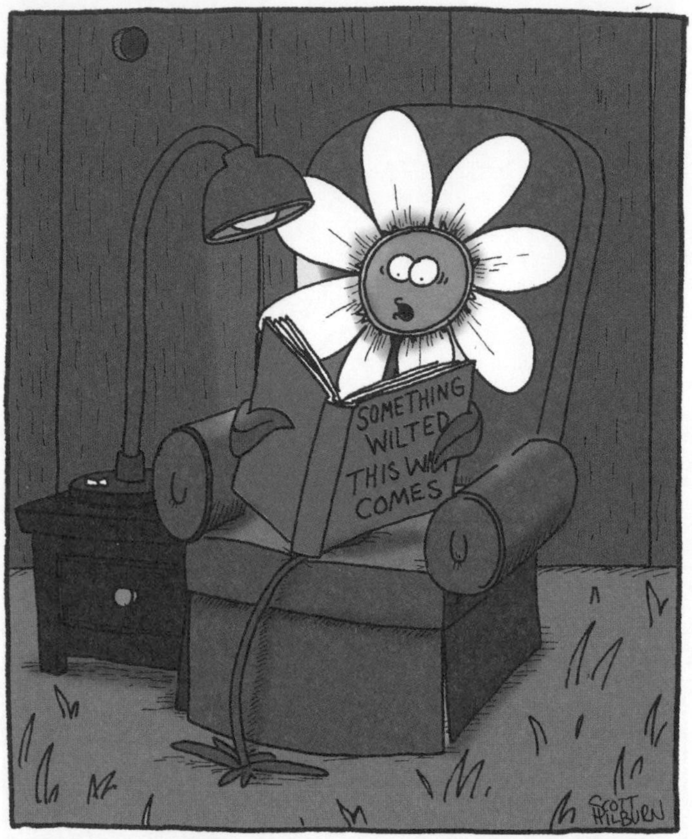
SOMETHING WILTED THIS
COMES
SCOTT HILBURN

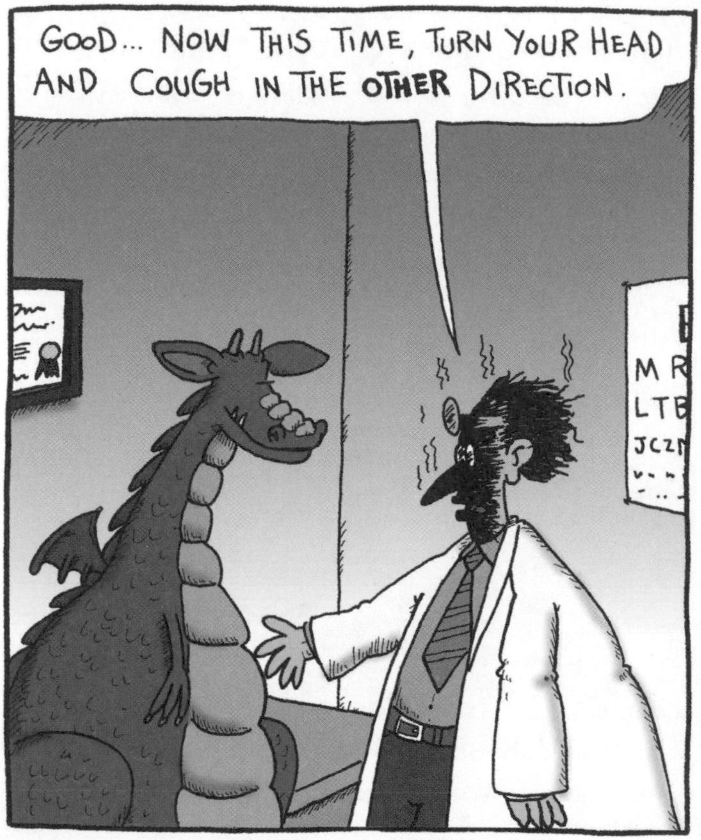
GOOD... NOW THIS TIME, TURN YOUR HEAD AND COUGH IN THE **OTHER** DIRECTION.

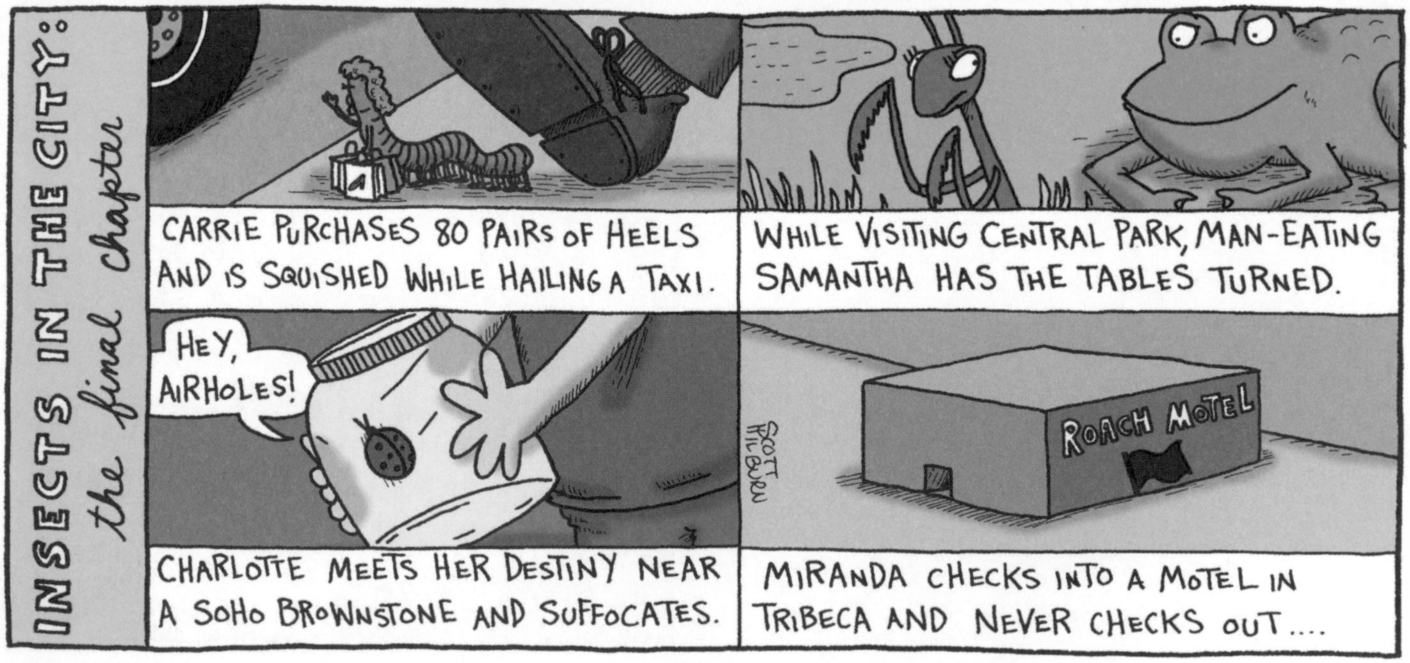
INSECTS IN THE CITY: *the final chapter*
CARRIE PURCHASES 80 PAIRS OF HEELS AND IS SQUISHED WHILE HAILING A TAXI.
WHILE VISITING CENTRAL PARK, MAN-EATING SAMANTHA HAS THE TABLES TURNED.
HEY, AIRHOLES!
CHARLOTTE MEETS HER DESTINY NEAR A SOHO BROWNSTONE AND SUFFOCATES.
SCOTT HILBURN
ROACH MOTEL
MIRANDA CHECKS INTO A MOTEL IN TRIBECA AND NEVER CHECKS OUT....

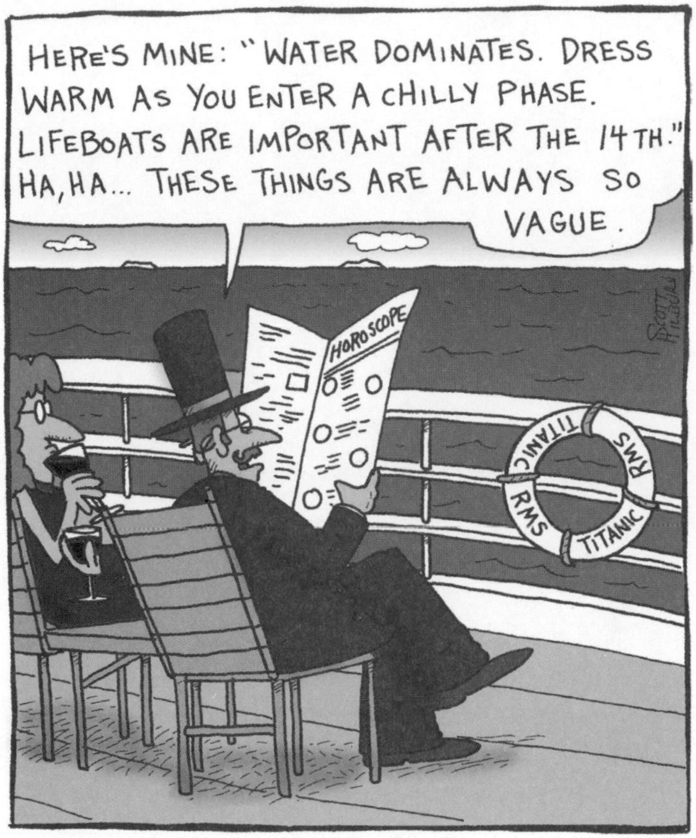
HERE'S MINE: "WATER DOMINATES. DRESS WARM AS YOU ENTER A CHILLY PHASE. LIFEBOATS ARE IMPORTANT AFTER THE 14TH." HA, HA... THESE THINGS ARE ALWAYS SO VAGUE.
HOROSCOPE
RMS TITANIC
RMS TITANIC
SCOTT HILBURN

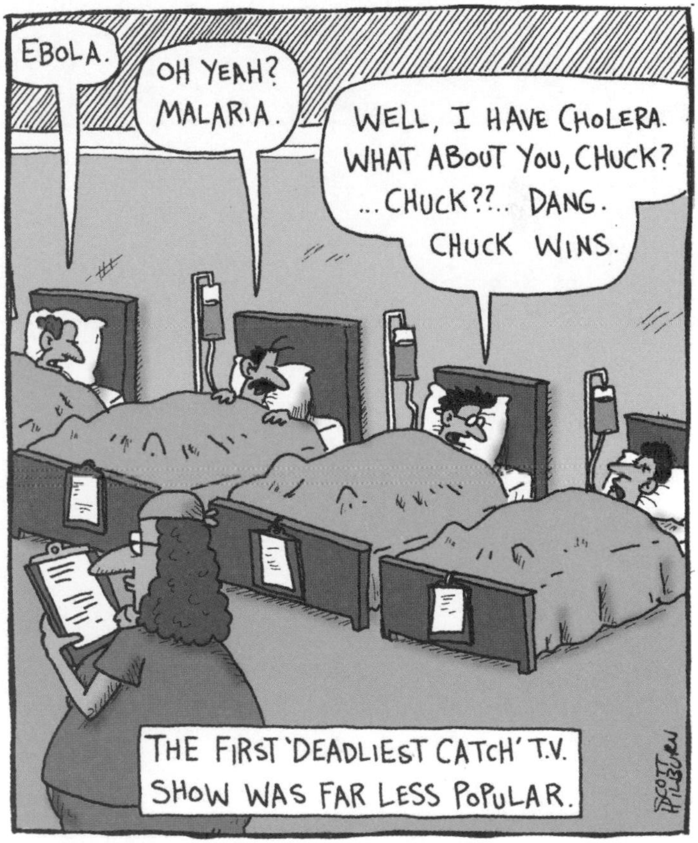
EBOLA.
OH YEAH? MALARIA.
WELL, I HAVE CHOLERA. WHAT ABOUT YOU, CHUCK? ...CHUCK??.. DANG. CHUCK WINS.
SCOTT HILBURN

THE FIRST 'DEADLIEST CATCH' T.V. SHOW WAS FAR LESS POPULAR.

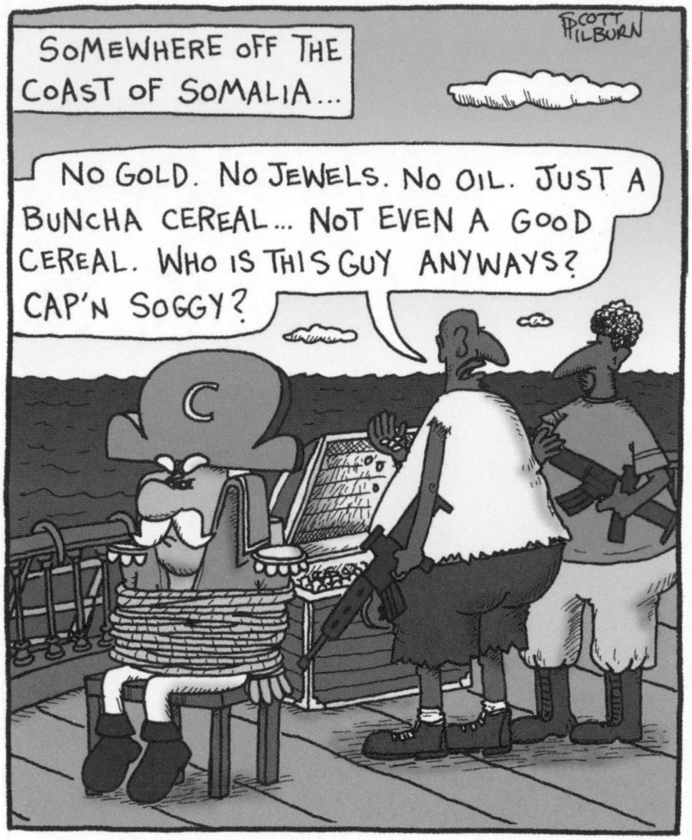
SCOTT HILBURN
SOMEWHERE OFF THE COAST OF SOMALIA...
NO GOLD. NO JEWELS. NO OIL. JUST A BUNCHA CEREAL... NOT EVEN A GOOD CEREAL. WHO IS THIS GUY ANYWAYS? CAP'N SOGGY?

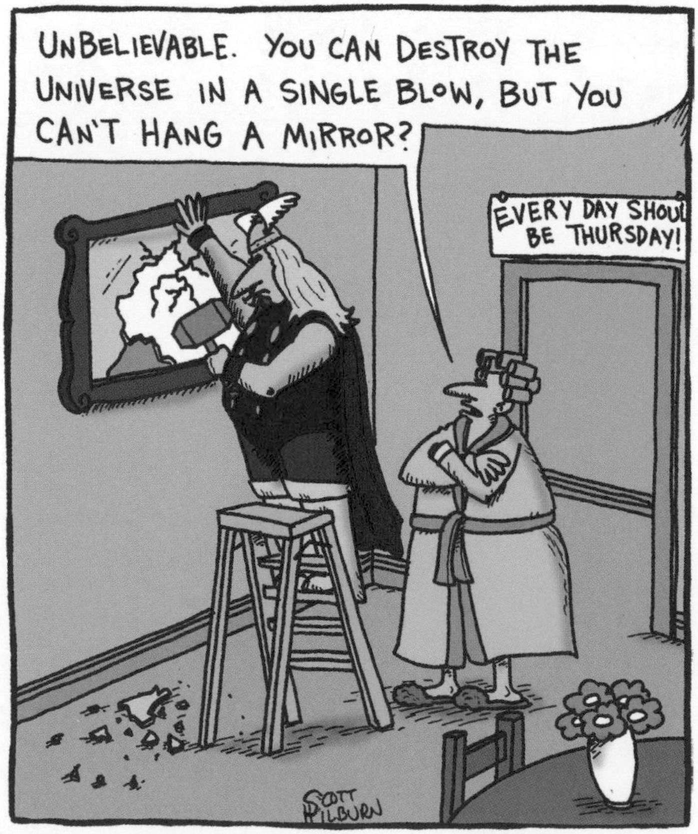
UNBELIEVABLE. YOU CAN DESTROY THE UNIVERSE IN A SINGLE BLOW, BUT YOU CAN'T HANG A MIRROR?
EVERY DAY SHOU BE THURSDAY!
SCOTT HILBURN

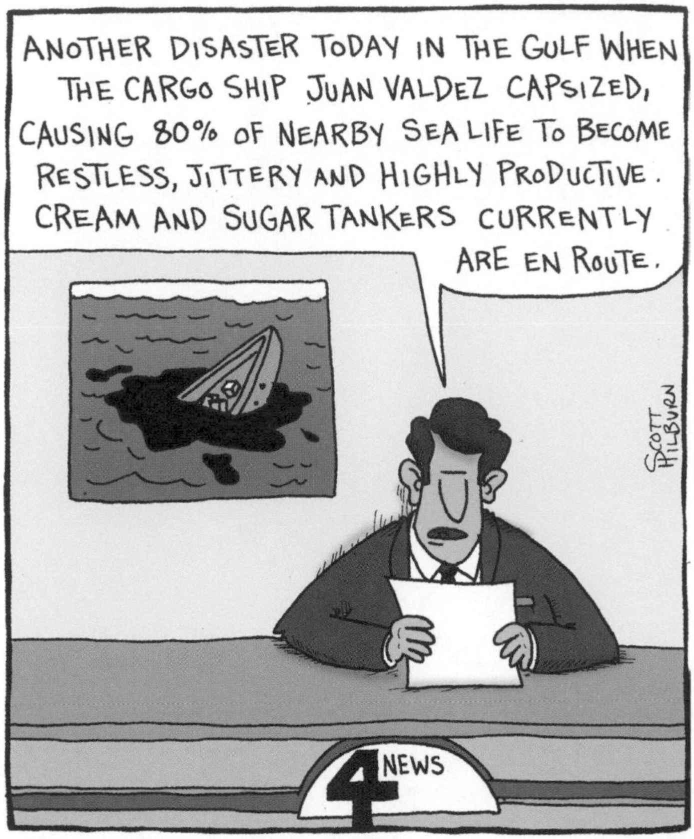
ANOTHER DISASTER TODAY IN THE GULF WHEN THE CARGO SHIP JUAN VALDEZ CAPSIZED, CAUSING 80% OF NEARBY SEA LIFE TO BECOME RESTLESS, JITTERY AND HIGHLY PRODUCTIVE. CREAM AND SUGAR TANKERS CURRENTLY ARE EN ROUTE.
SCOTT HILBURN
4 NEWS

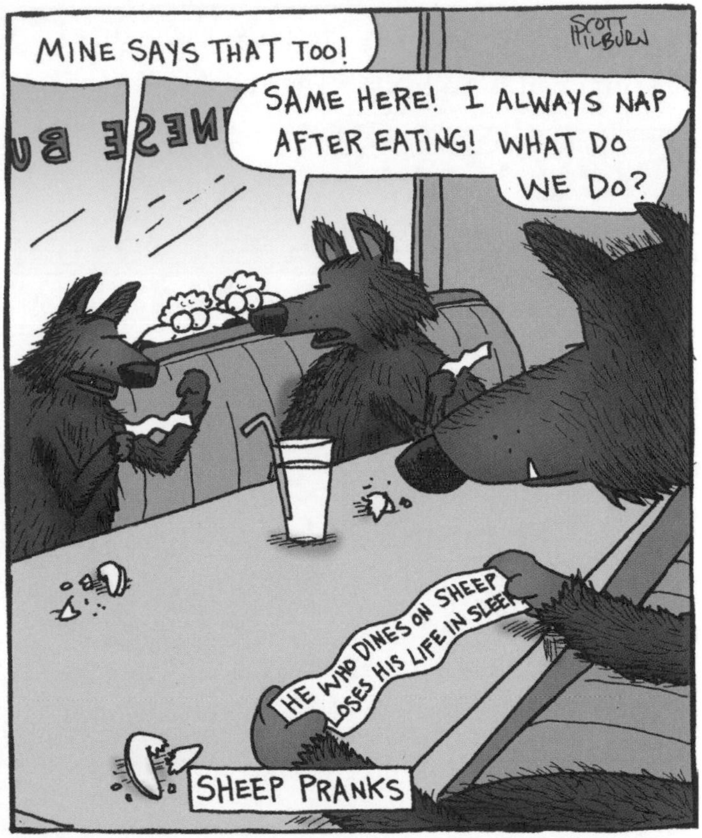
MINE SAYS THAT TOO!
SAME HERE! I ALWAYS NAP AFTER EATING! WHAT DO WE DO?
SCOTT HILBURN
HE WHO DINES ON SHEEP LOSES HIS LIFE IN SLEEP
SHEEP PRANKS

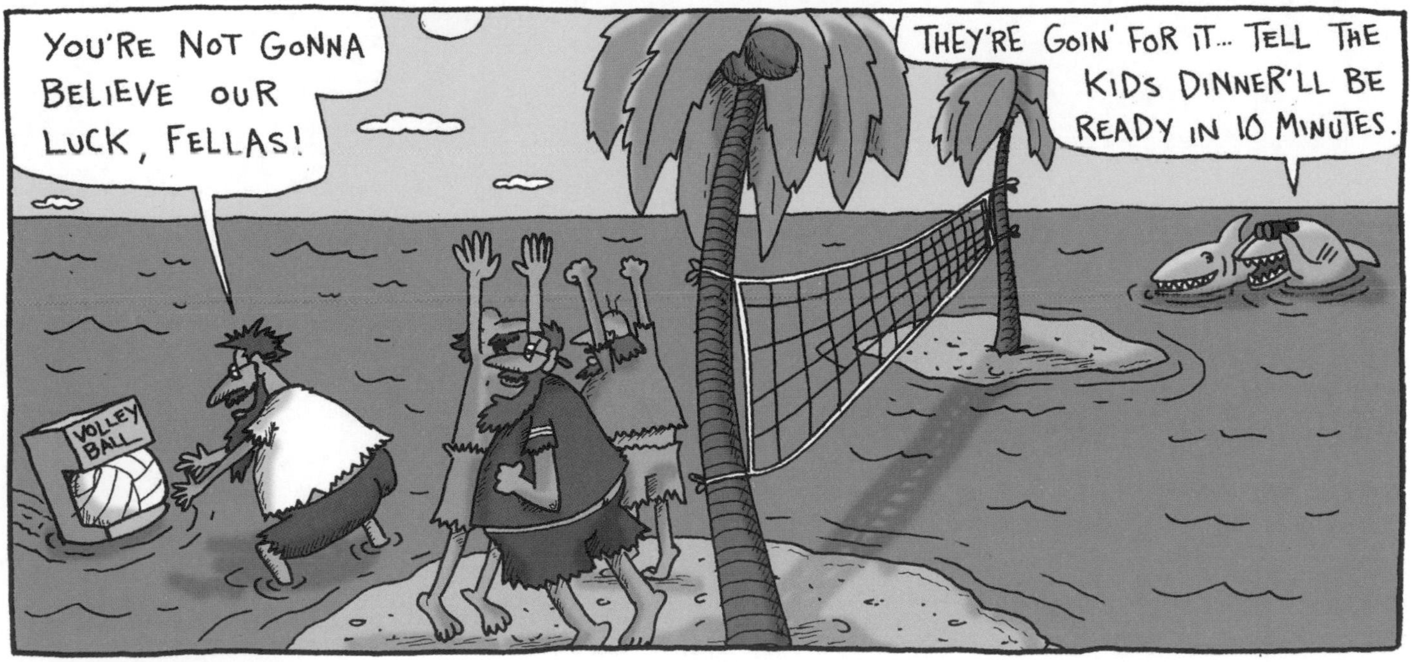
YOU'RE NOT GONNA BELIEVE OUR LUCK, FELLAS!
THEY'RE GOIN' FOR IT... TELL THE KIDS DINNER'LL BE READY IN 10 MINUTES.
VOLLEY BALL

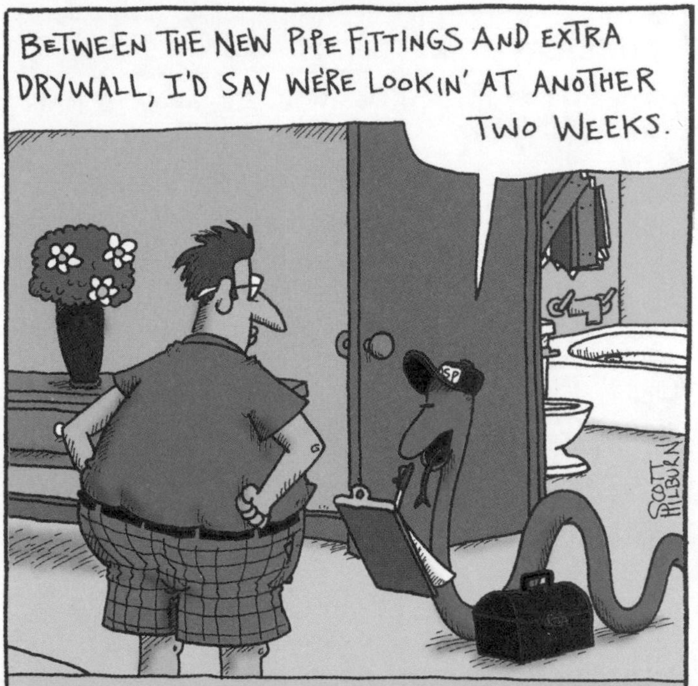
BETWEEN THE NEW PIPE FITTINGS AND EXTRA DRYWALL, I'D SAY WE'RE LOOKIN' AT ANOTHER TWO WEEKS.
SP
SCOTT HILBURN

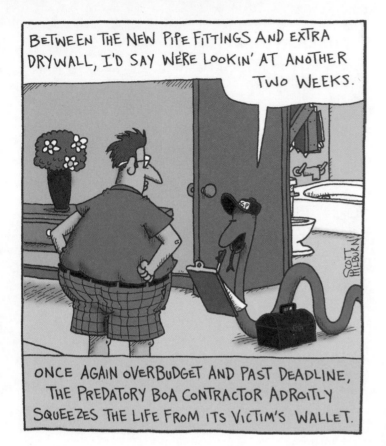

ONCE AGAIN OVERBUDGET AND PAST DEADLINE, THE PREDATORY BOA CONTRACTOR ADROITLY SQUEEZES THE LIFE FROM ITS VICTIM'S WALLET.

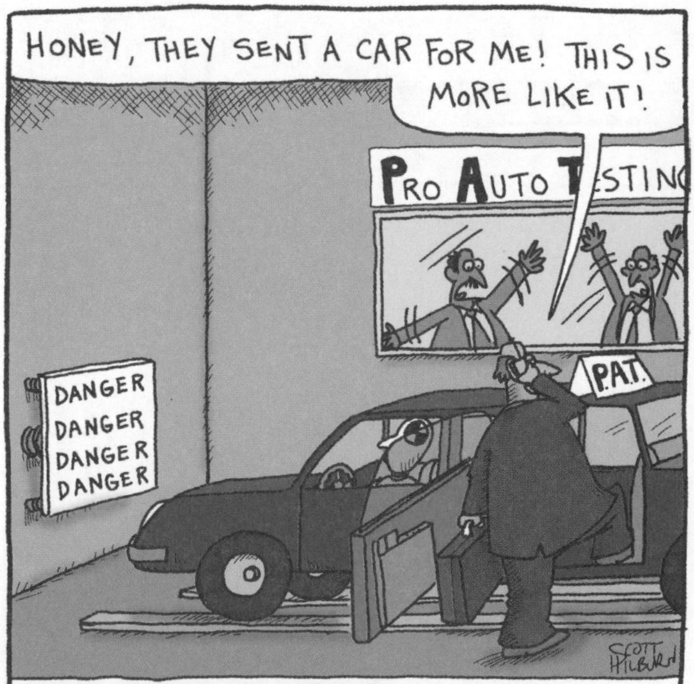
HONEY, THEY SENT A CAR FOR ME! THIS IS MORE LIKE IT!
PRO AUTO
P.A.T.
DANGER
DANGER
DANGER
DANGER
SCOTT HILBURN

DISORIENTED WHILE TALKING ON HIS CELL PHONE, PAT MADE A SERIES OF WRONG TURNS IN THE UNFAMILIAR OFFICE PARK.

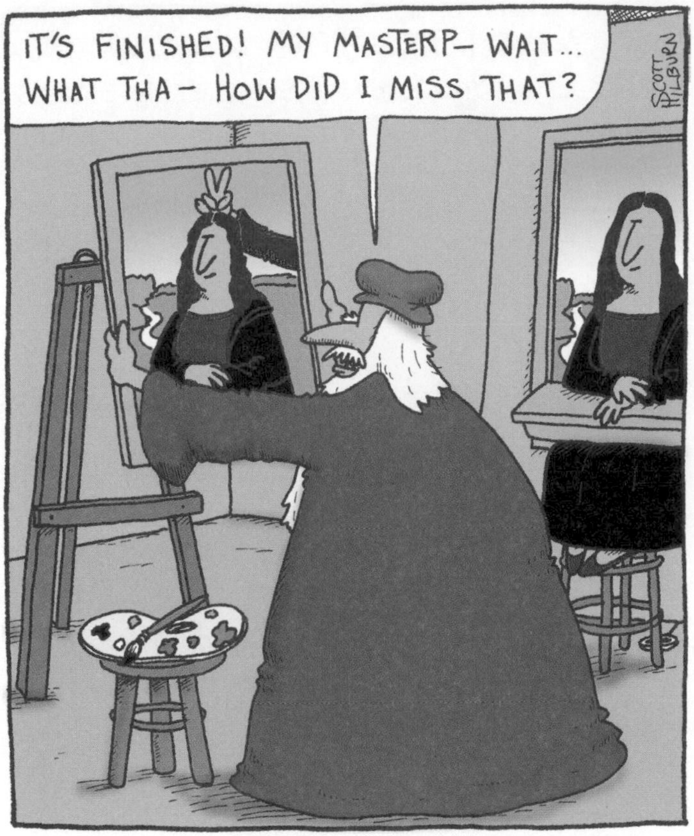
IT'S FINISHED! MY MASTERP– WAIT... WHAT THA– HOW DID I MISS THAT?
SCOTT HILBURN

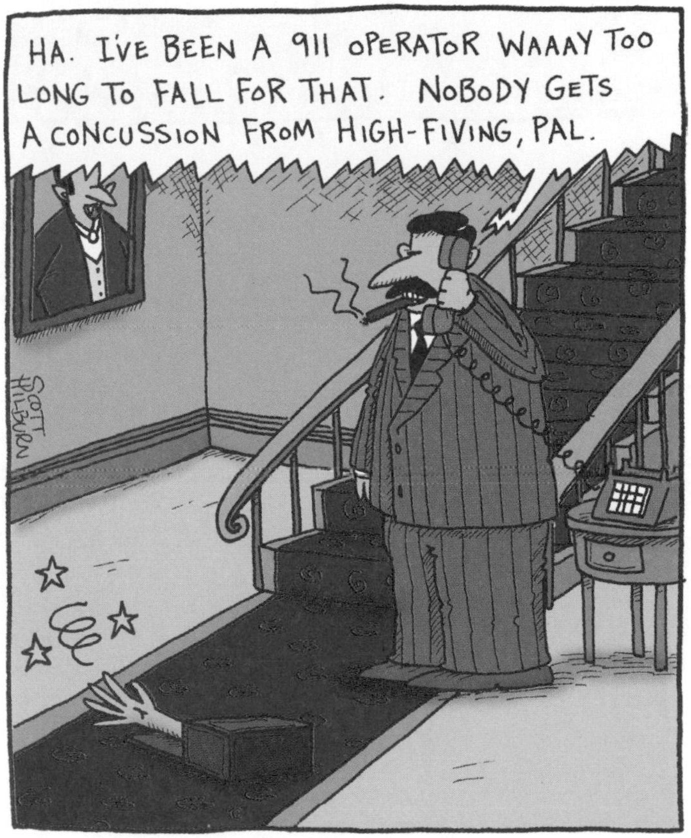
HA. I'VE BEEN A 911 OPERATOR WAAAY TOO LONG TO FALL FOR THAT. NOBODY GETS A CONCUSSION FROM HIGH-FIVING, PAL.
SCOTT HILBURN

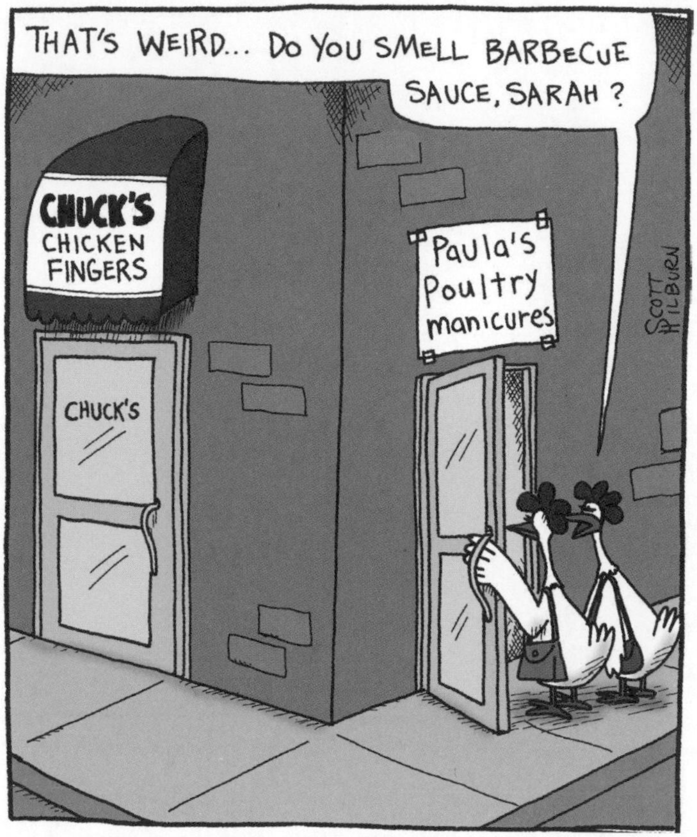
THAT'S WEIRD... DO YOU SMELL BARBECUE SAUCE, SARAH?
CHUCK'S CHICKEN FINGERS
CHUCK'S
Paula's Poultry manicures
SCOTT HILBURN

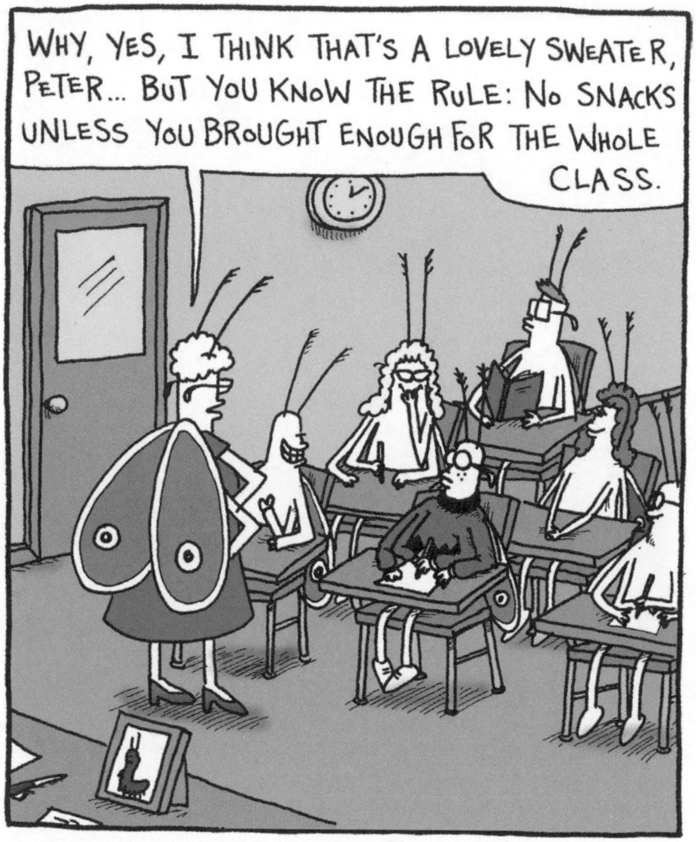
WHY, YES, I THINK THAT'S A LOVELY SWEATER, PETER... BUT YOU KNOW THE RULE: NO SNACKS UNLESS YOU BROUGHT ENOUGH FOR THE WHOLE CLASS.

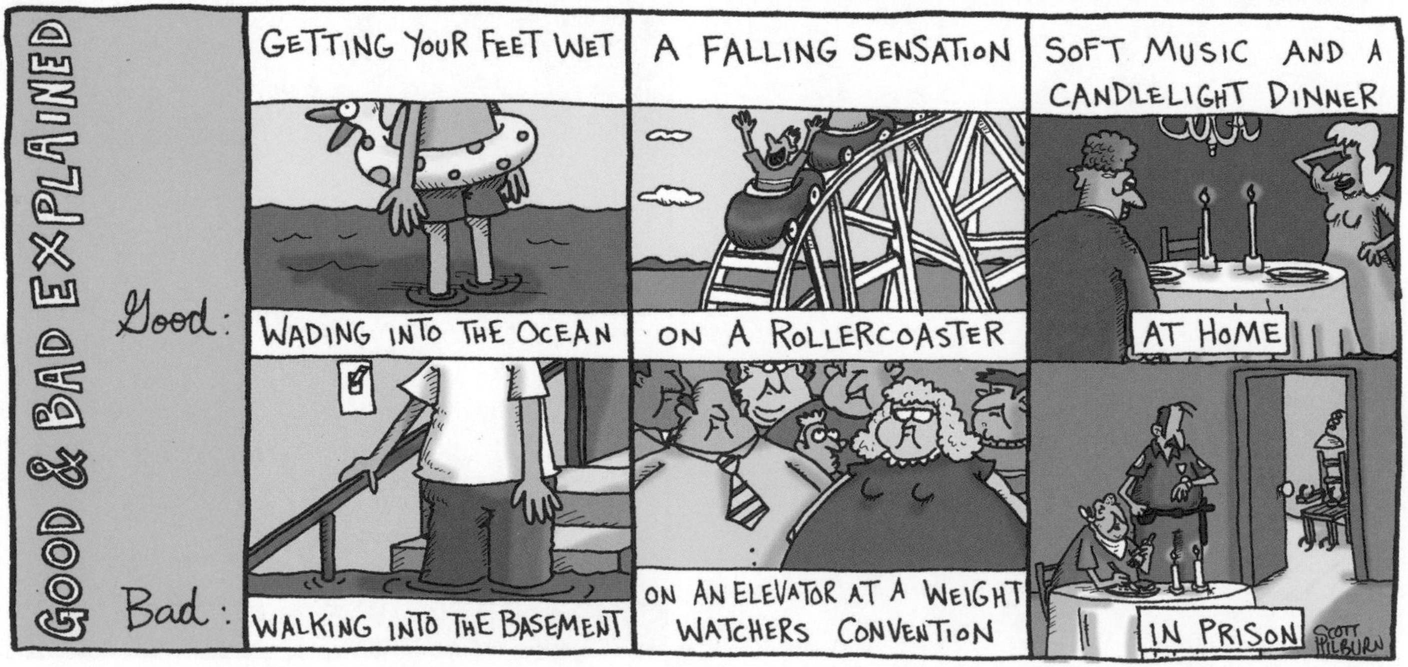
GOOD & BAD EXPLAINED
Good:
Bad:
GETTING YOUR FEET WET
WADING INTO THE OCEAN
WALKING INTO THE BASEMENT
A FALLING SENSATION
ON A ROLLERCOASTER
ON AN ELEVATOR AT A WEIGHT WATCHERS CONVENTION
SOFT MUSIC AND A CANDLELIGHT DINNER
AT HOME
IN PRISON
SCOTT HILBURN

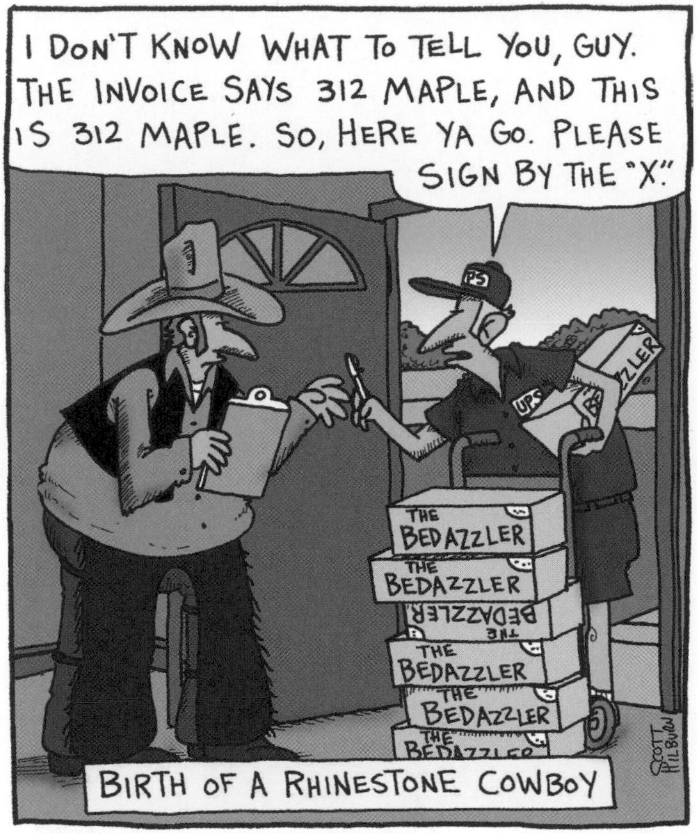
I DON'T KNOW WHAT TO TELL YOU, GUY. THE INVOICE SAYS 312 MAPLE, AND THIS IS 312 MAPLE. SO, HERE YA GO. PLEASE SIGN BY THE "X."
UPS
UPS
THE BEDAZZLER
THE BEDAZZLER
THE BEDAZZLER
THE BEDAZZLER
THE BEDAZZLER
SCOTT HILBURN
BIRTH OF A RHINESTONE COWBOY

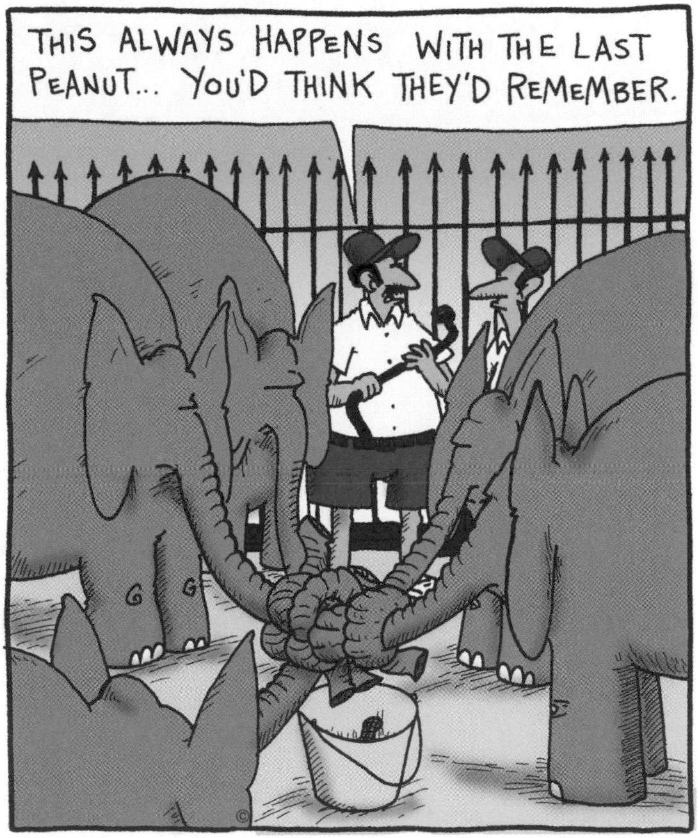
THIS ALWAYS HAPPENS WITH THE LAST PEANUT... YOU'D THINK THEY'D REMEMBER.

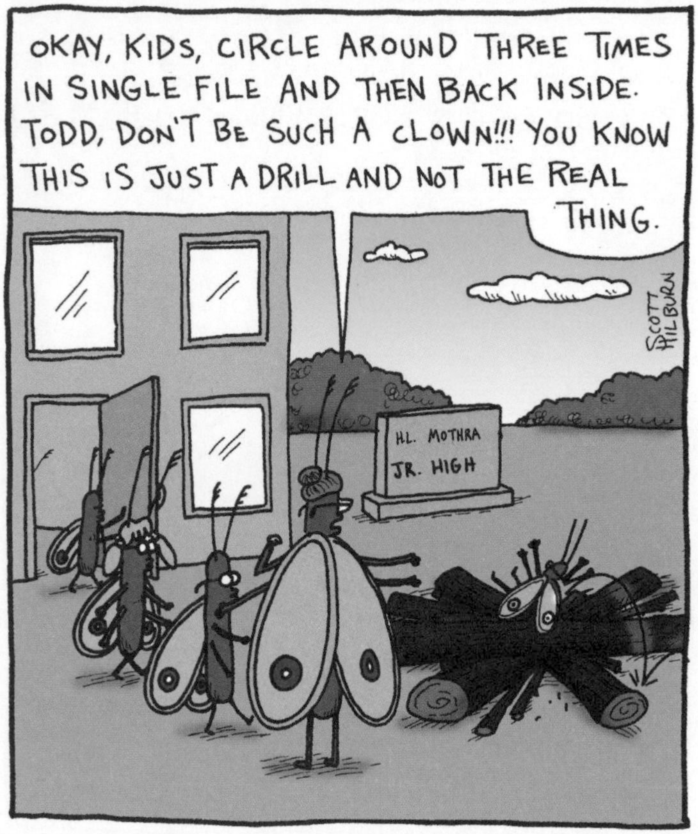
OKAY, KIDS, CIRCLE AROUND THREE TIMES IN SINGLE FILE AND THEN BACK INSIDE. TODD, DON'T BE SUCH A CLOWN!!! YOU KNOW THIS IS JUST A DRILL AND NOT THE REAL THING.
H.L. MOTHRA JR. HIGH
SCOTT HILBURN

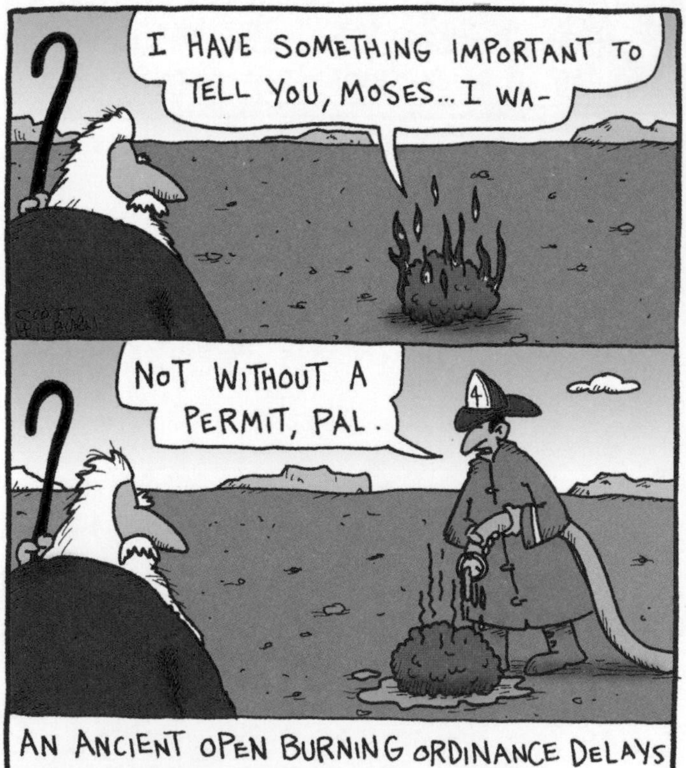
I HAVE SOMETHING IMPORTANT TO TELL YOU, MOSES... I WA-
NOT WITHOUT A PERMIT, PAL.
4
AN ANCIENT OPEN BURNING ORDINANCE DELAYS MOSES FROM FREEING HIS PEOPLE

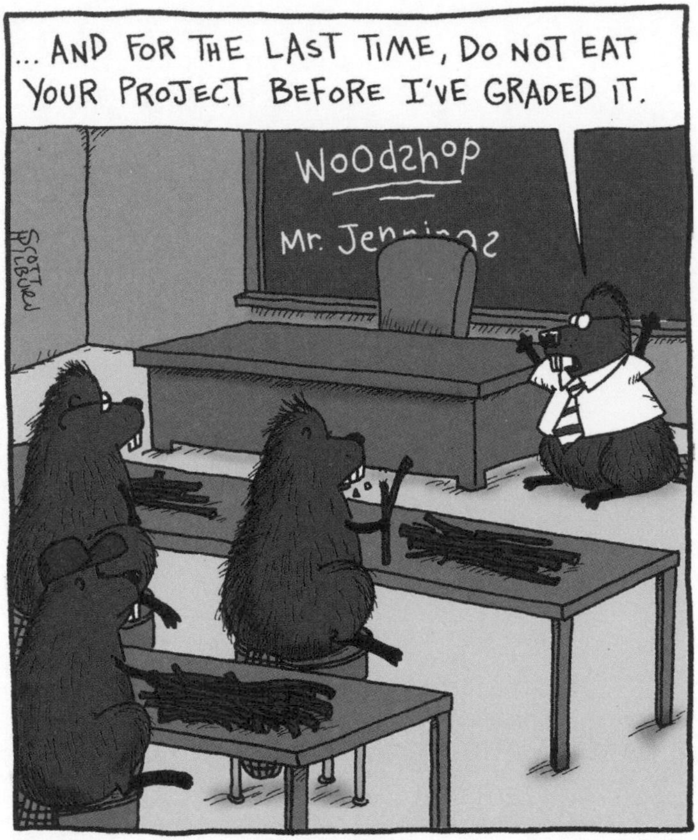
... AND FOR THE LAST TIME, DO NOT EAT YOUR PROJECT BEFORE I'VE GRADED IT.
WOODSHOP
Mr. Jennings
SCOTT HILBURN

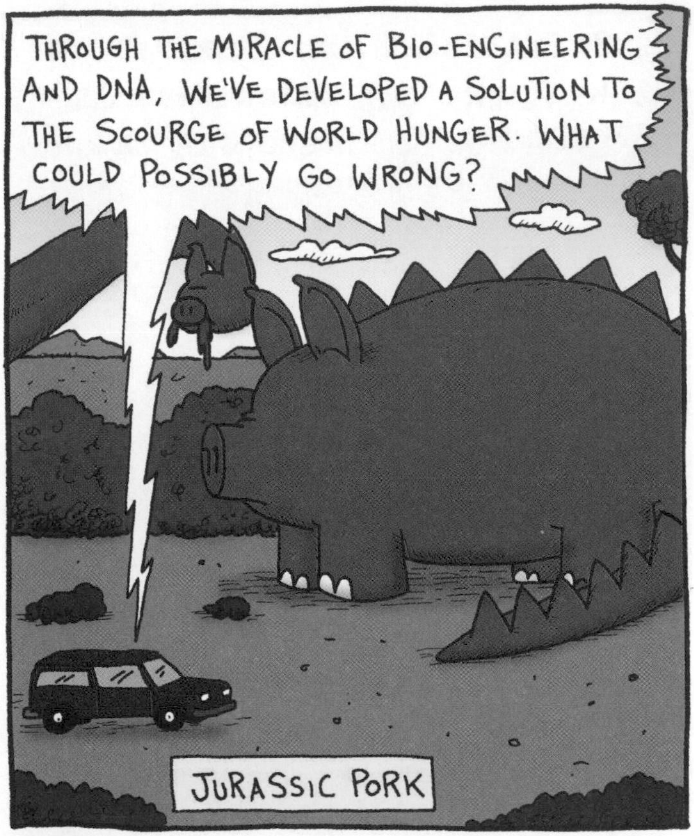
THROUGH THE MIRACLE OF BIO-ENGINEERING AND DNA, WE'VE DEVELOPED A SOLUTION TO THE SCOURGE OF WORLD HUNGER. WHAT COULD POSSIBLY GO WRONG?

JURASSIC PORK

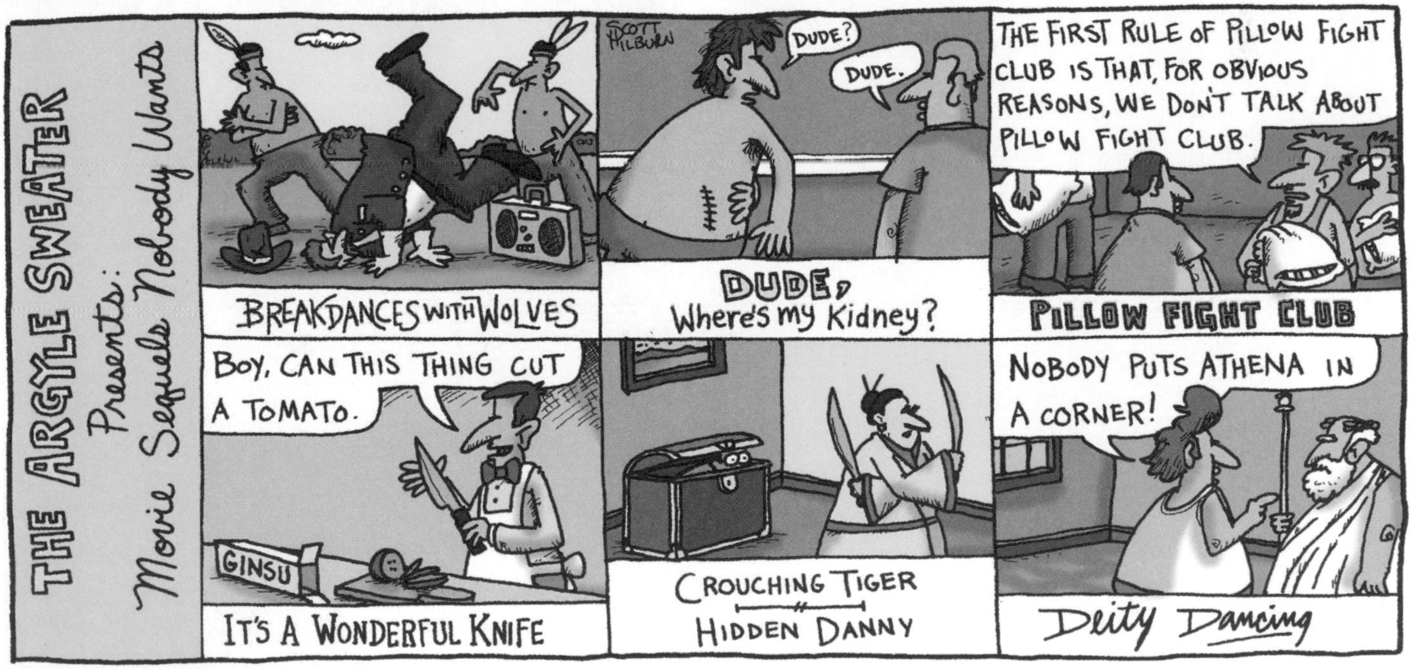
THE ARGYLE SWEATER
Presents:
Movie Sequels Nobody Wants
BREAKDANCES WITH WOLVES
SCOTT HILBURN
DUDE?
DUDE.
DUDE, Where's my Kidney?
THE FIRST RULE OF PILLOW FIGHT CLUB IS THAT, FOR OBVIOUS REASONS, WE DON'T TALK ABOUT PILLOW FIGHT CLUB.
PILLOW FIGHT CLUB
BOY, CAN THIS THING CUT A TOMATO.
GINSU
IT'S A WONDERFUL KNIFE
CROUCHING TIGER HIDDEN DANNY
NOBODY PUTS ATHENA IN A CORNER!
Deity Dancing

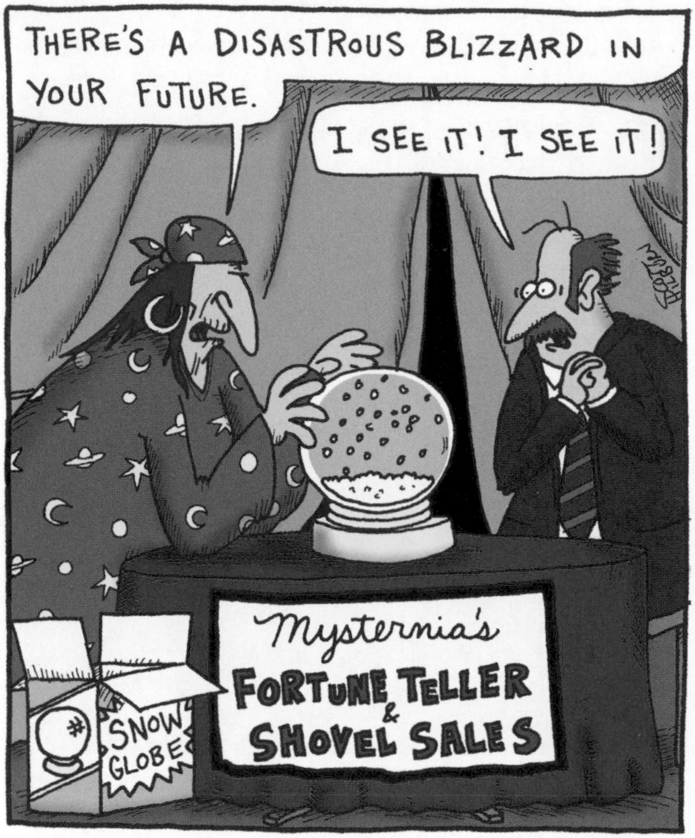
THERE'S A DISASTROUS BLIZZARD IN YOUR FUTURE.
I SEE IT! I SEE IT!
Mysternia's
FORTUNE TELLER & SHOVEL SALES
SNOW GLOBE

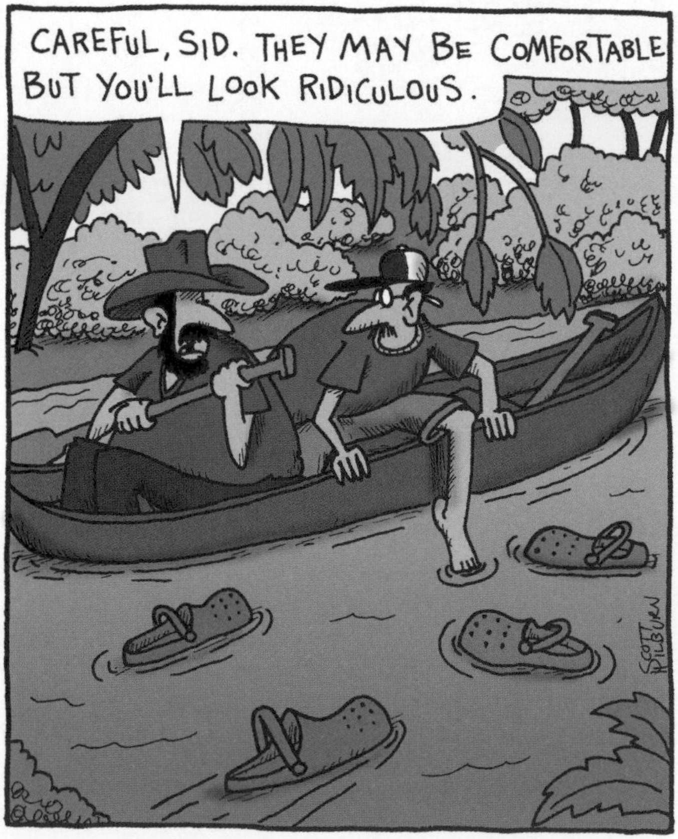
CAREFUL, SID. THEY MAY BE COMFORTABLE BUT YOU'LL LOOK RIDICULOUS.
SCOTT HILBURN

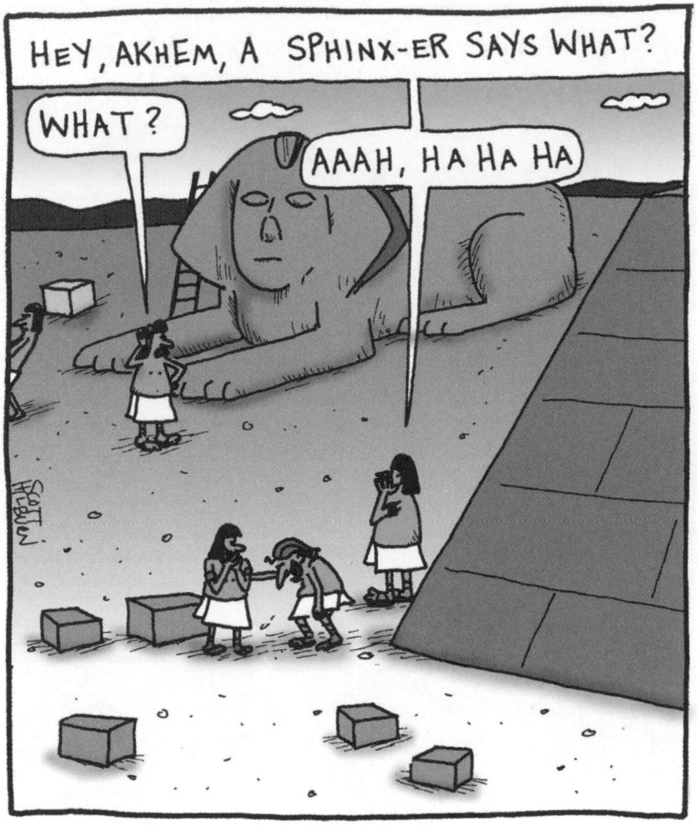
HEY, AKHEM, A SPHINX-ER SAYS WHAT?
WHAT?
AAAH, HA HA HA

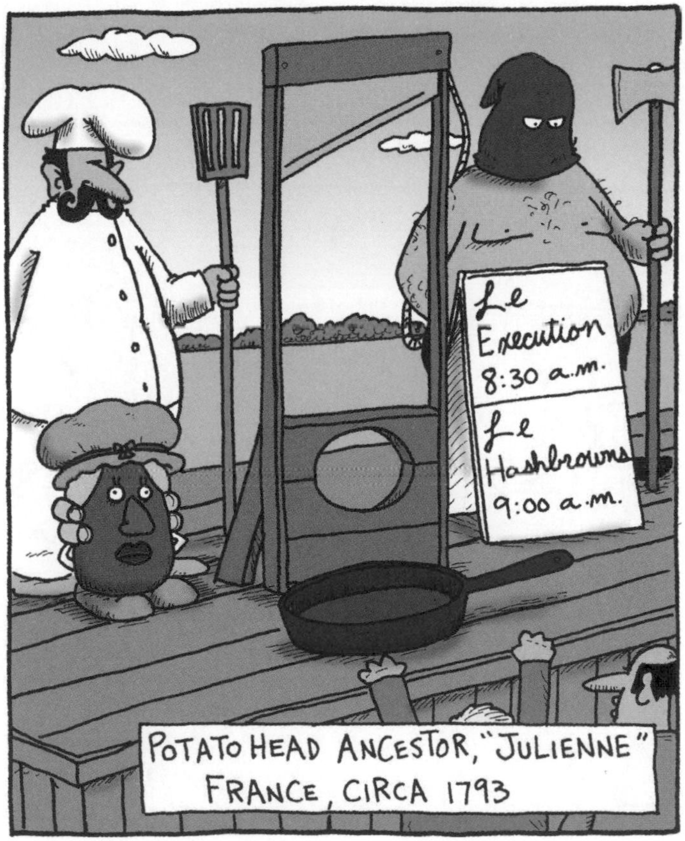
Le Execution 8:30 a.m.
Le Hashbrowns 9:00 a.m.
POTATO HEAD ANCESTOR, "JULIENNE"
FRANCE, CIRCA 1793

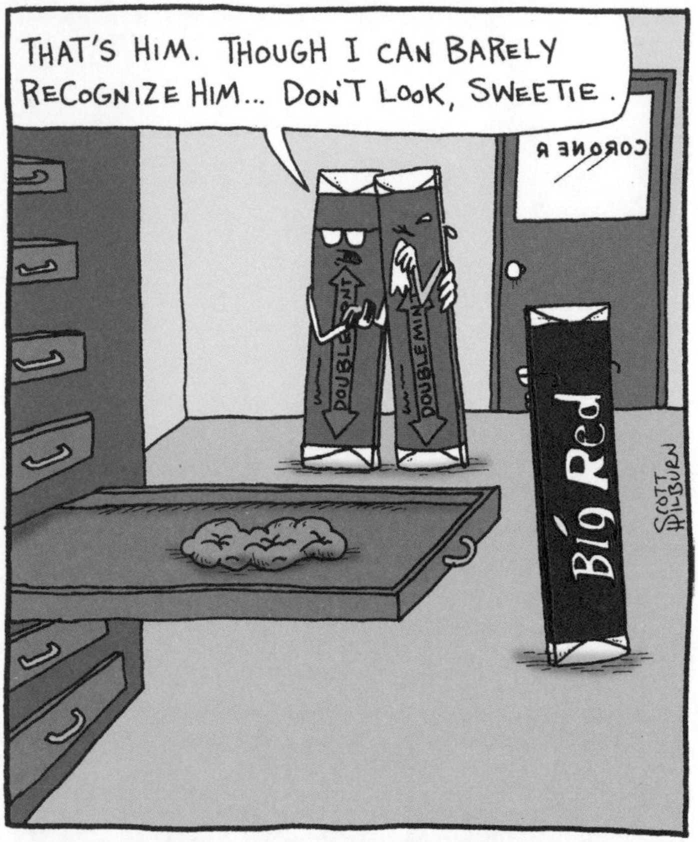
THAT'S HIM. THOUGH I CAN BARELY RECOGNIZE HIM... DON'T LOOK, SWEETIE.
DOUBLEMINT
DOUBLEMINT
Big Red
SCOTT HILBURN

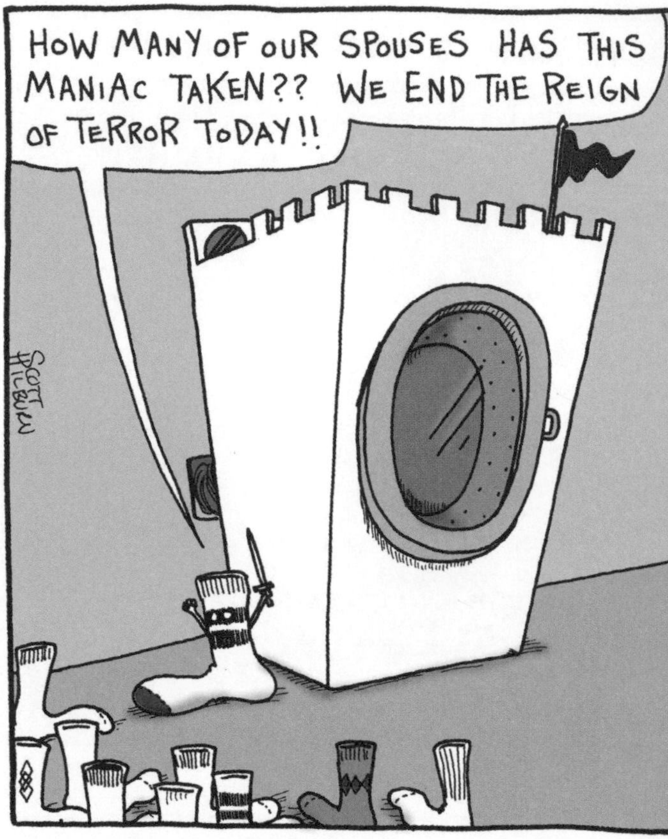
HOW MANY OF OUR SPOUSES HAS THIS MANIAC TAKEN?? WE END THE REIGN OF TERROR TODAY!!
SCOTT HILBURN

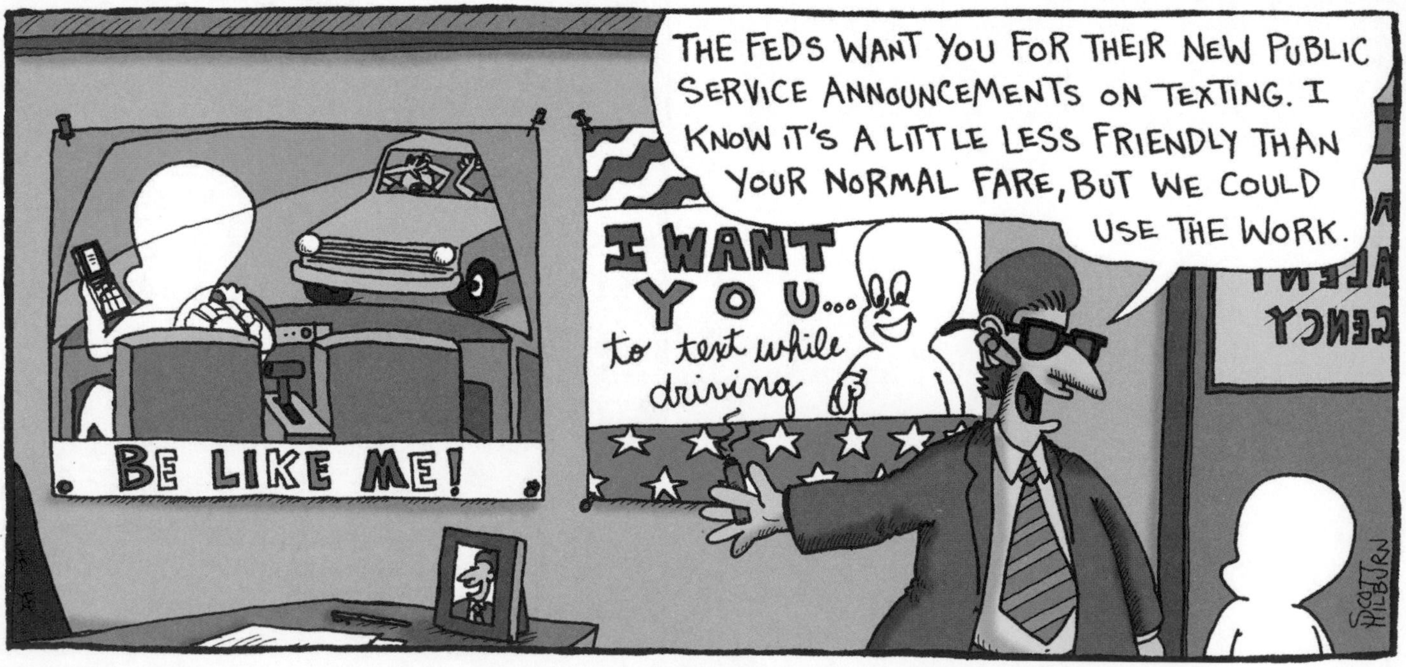
THE FEDS WANT YOU FOR THEIR NEW PUBLIC SERVICE ANNOUNCEMENTS ON TEXTING. I KNOW IT'S A LITTLE LESS FRIENDLY THAN YOUR NORMAL FARE, BUT WE COULD USE THE WORK.
BE LIKE ME!
I WANT YOU...
to text while driving
SCOTT HILBURN

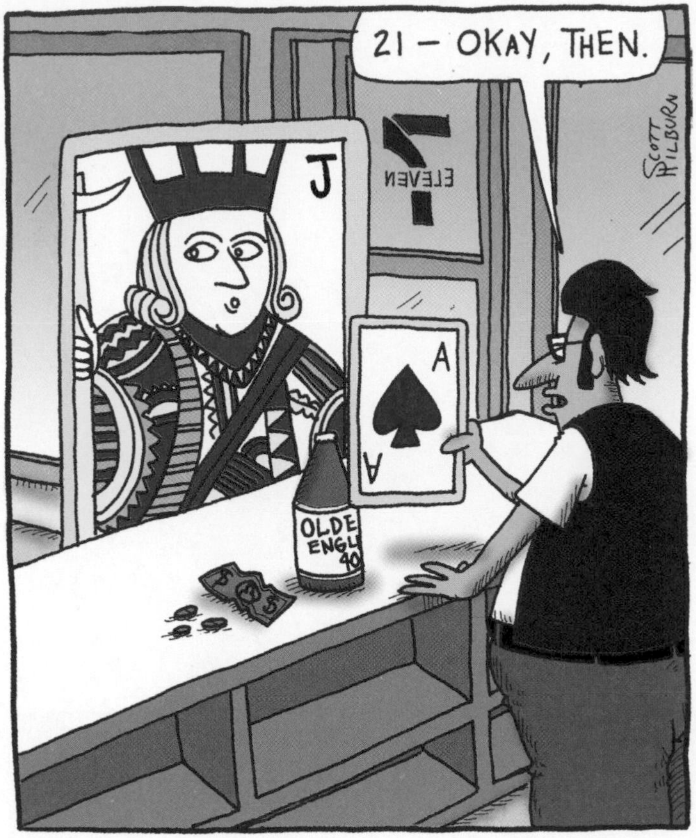
21 – OKAY, THEN.
ELEVEN
SCOTT HILBURN
OLDE ENGL 40

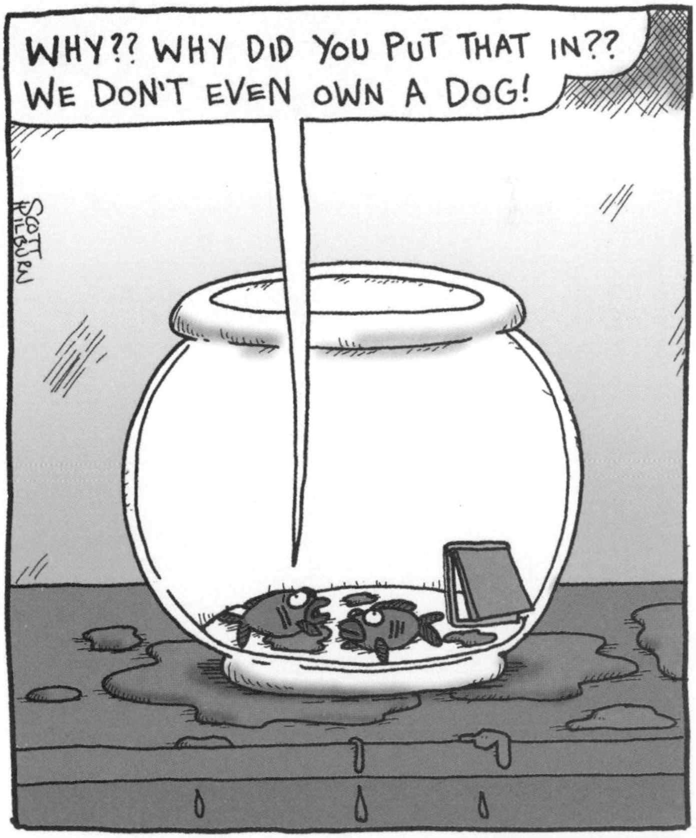
WHY?? WHY DID YOU PUT THAT IN?? WE DON'T EVEN OWN A DOG!
SCOTT HILBURN

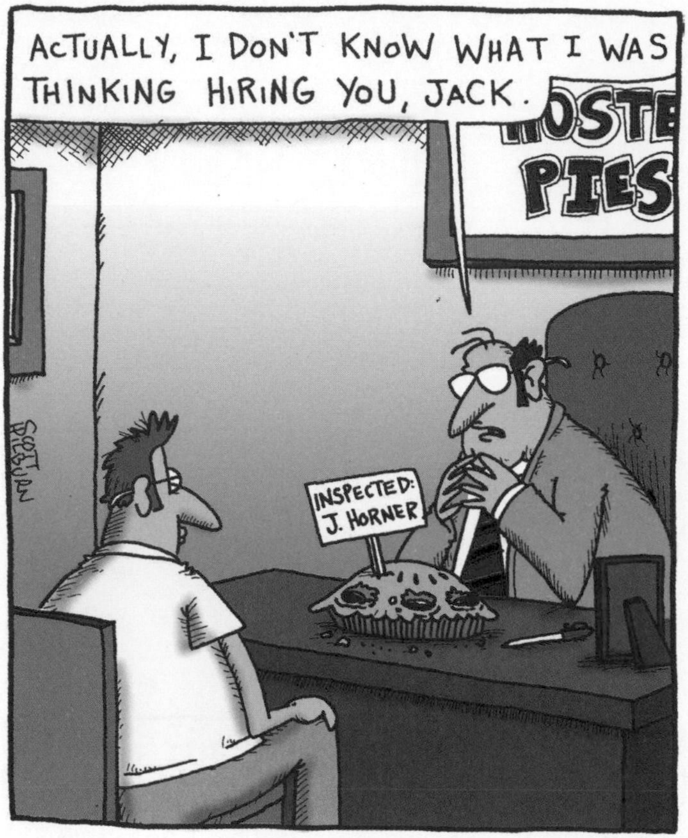
ACTUALLY, I DON'T KNOW WHAT I WAS THINKING HIRING YOU, JACK.
HOSTE
PIES
INSPECTED: J. HORNER
SCOTT HILBURN

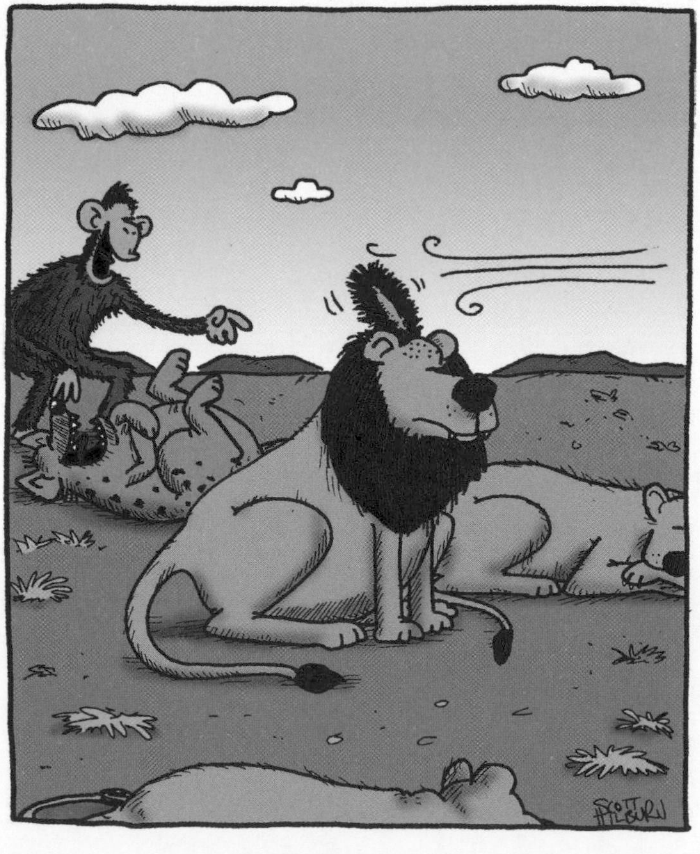
SCOTT HILBURN

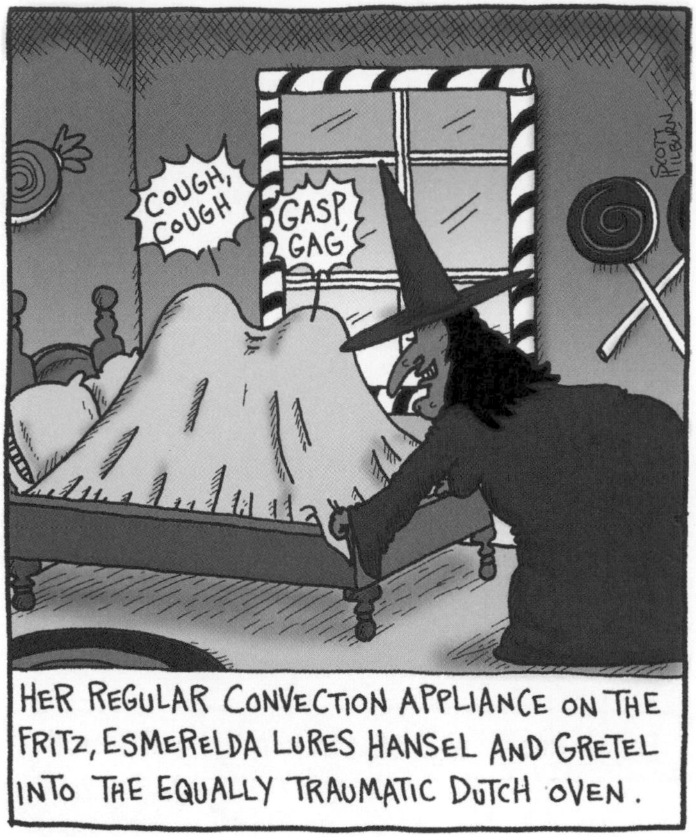
COUGH, COUGH
GASP, GAG
HER REGULAR CONVECTION APPLIANCE ON THE FRITZ, ESMERELDA LURES HANSEL AND GRETEL INTO THE EQUALLY TRAUMATIC DUTCH OVEN.

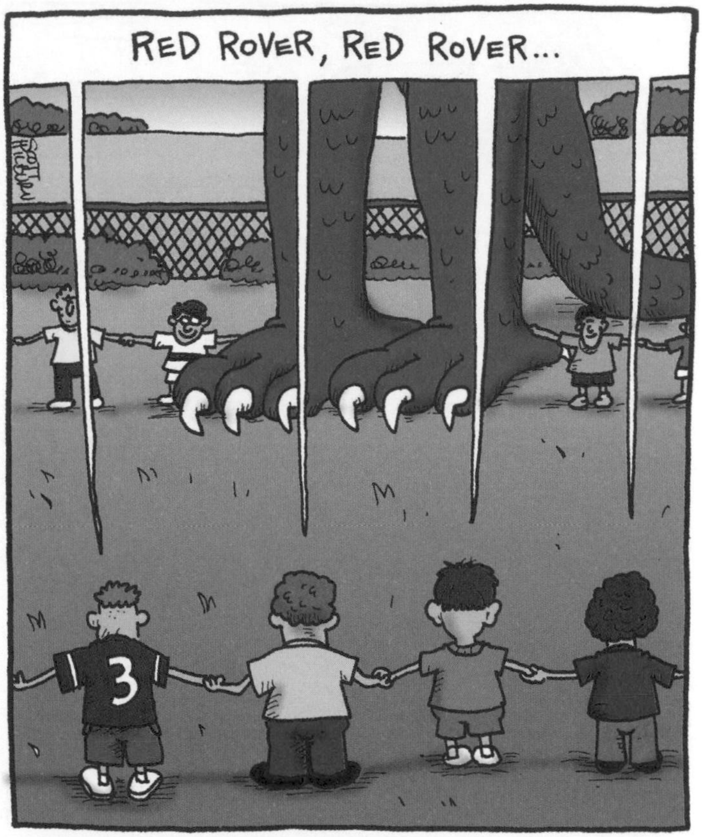
RED ROVER, RED ROVER...
3

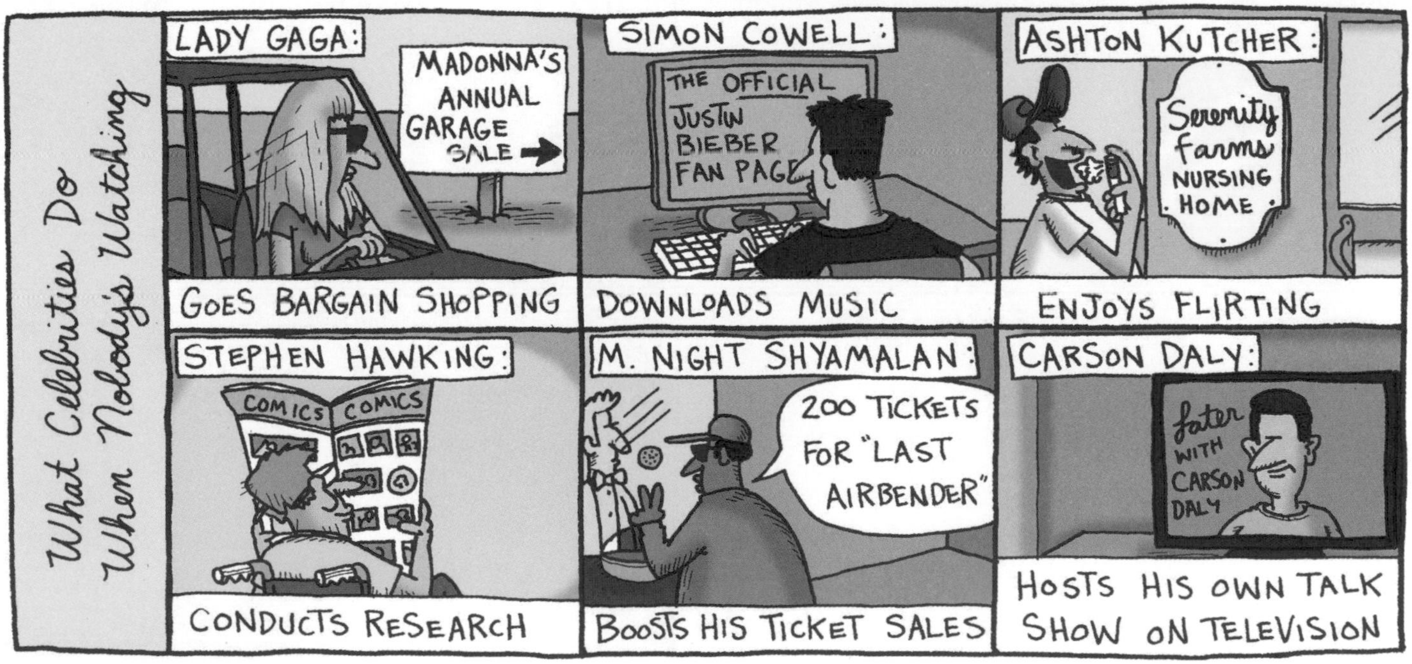
What Celebrities Do When Nobody's Watching
LADY GAGA:
MADONNA'S ANNUAL GARAGE SALE
GOES BARGAIN SHOPPING
SIMON COWELL:
THE OFFICIAL JUSTIN BIEBER FAN PAGE
DOWNLOADS MUSIC
ASHTON KUTCHER:
Serenity Farms NURSING HOME
ENJOYS FLIRTING
STEPHEN HAWKING:
COMICS COMICS
CONDUCTS RESEARCH
M. NIGHT SHYAMALAN:
200 TICKETS FOR "LAST AIRBENDER"
BOOSTS HIS TICKET SALES
CARSON DALY:
Later WITH CARSON DALY
HOSTS HIS OWN TALK SHOW ON TELEVISION

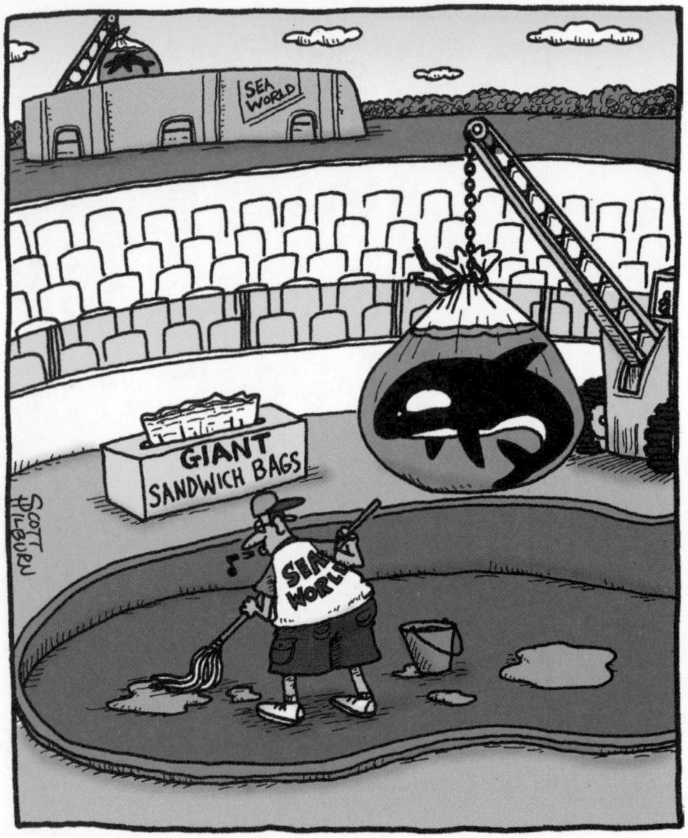
SEA WORLD
GIANT SANDWICH BAGS
SEA WORLD

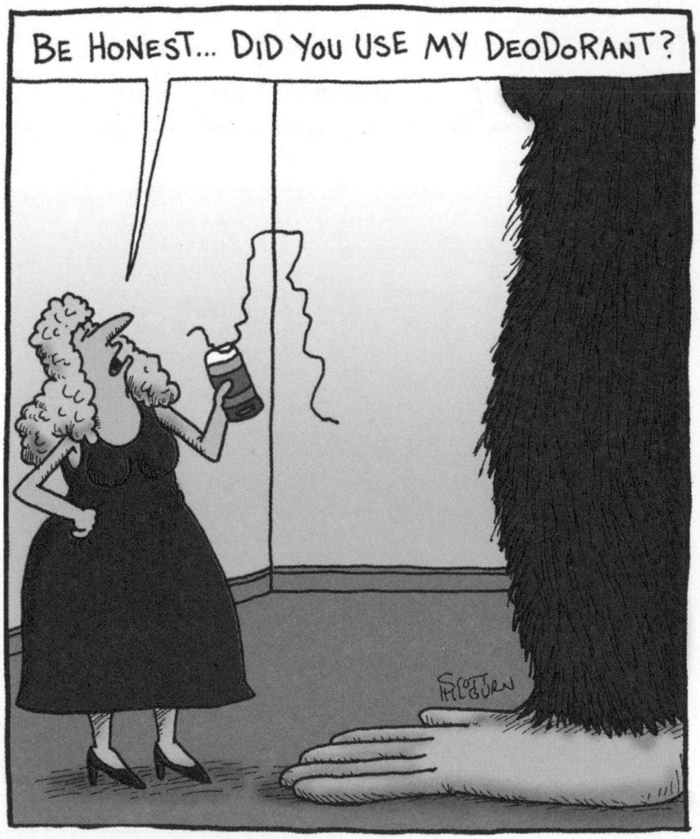
BE HONEST... DID YOU USE MY DEODORANT?

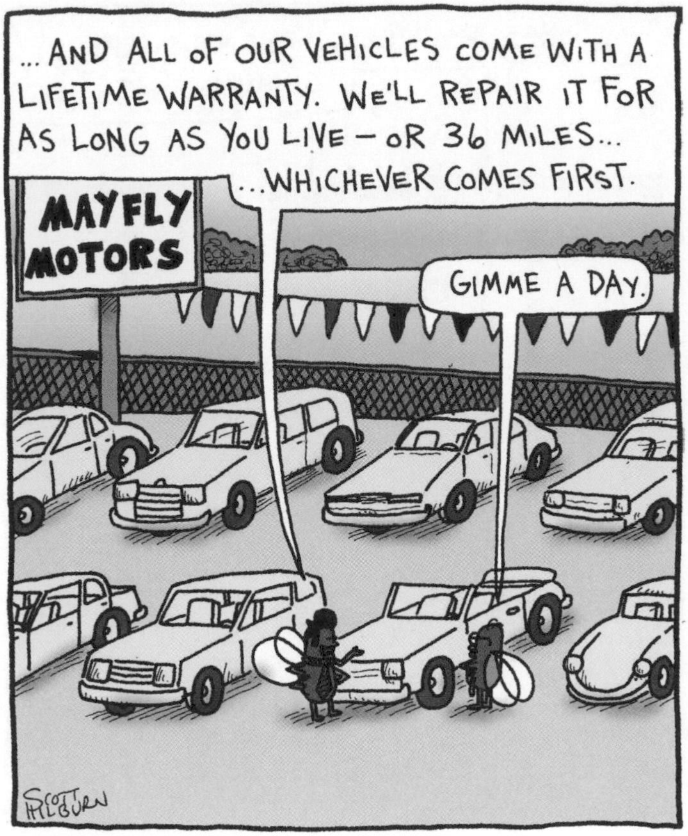
...AND ALL OF OUR VEHICLES COME WITH A LIFETIME WARRANTY. WE'LL REPAIR IT FOR AS LONG AS YOU LIVE – OR 36 MILES...
...WHICHEVER COMES FIRST.
MAYFLY MOTORS
GIMME A DAY.
SCOTT HILBURN

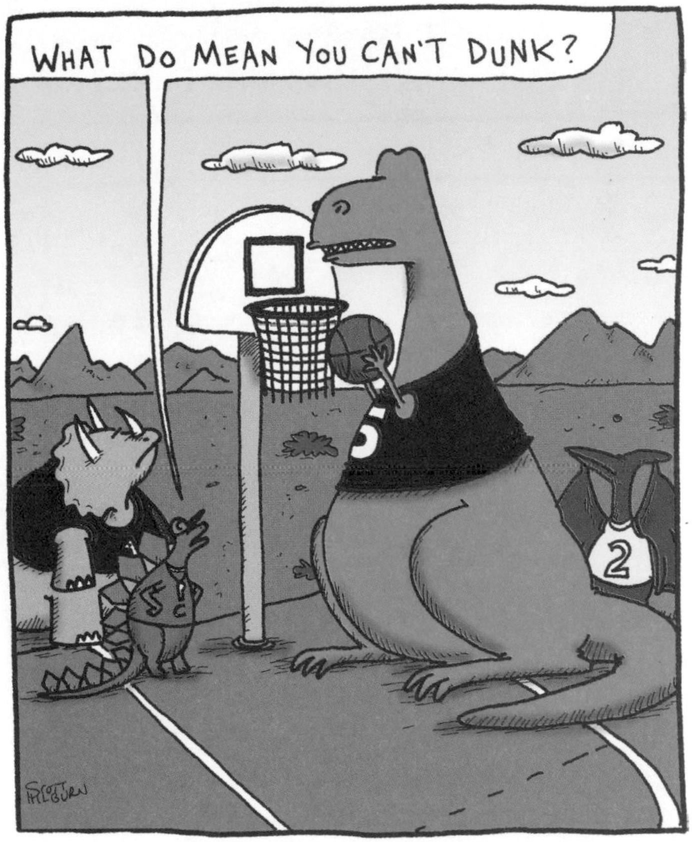
WHAT DO MEAN YOU CAN'T DUNK?
2
SCOTT HILBURN

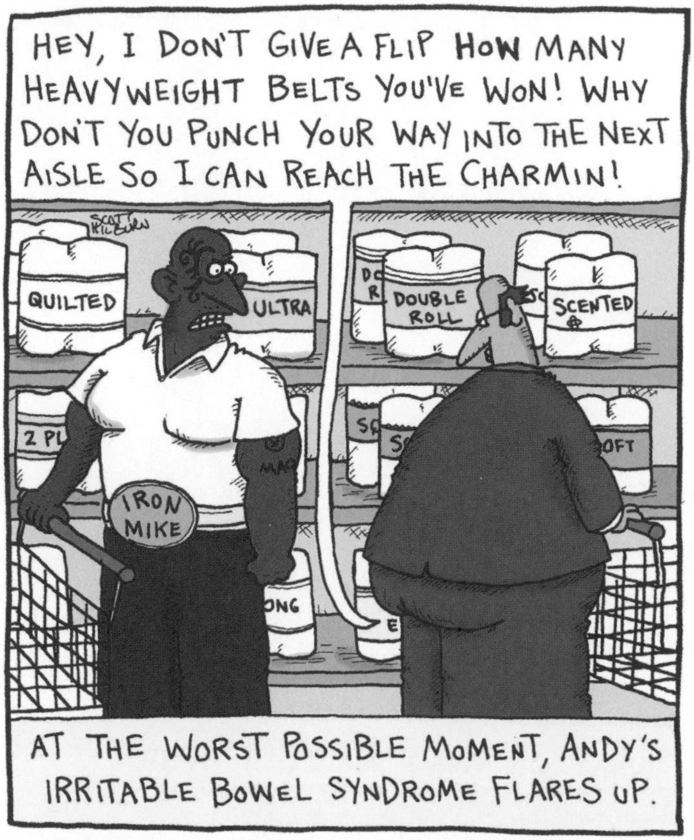
HEY, I DON'T GIVE A FLIP HOW MANY HEAVYWEIGHT BELTS YOU'VE WON! WHY DON'T YOU PUNCH YOUR WAY INTO THE NEXT AISLE SO I CAN REACH THE CHARMIN!
QUILTED
ULTRA
DOUBLE ROLL
SCENTED
IRON MIKE

AT THE WORST POSSIBLE MOMENT, ANDY'S IRRITABLE BOWEL SYNDROME FLARES UP.

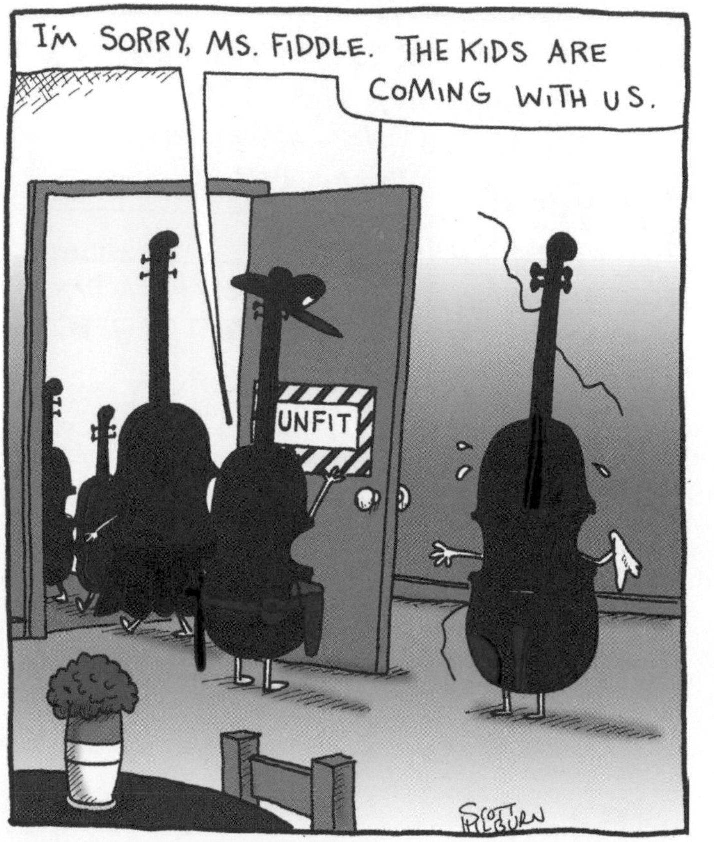
I'M SORRY, MS. FIDDLE. THE KIDS ARE COMING WITH US.
UNFIT

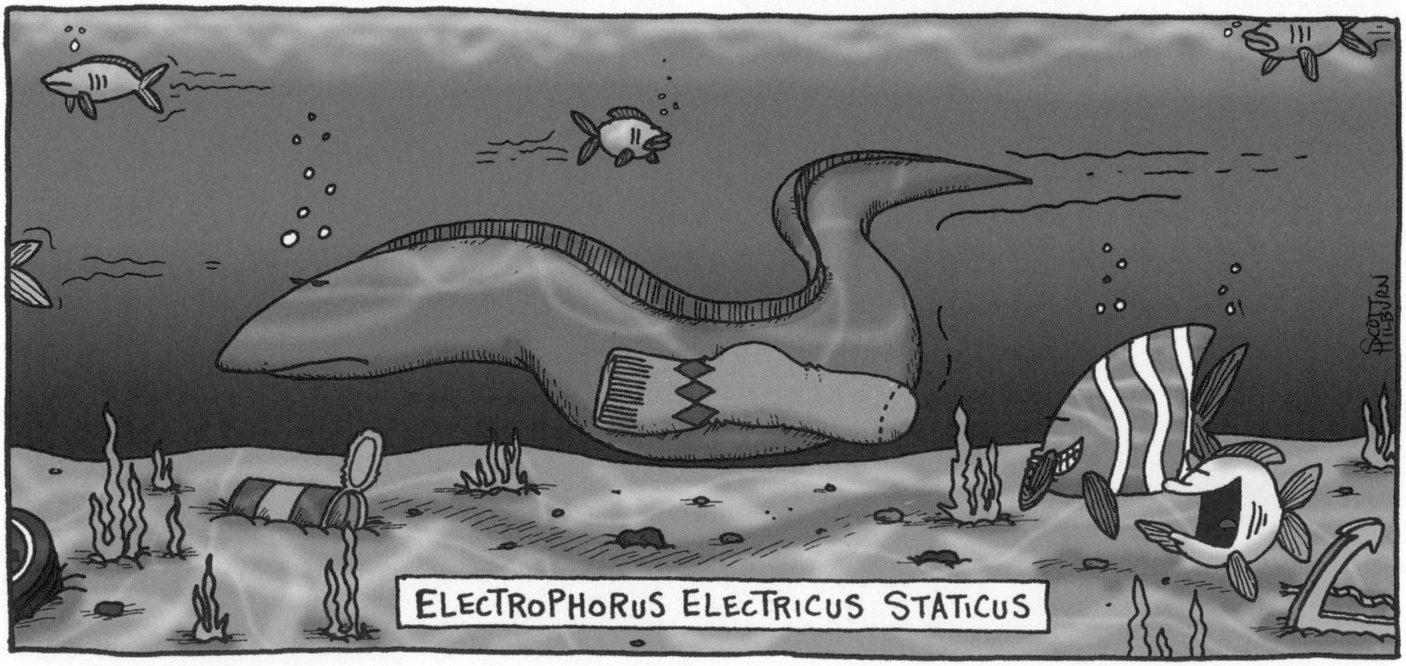

ELECTROPHORUS ELECTRICUS STATICUS

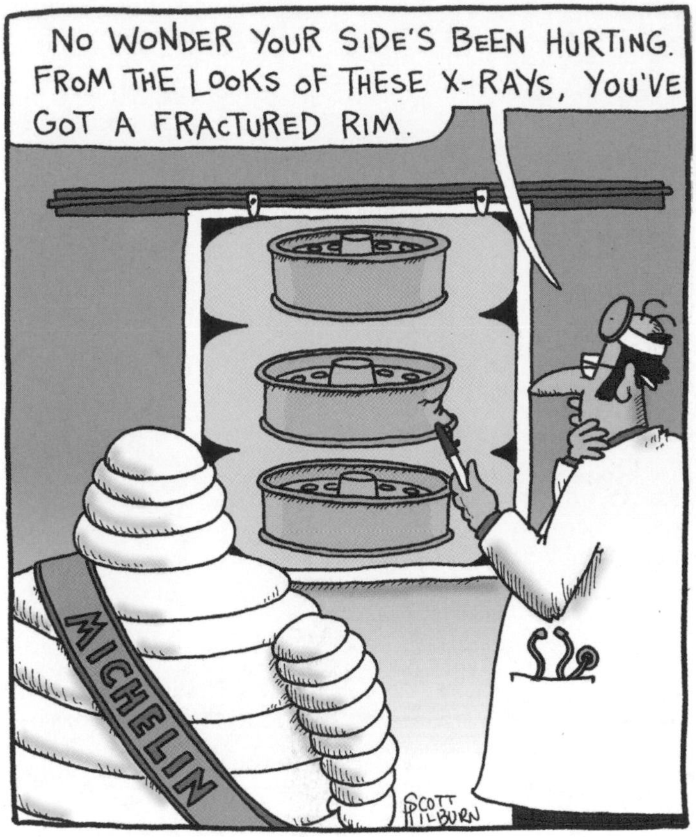
NO WONDER YOUR SIDE'S BEEN HURTING. FROM THE LOOKS OF THESE X-RAYS, YOU'VE GOT A FRACTURED RIM.
MICHELIN
SCOTT HILBURN

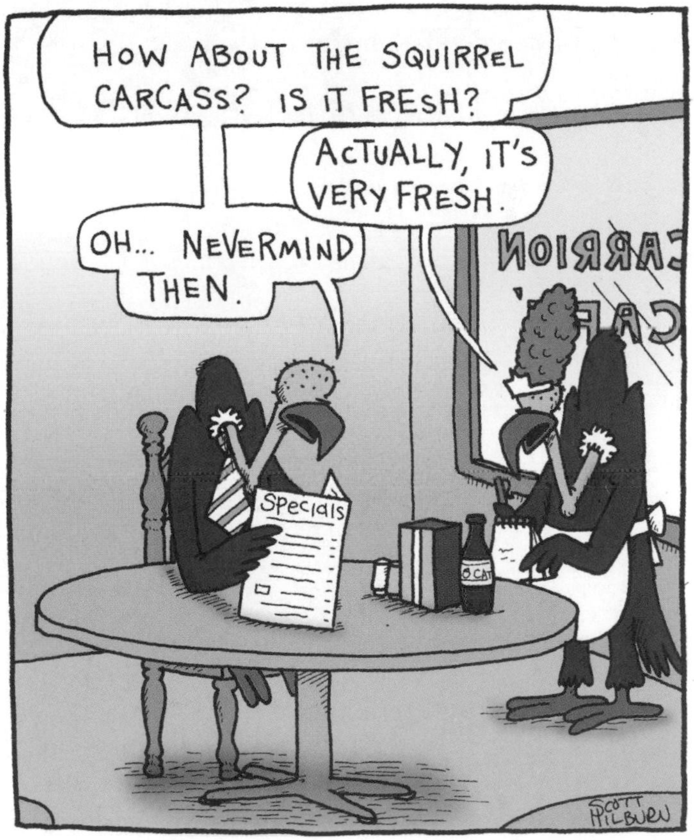
HOW ABOUT THE SQUIRREL CARCASS? IS IT FRESH?
ACTUALLY, IT'S VERY FRESH.
OH... NEVERMIND THEN.
Specials
SCOTT HILBURN

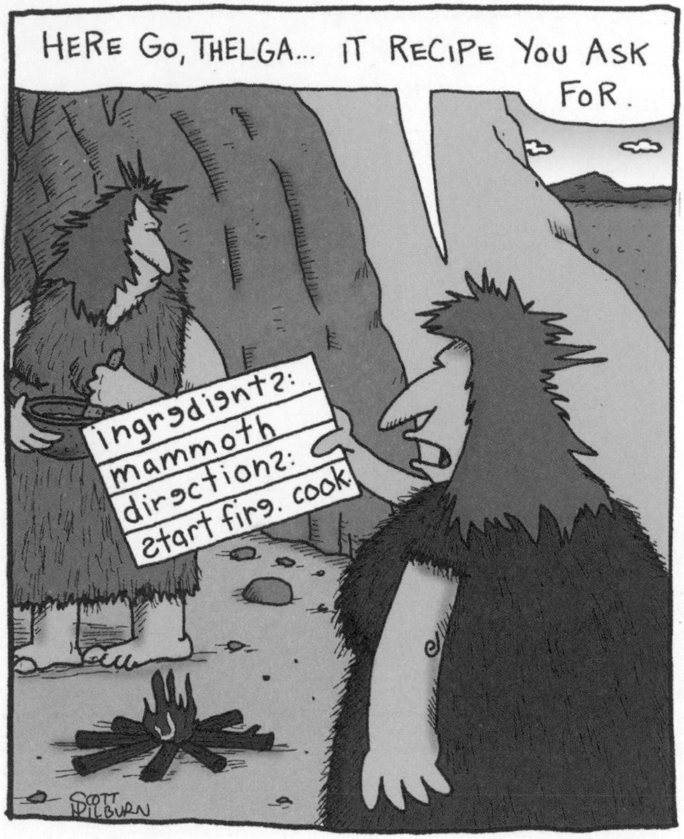
HERE GO, THELGA... IT RECIPE YOU ASK FOR.
ingredientz:
mammoth
directionz:
start fire. cook
SCOTT HILBURN

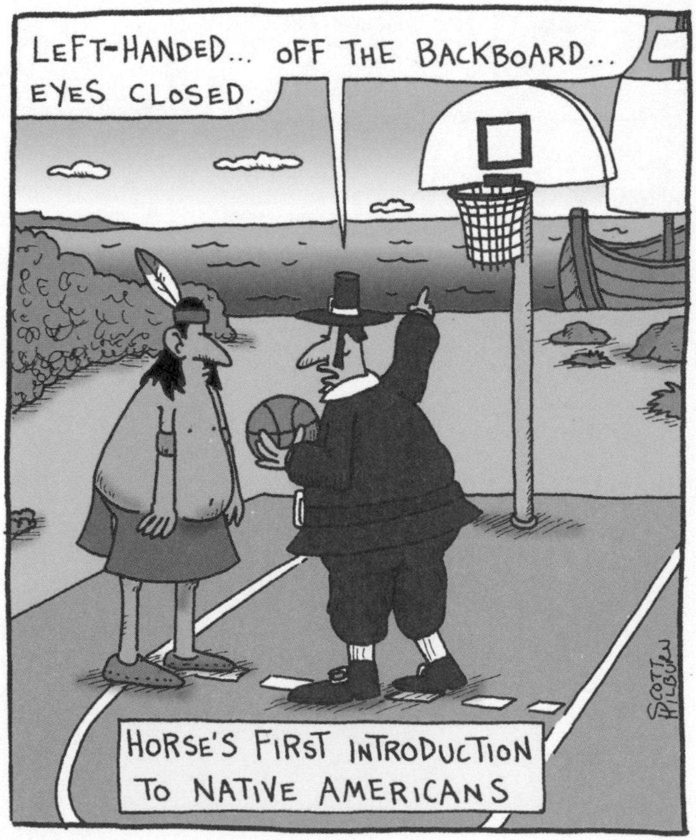
LEFT-HANDED... OFF THE BACKBOARD... EYES CLOSED.
SCOTT HILBURN
HORSE'S FIRST INTRODUCTION TO NATIVE AMERICANS

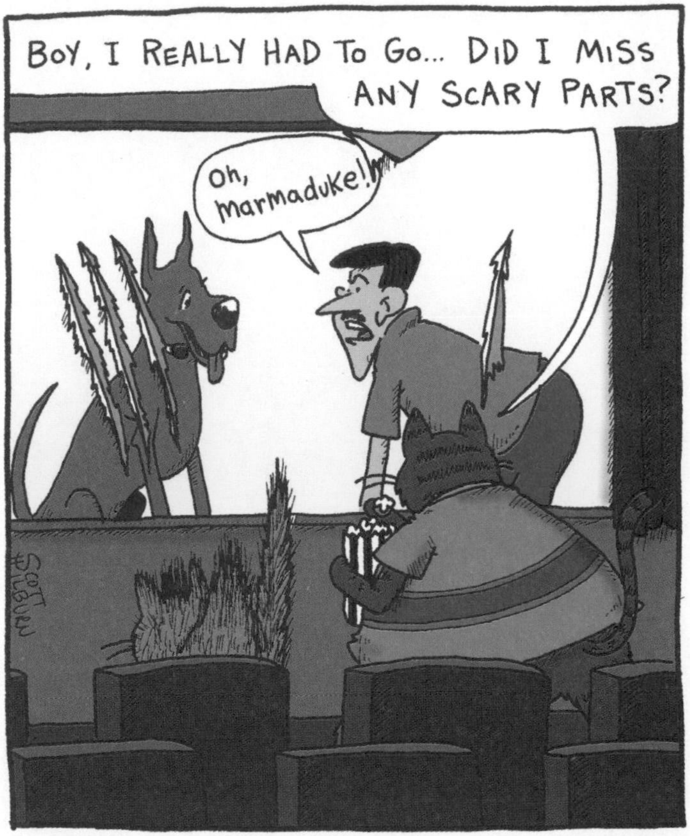
BOY, I REALLY HAD TO GO... DID I MISS ANY SCARY PARTS?
Oh, marmaduke!

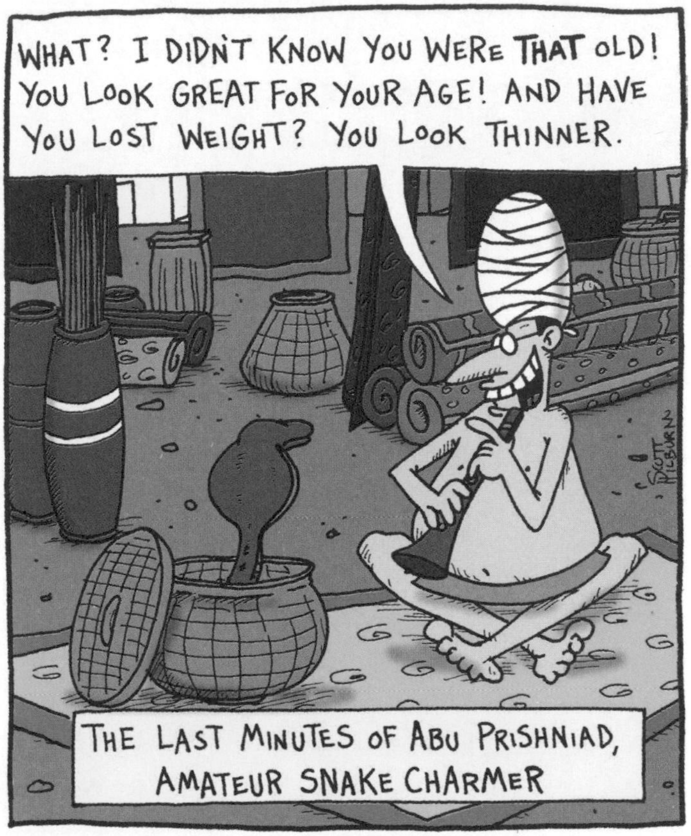
WHAT? I DIDN'T KNOW YOU WERE THAT OLD! YOU LOOK GREAT FOR YOUR AGE! AND HAVE YOU LOST WEIGHT? YOU LOOK THINNER.
THE LAST MINUTES OF ABU PRISHNIAD, AMATEUR SNAKE CHARMER

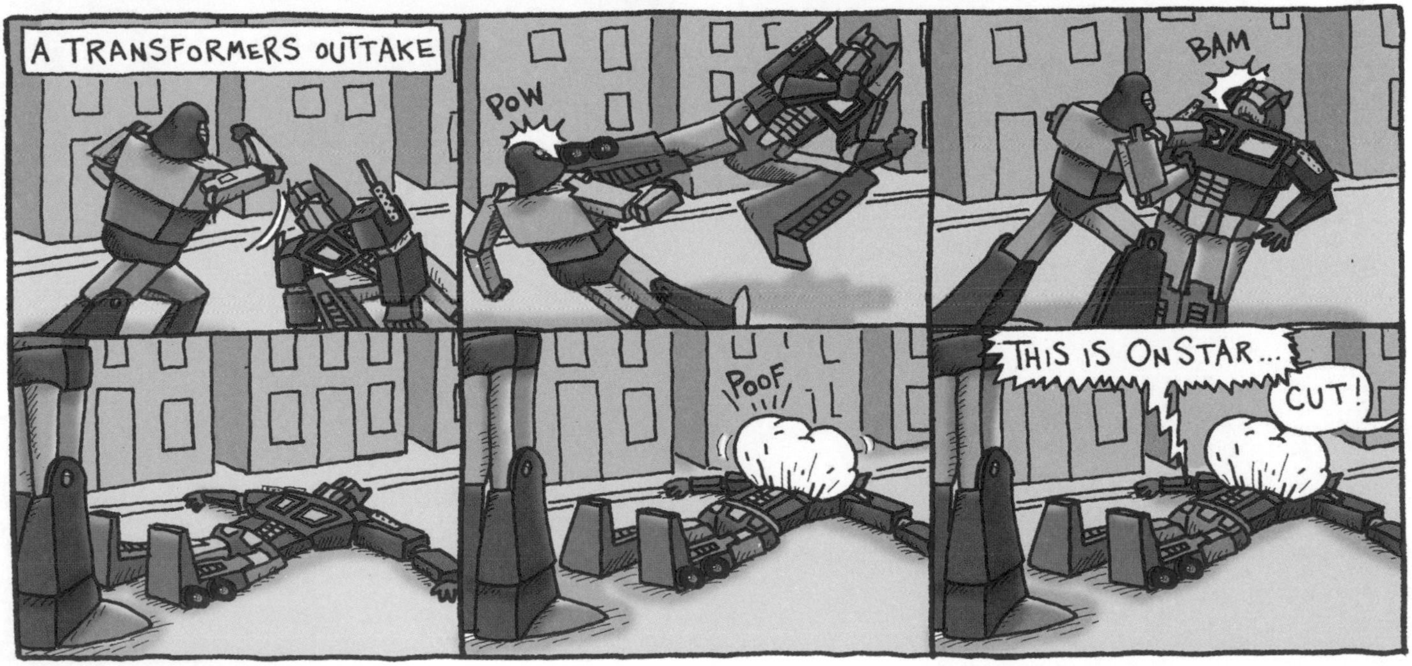
A TRANSFORMERS OUTTAKE
POW
BAM
POOF
THIS IS ONSTAR...
CUT!

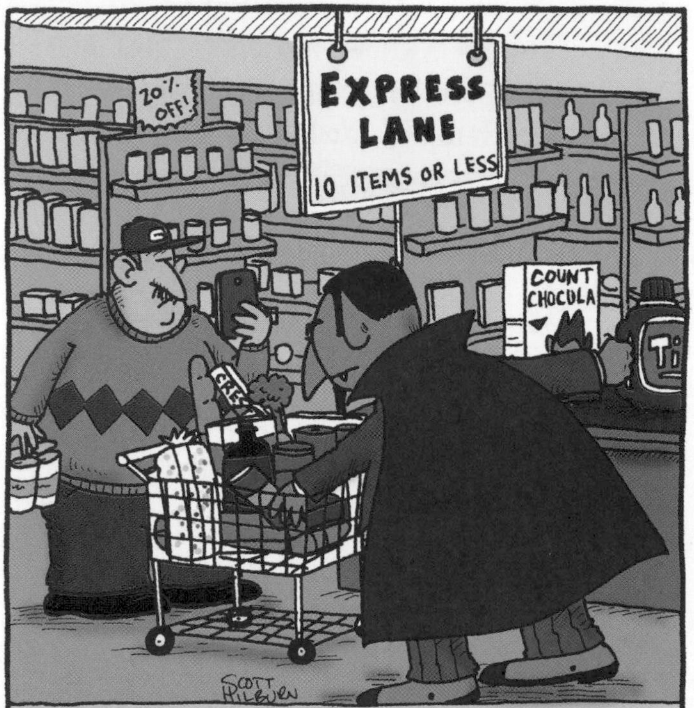
20% OFF!
EXPRESS LANE
10 ITEMS OR LESS
COUNT CHOCULA
SCOTT HILBURN

SCANDAL HITS WHEN THE PAPARAZZI CATCH THE COUNT WITH 25 ITEMS.

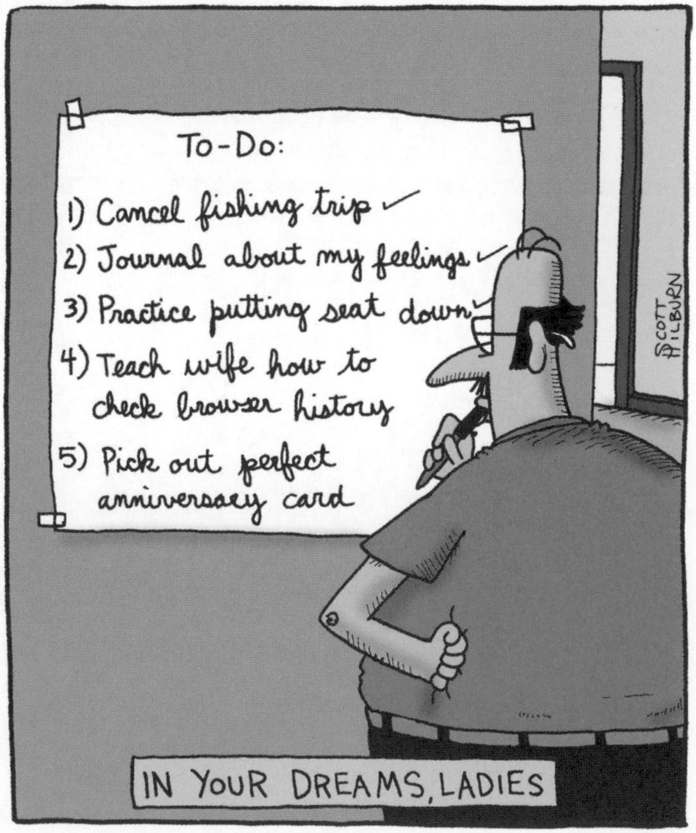
To-Do:
1) Cancel fishing trip ✓
2) Journal about my feelings ✓
3) Practice putting seat down ✓
4) Teach wife how to check browser history
5) Pick out perfect anniversary card
SCOTT HILBURN

IN YOUR DREAMS, LADIES

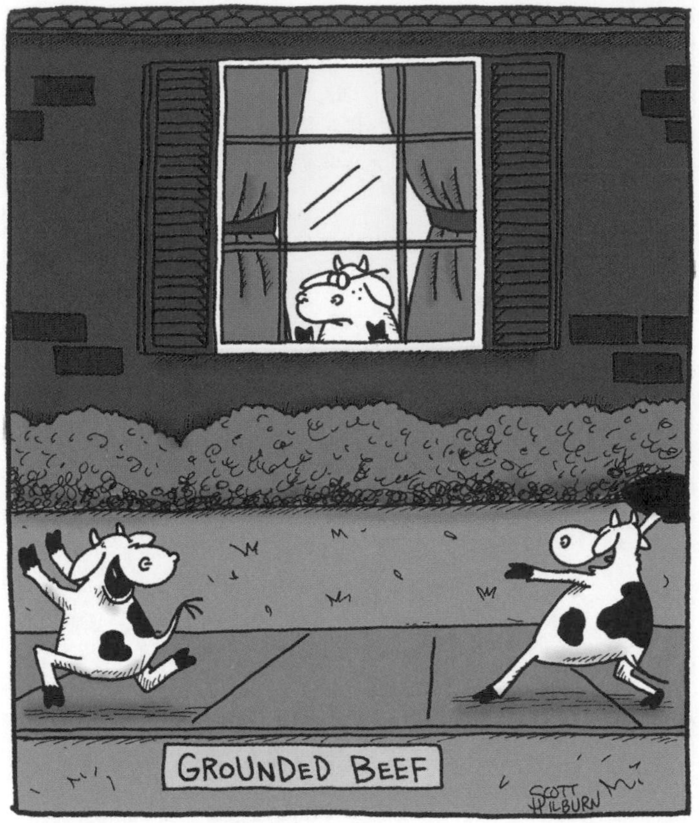
GROUNDED BEEF
SCOTT HILBURN

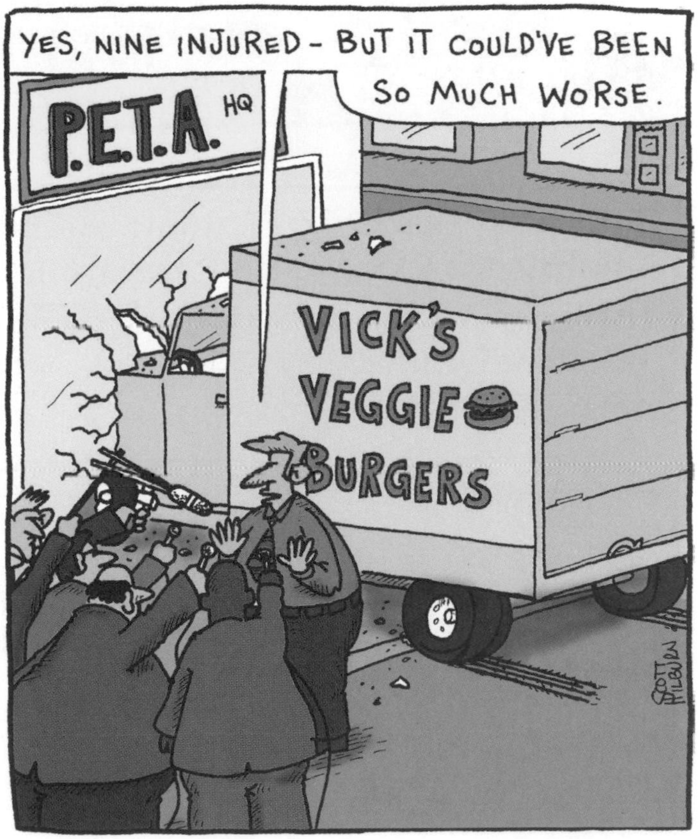
YES, NINE INJURED - BUT IT COULD'VE BEEN SO MUCH WORSE.
P.E.T.A. HQ
VICK'S VEGGIE BURGERS
SCOTT HILBURN

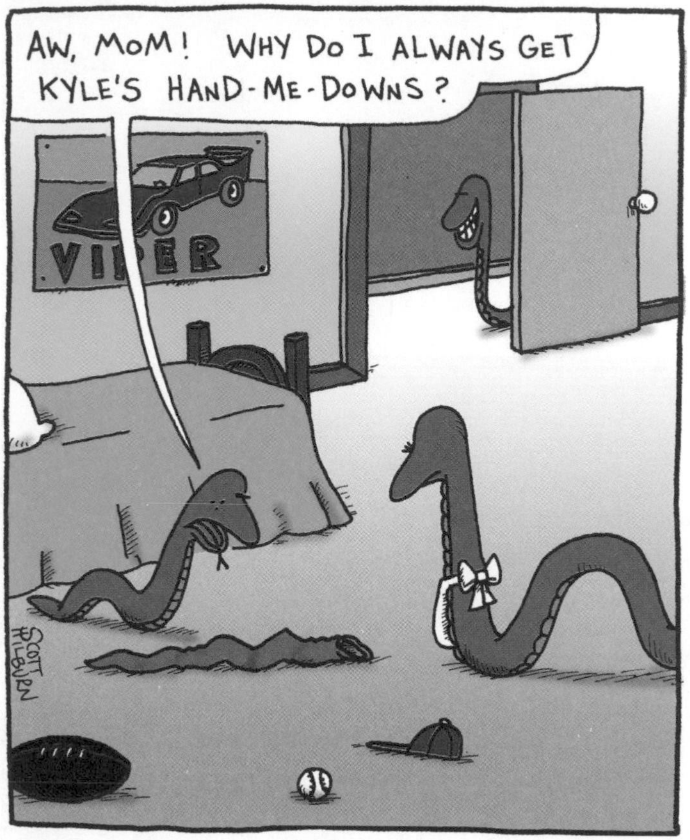
AW, MOM! WHY DO I ALWAYS GET KYLE'S HAND-ME-DOWNS?
VIPER
SCOTT HILBURN

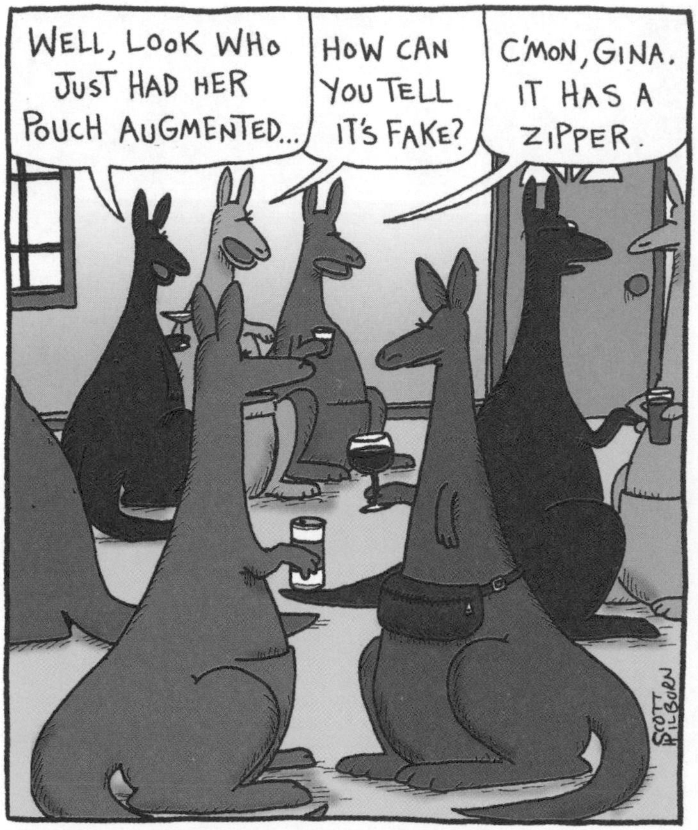
WELL, LOOK WHO JUST HAD HER POUCH AUGMENTED...
HOW CAN YOU TELL IT'S FAKE?
C'MON, GINA. IT HAS A ZIPPER.
SCOTT HILBURN

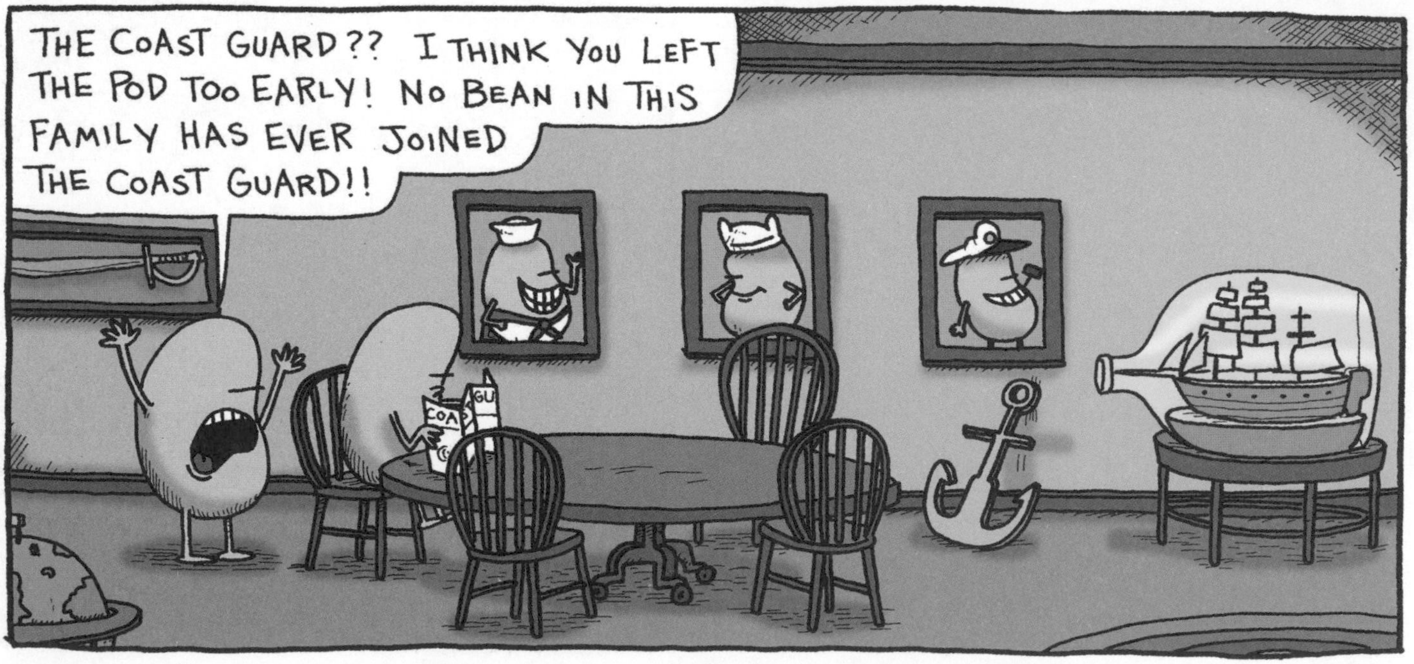
THE COAST GUARD?? I THINK YOU LEFT THE POD TOO EARLY! NO BEAN IN THIS FAMILY HAS EVER JOINED THE COAST GUARD!!

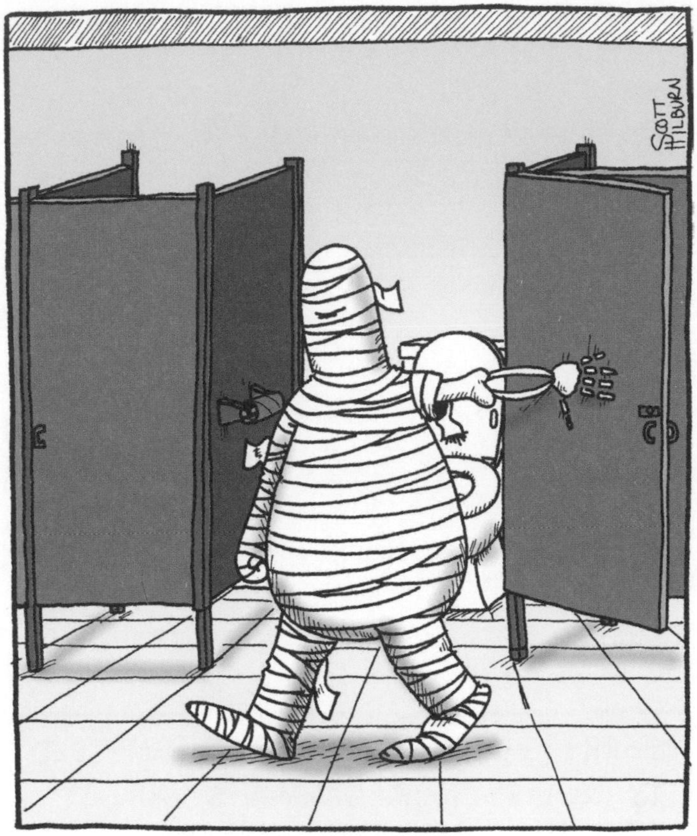
SCOTT HILBURN

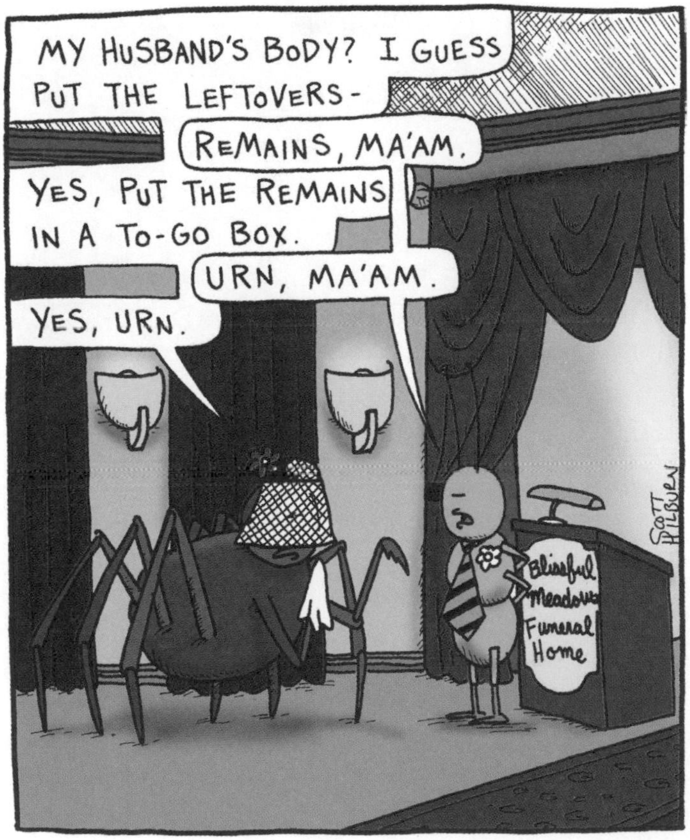
MY HUSBAND'S BODY? I GUESS PUT THE LEFTOVERS-
REMAINS, MA'AM.
YES, PUT THE REMAINS IN A TO-GO BOX.
URN, MA'AM.
YES, URN.
Blissful Meadows Funeral Home
SCOTT HILBURN

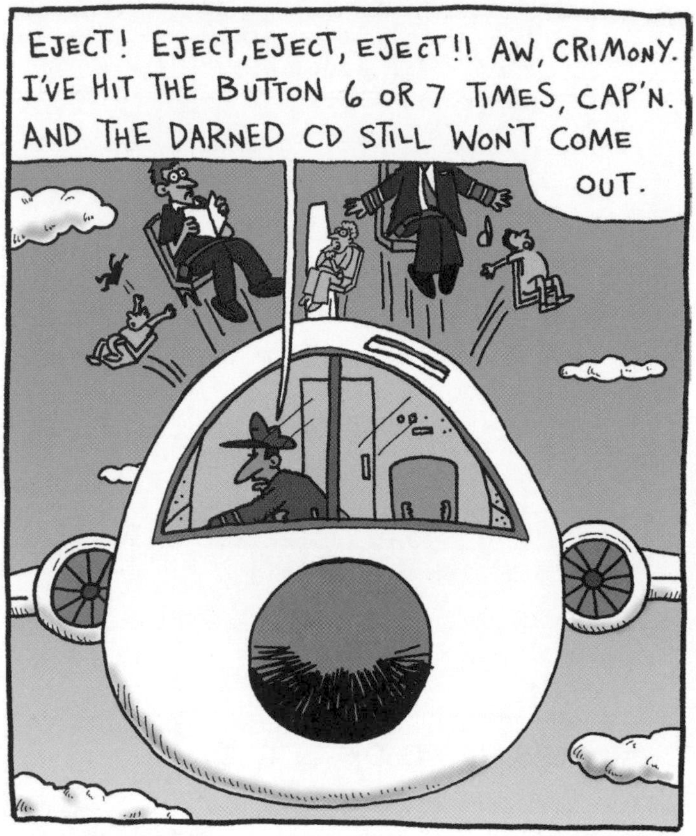
EJECT! EJECT, EJECT, EJECT!! AW, CRIMONY. I'VE HIT THE BUTTON 6 OR 7 TIMES, CAP'N. AND THE DARNED CD STILL WON'T COME OUT.

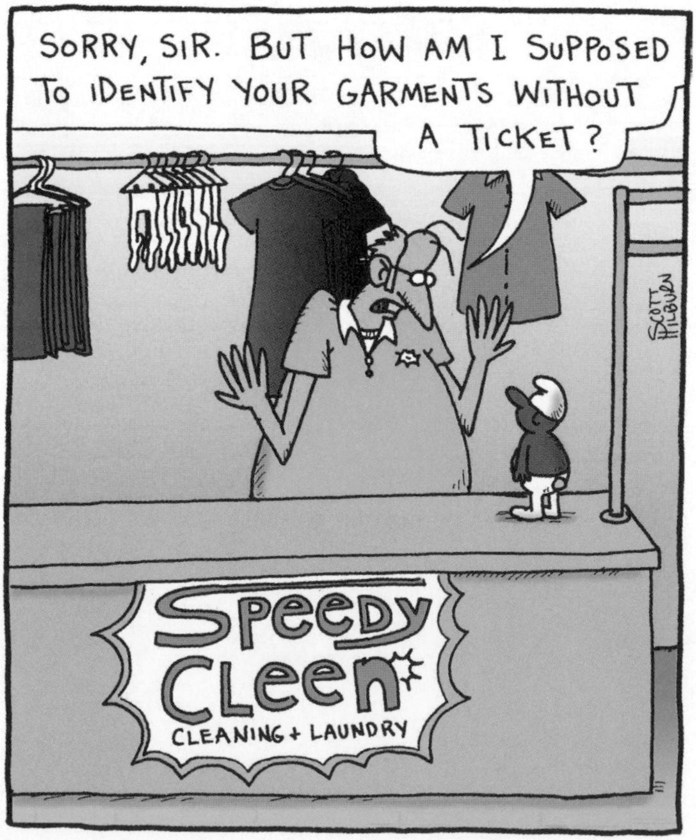
SORRY, SIR. BUT HOW AM I SUPPOSED TO IDENTIFY YOUR GARMENTS WITHOUT A TICKET?
SCOTT HILBURN
Speedy Cleen
CLEANING + LAUNDRY

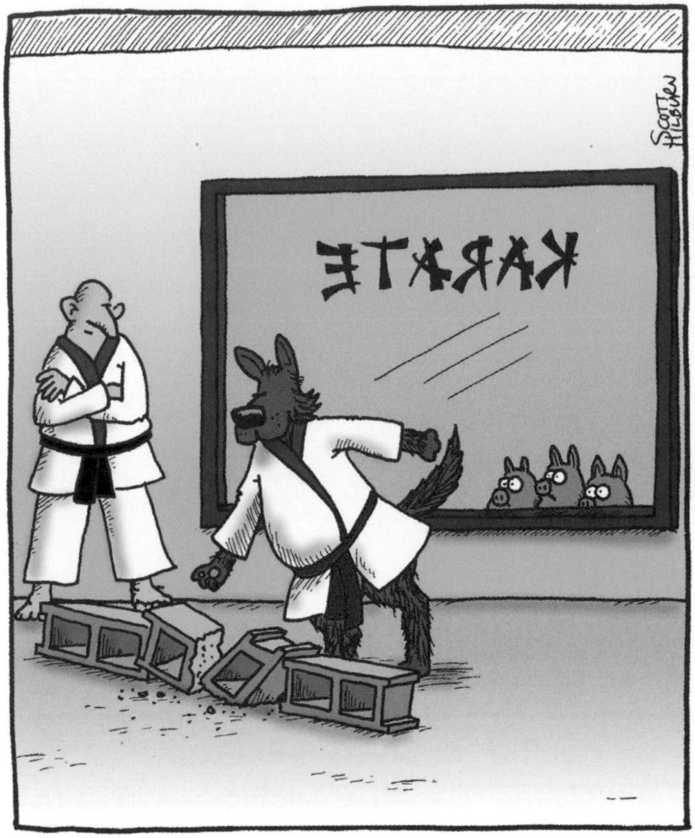
SCOTT HILBURN

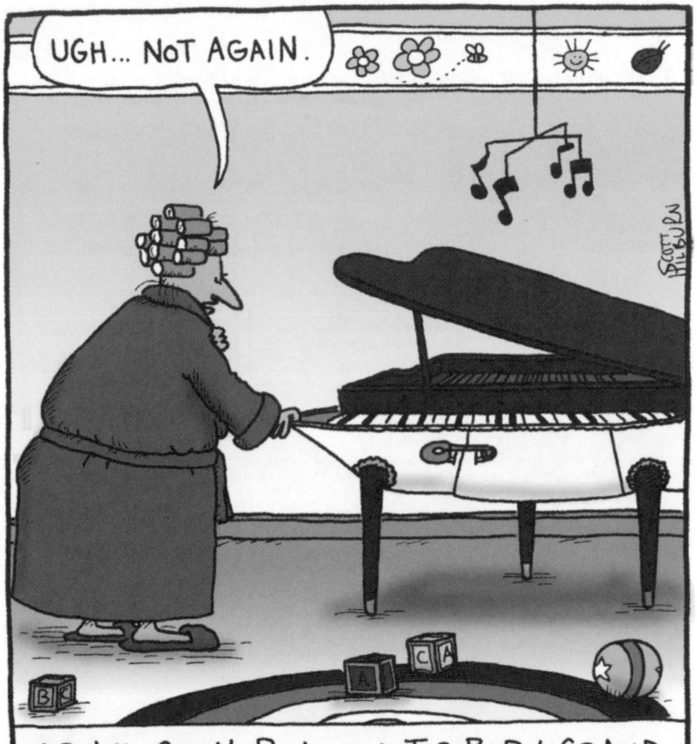
UGH... NOT AGAIN.
SCOTT HILBURN

MIRIAM SOON REALIZED THE BABY GRAND WAS MORE THAN SHE BARGAINED FOR.

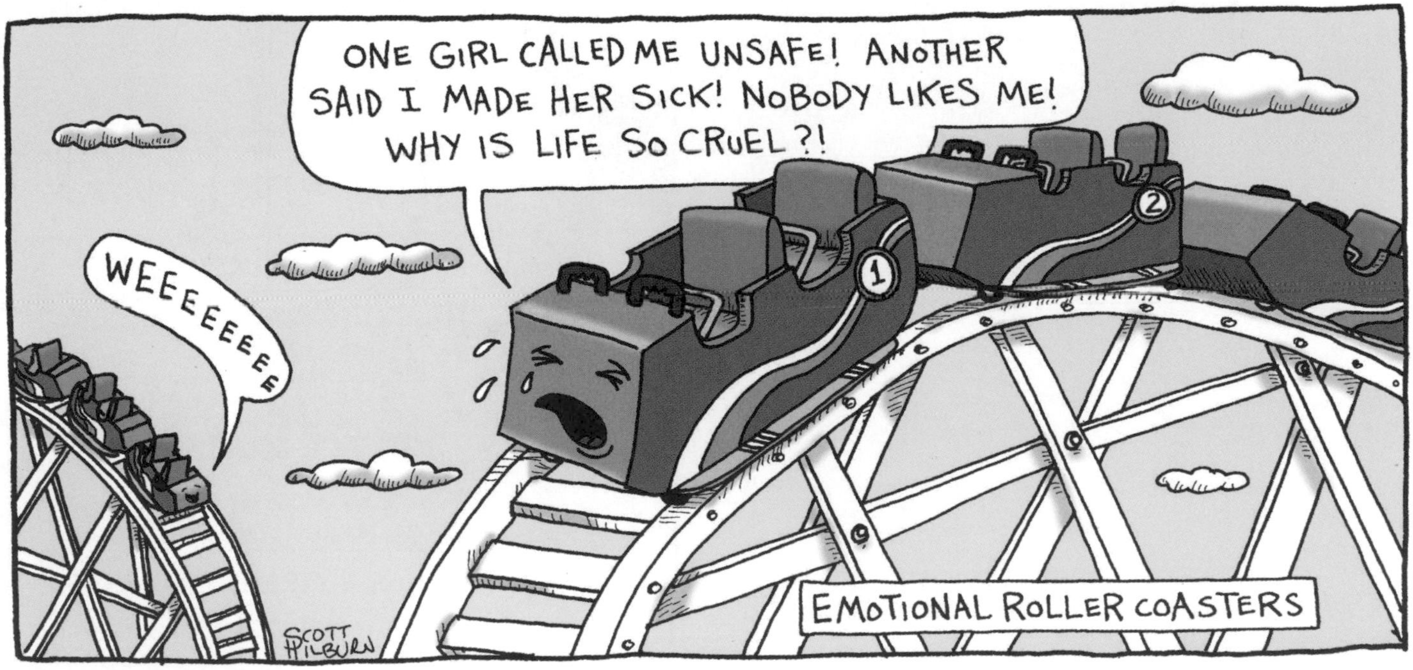
ONE GIRL CALLED ME UNSAFE! ANOTHER SAID I MADE HER SICK! NOBODY LIKES ME! WHY IS LIFE SO CRUEL?!
WEEEEEEEEE
1
2
SCOTT HILBURN

EMOTIONAL ROLLER COASTERS

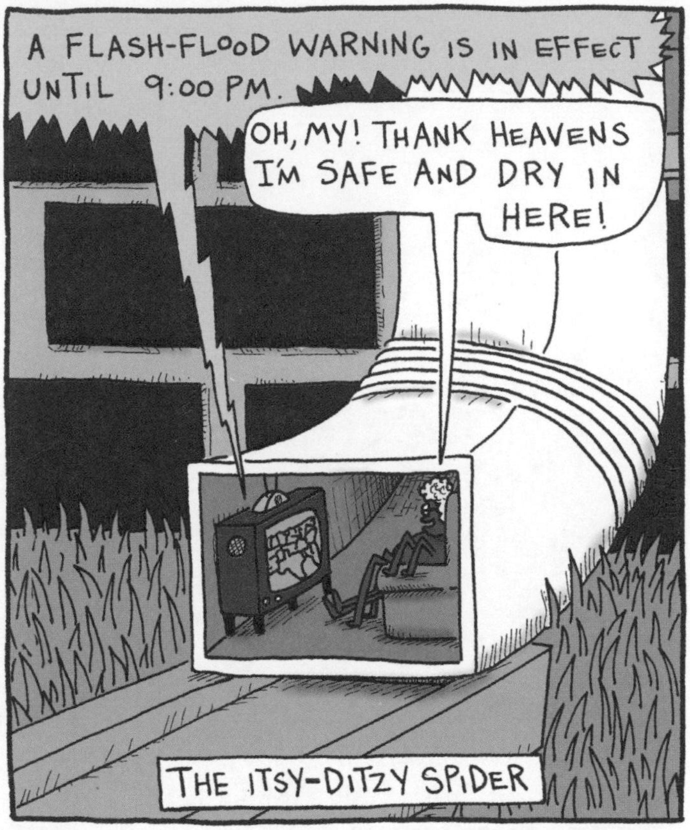
A FLASH-FLOOD WARNING IS IN EFFECT UNTIL 9:00 PM.
OH, MY! THANK HEAVENS I'M SAFE AND DRY IN HERE!

THE ITSY-DITZY SPIDER

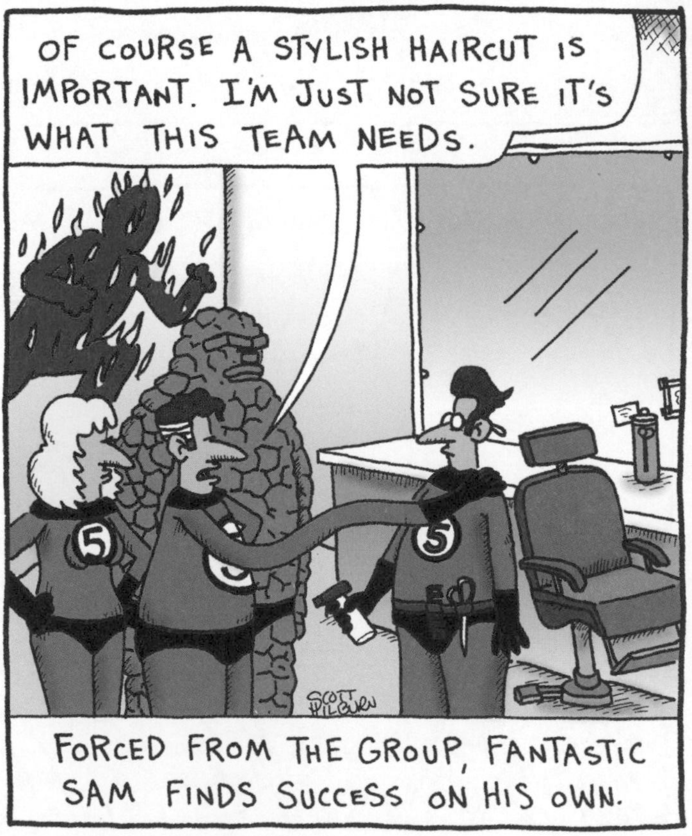
OF COURSE A STYLISH HAIRCUT IS IMPORTANT. I'M JUST NOT SURE IT'S WHAT THIS TEAM NEEDS.
SCOTT HILBURN

FORCED FROM THE GROUP, FANTASTIC SAM FINDS SUCCESS ON HIS OWN.

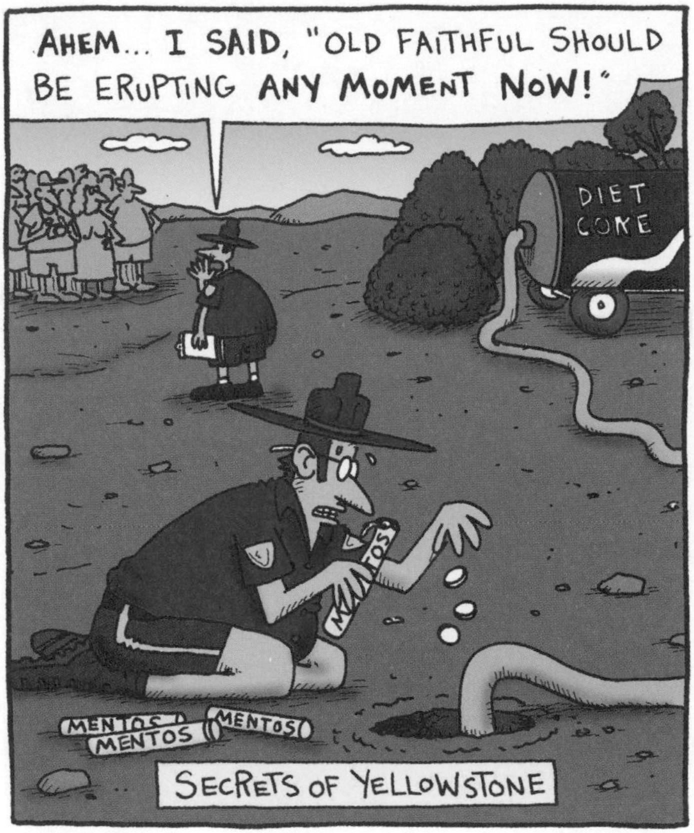
AHEM... I SAID, "OLD FAITHFUL SHOULD BE ERUPTING ANY MOMENT NOW!"
DIET COKE
MENTOS
MENTOS
MENTOS

SECRETS OF YELLOWSTONE

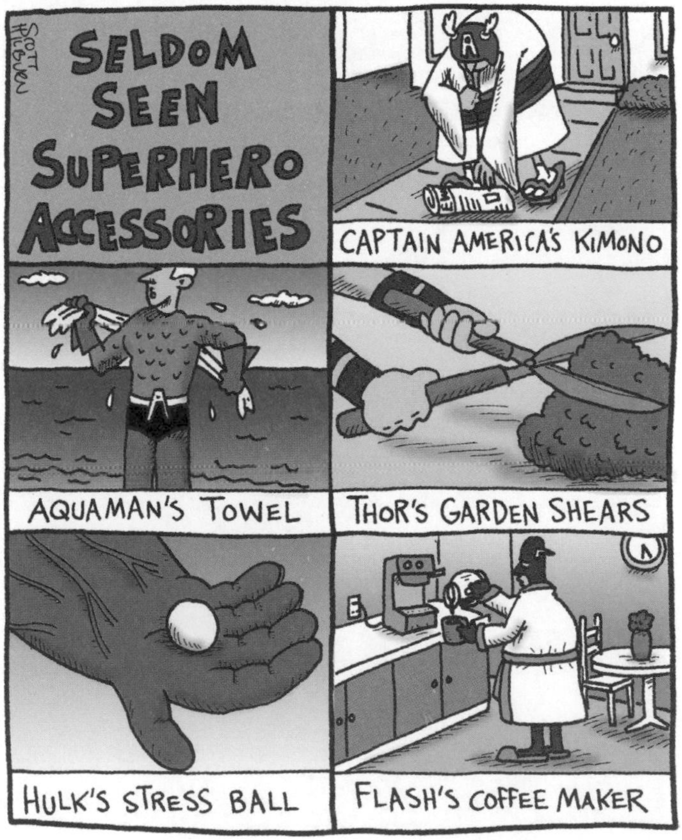
SELDOM SEEN SUPERHERO ACCESSORIES
CAPTAIN AMERICA'S KIMONO
AQUAMAN'S TOWEL
THOR'S GARDEN SHEARS
HULK'S STRESS BALL
FLASH'S COFFEE MAKER

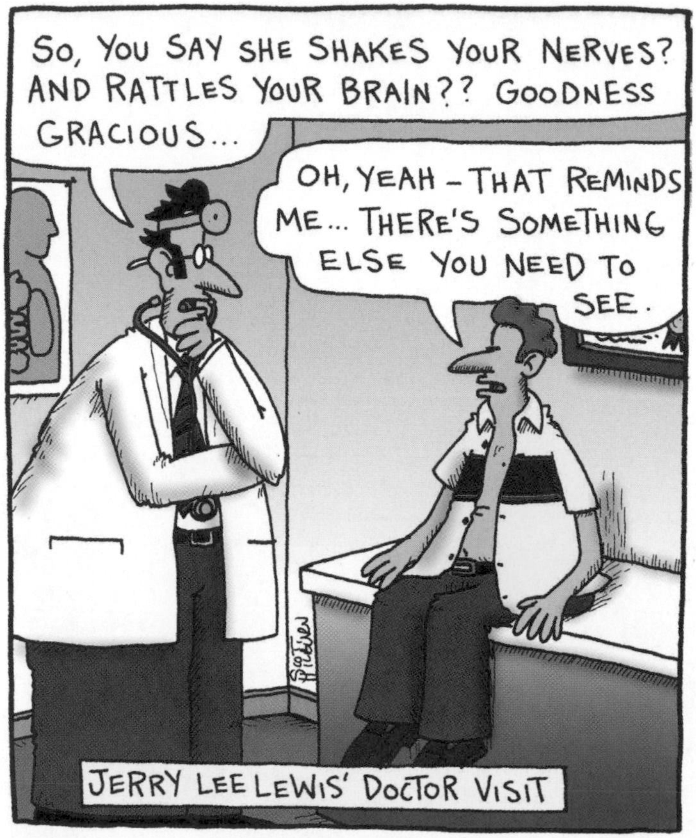
So, YOU SAY SHE SHAKES YOUR NERVES? AND RATTLES YOUR BRAIN?? GOODNESS GRACIOUS...
OH, YEAH – THAT REMINDS ME... THERE'S SOMETHING ELSE YOU NEED TO SEE.
JERRY LEE LEWIS' DOCTOR VISIT

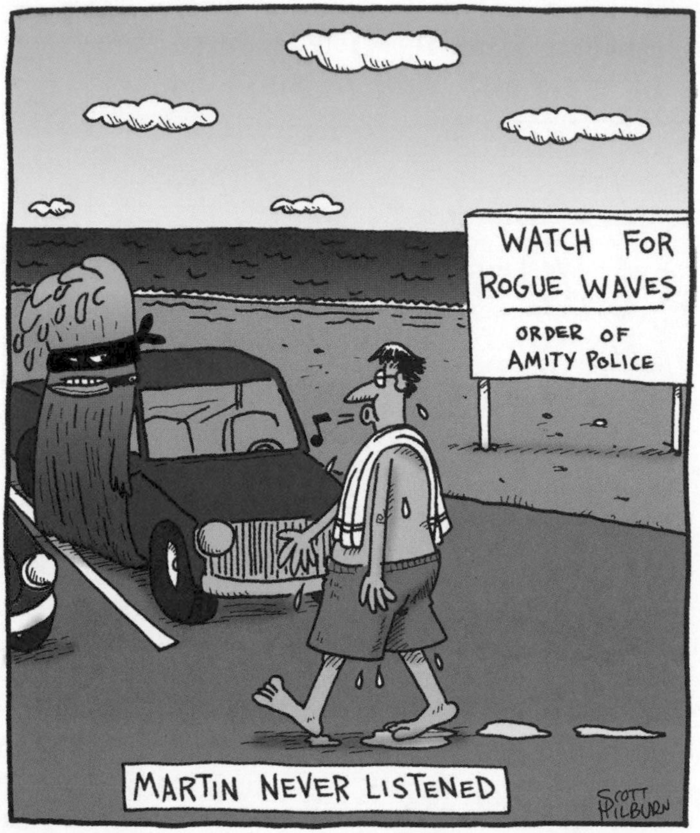
WATCH FOR ROGUE WAVES
ORDER OF AMITY POLICE
MARTIN NEVER LISTENED
SCOTT HILBURN

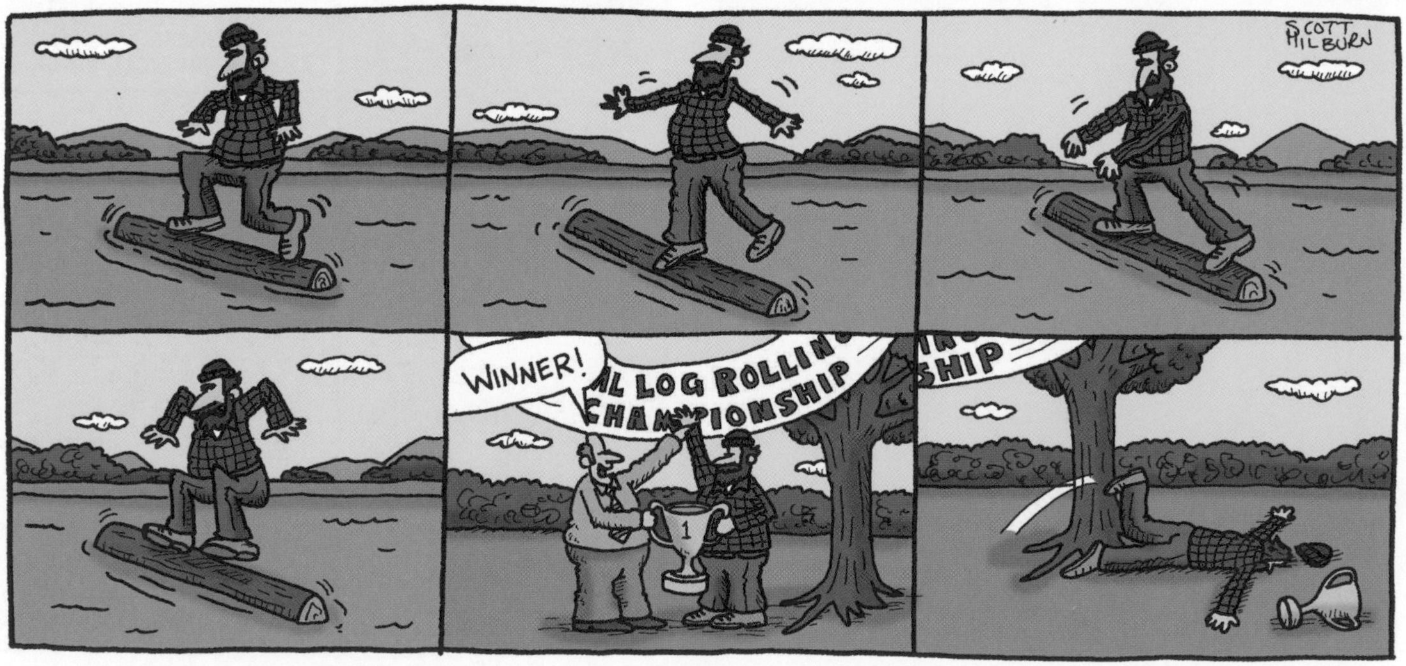
SCOTT HILBURN
WINNER!
L LOG ROLLIN
CHAMPIONSHIP
SHIP

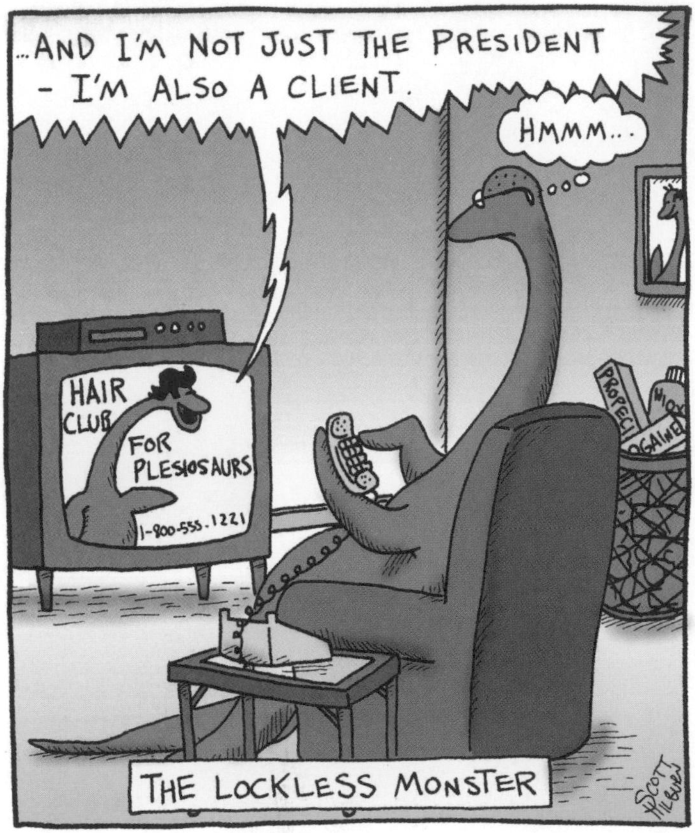
...AND I'M NOT JUST THE PRESIDENT - I'M ALSO A CLIENT.
HMMM...
HAIR CLUB FOR PLESIOSAURS
1-800-555-1221
THE LOCKLESS MONSTER

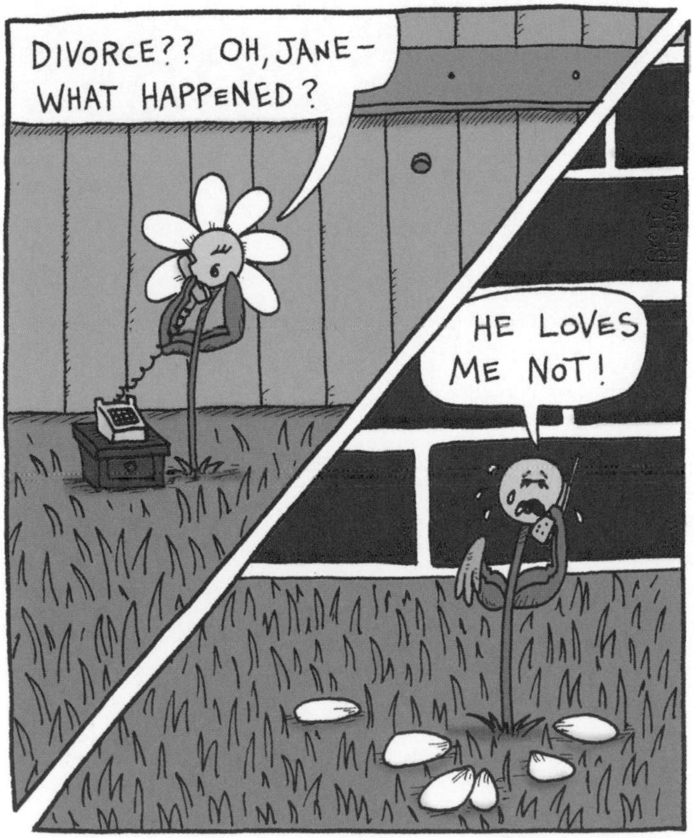
DIVORCE?? OH, JANE- WHAT HAPPENED?
HE LOVES ME NOT!

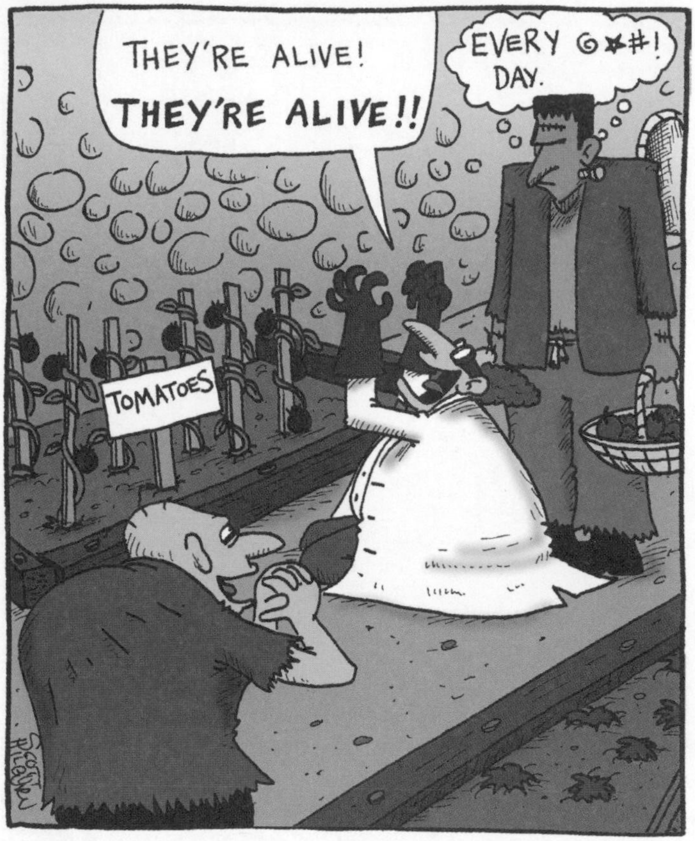
THEY'RE ALIVE!
THEY'RE ALIVE!!
EVERY @*#! DAY.
TOMATOES
SCOTT HILBURN

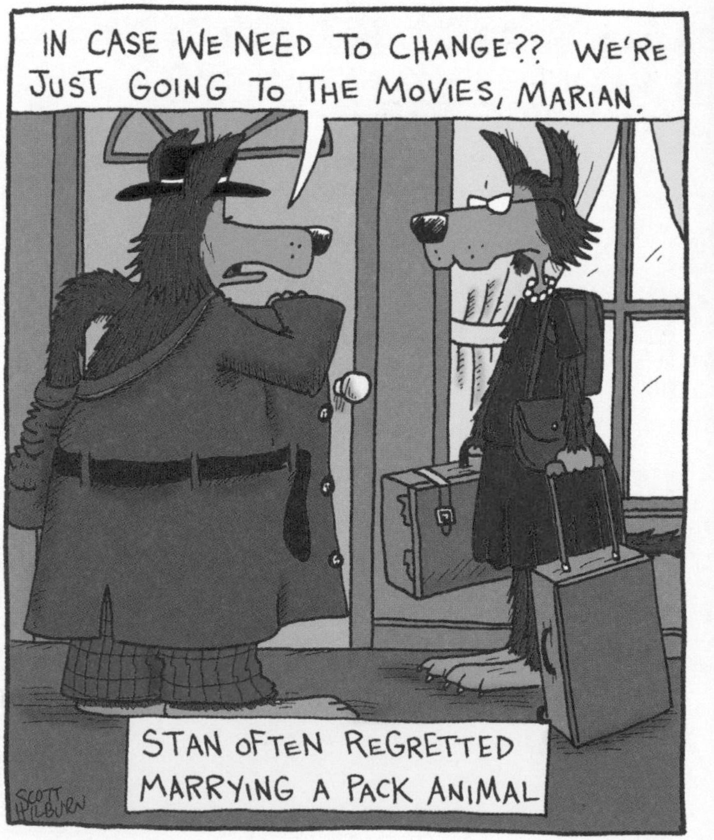
IN CASE WE NEED TO CHANGE?? WE'RE JUST GOING TO THE MOVIES, MARIAN.
STAN OFTEN REGRETTED MARRYING A PACK ANIMAL
SCOTT HILBURN

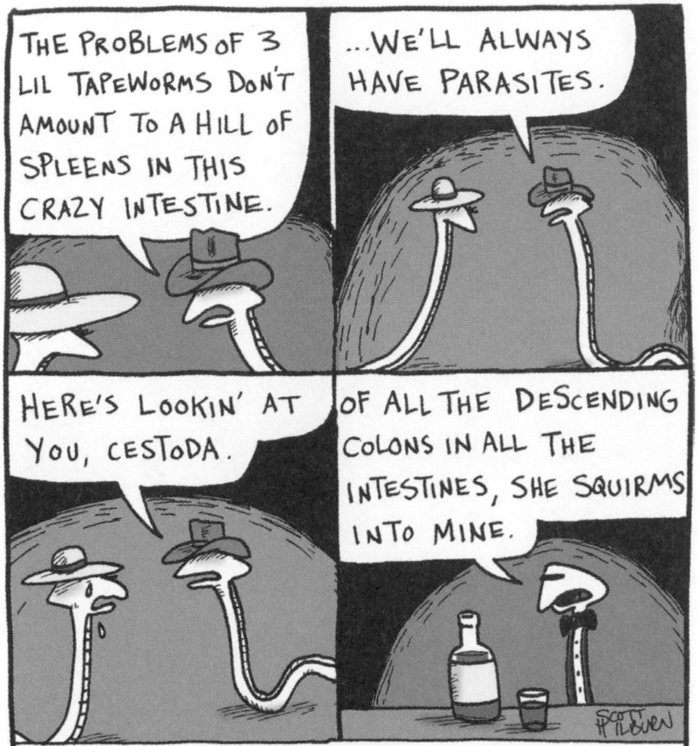
THE PROBLEMS OF 3 LIL TAPEWORMS DON'T AMOUNT TO A HILL OF SPLEENS IN THIS CRAZY INTESTINE.
...WE'LL ALWAYS HAVE PARASITES.
HERE'S LOOKIN' AT YOU, CESTODA.
OF ALL THE DESCENDING COLONS IN ALL THE INTESTINES, SHE SQUIRMS INTO MINE.
SCOTT HILBURN
CLASSIC SCENES FROM "COLONBLANCA."

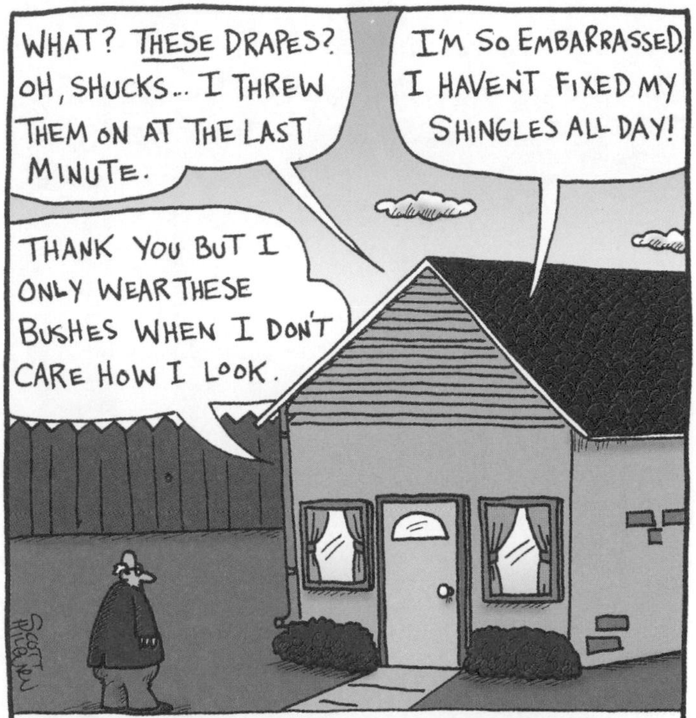
WHAT? THESE DRAPES? OH, SHUCKS... I THREW THEM ON AT THE LAST MINUTE.
I'M SO EMBARRASSED. I HAVEN'T FIXED MY SHINGLES ALL DAY!
THANK YOU BUT I ONLY WEAR THESE BUSHES WHEN I DON'T CARE HOW I LOOK.
SCOTT HILBURN
DESPITE HIS SUCCESS, FRANK LIVED IN A RATHER MODEST HOME

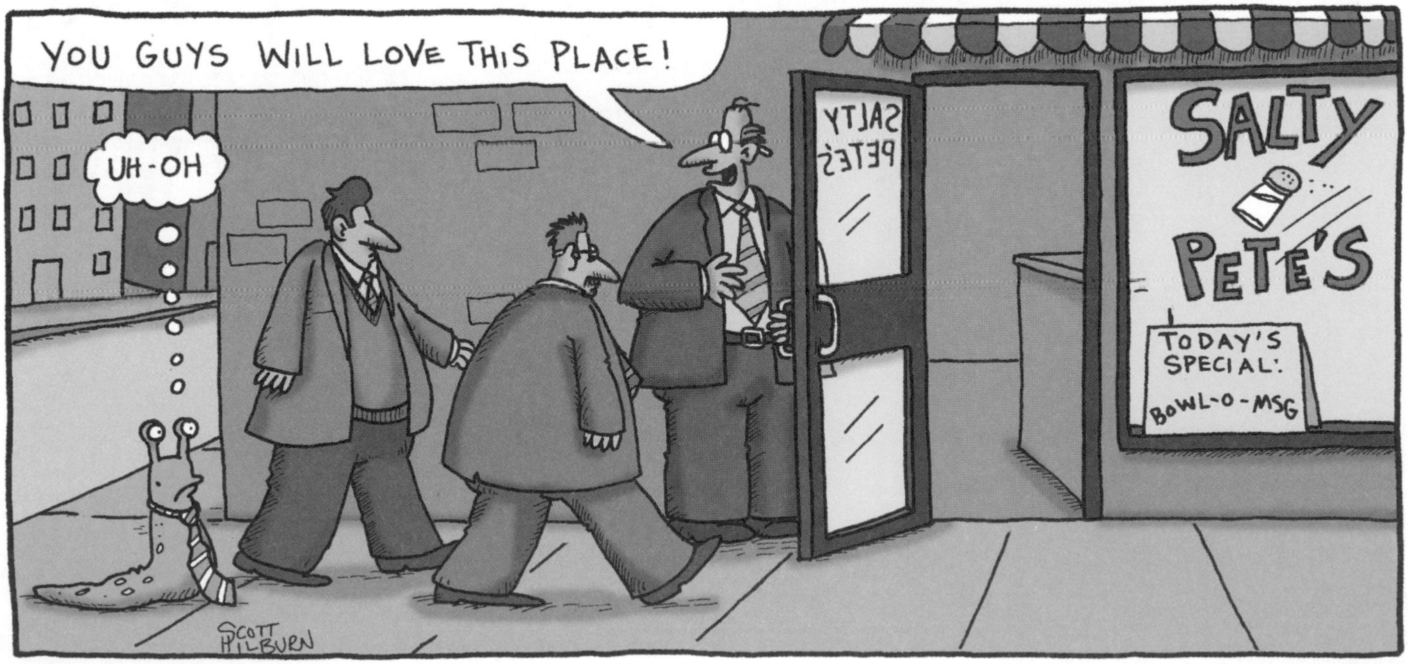
YOU GUYS WILL LOVE THIS PLACE!
UH-OH
SALTY PETE'S
SALTY PETE'S
TODAY'S SPECIAL: BOWL-O-MSG
SCOTT HILBURN

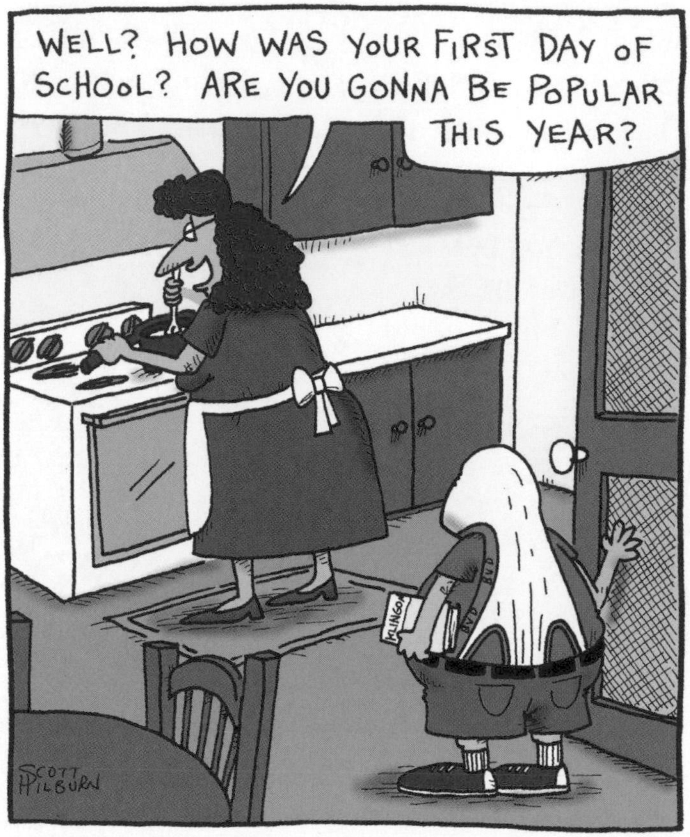
WELL? HOW WAS YOUR FIRST DAY OF SCHOOL? ARE YOU GONNA BE POPULAR THIS YEAR?
SCOTT HILBURN

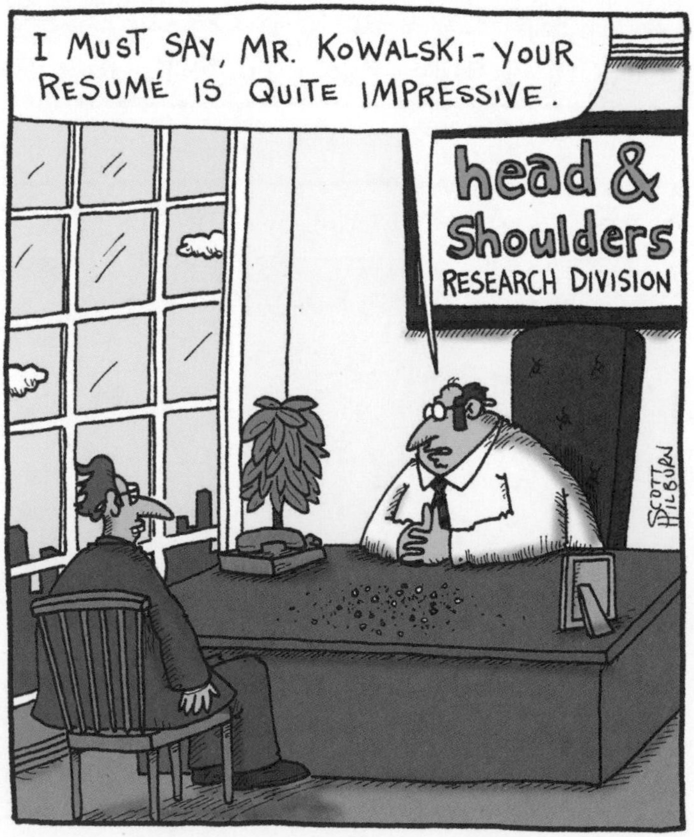
I MUST SAY, MR. KOWALSKI - YOUR RESUMÉ IS QUITE IMPRESSIVE.
head & Shoulders
RESEARCH DIVISION
SCOTT HILBURN

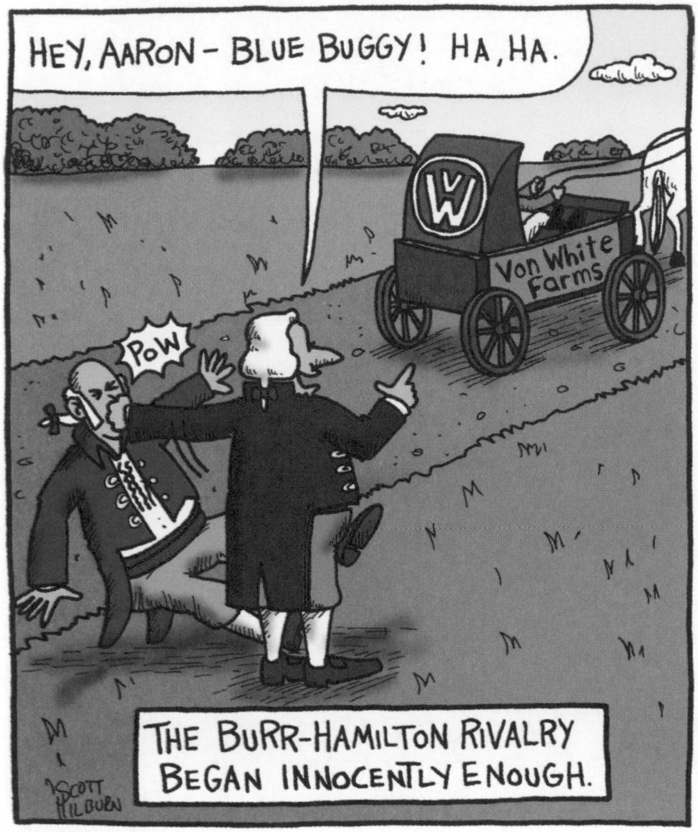
HEY, AARON - BLUE BUGGY! HA, HA.
POW
Von White Farms
SCOTT HILBURN

THE BURR-HAMILTON RIVALRY BEGAN INNOCENTLY ENOUGH.

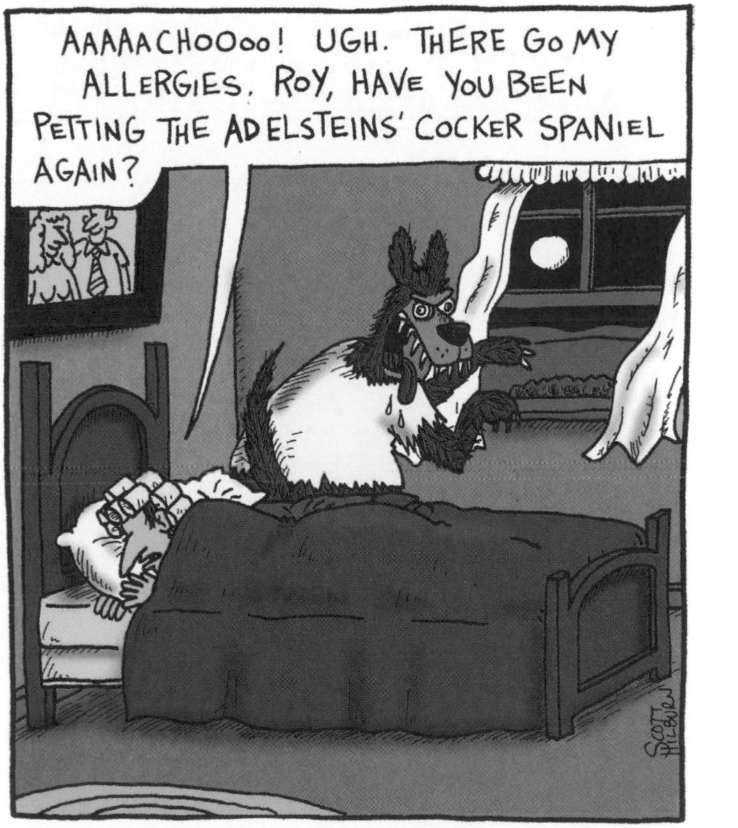
AAAAACHOOooo! UGH. THERE GO MY ALLERGIES. ROY, HAVE YOU BEEN PETTING THE ADELSTEINS' COCKER SPANIEL AGAIN?
SCOTT HILBURN

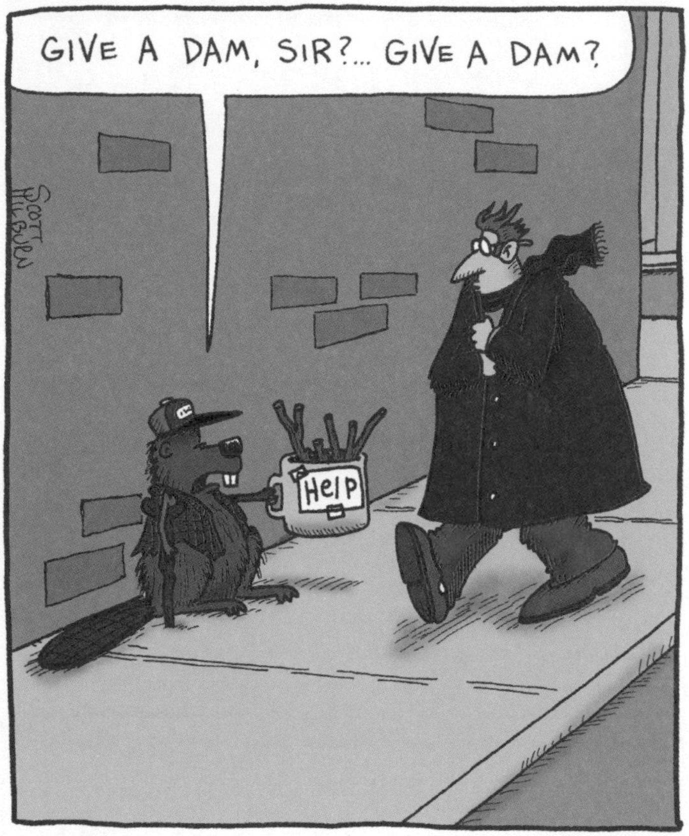
GIVE A DAM, SIR?... GIVE A DAM?
Help

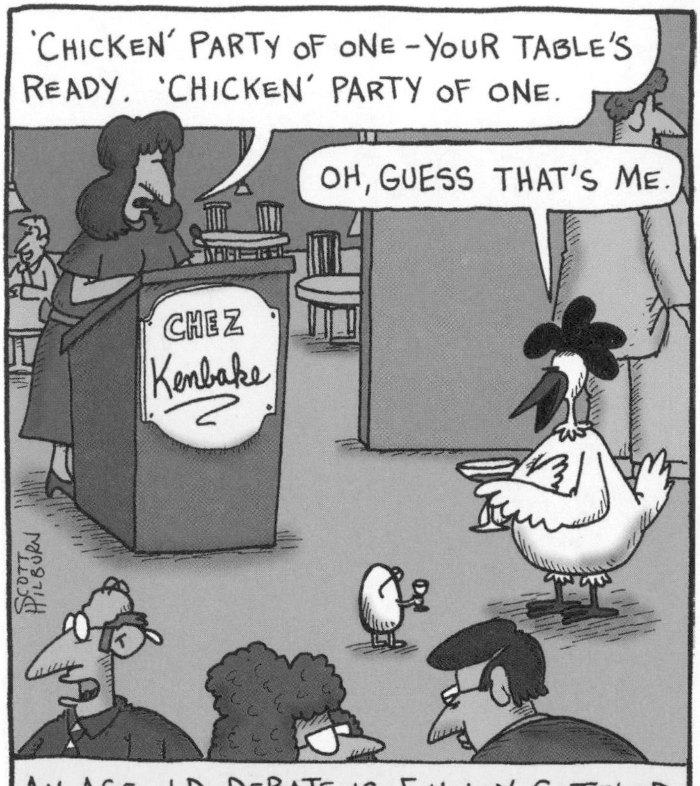
'CHICKEN' PARTY OF ONE - YOUR TABLE'S READY. 'CHICKEN' PARTY OF ONE.
OH, GUESS THAT'S ME.
CHEZ Kenbake

AN AGE-OLD DEBATE IS FINALLY SETTLED.

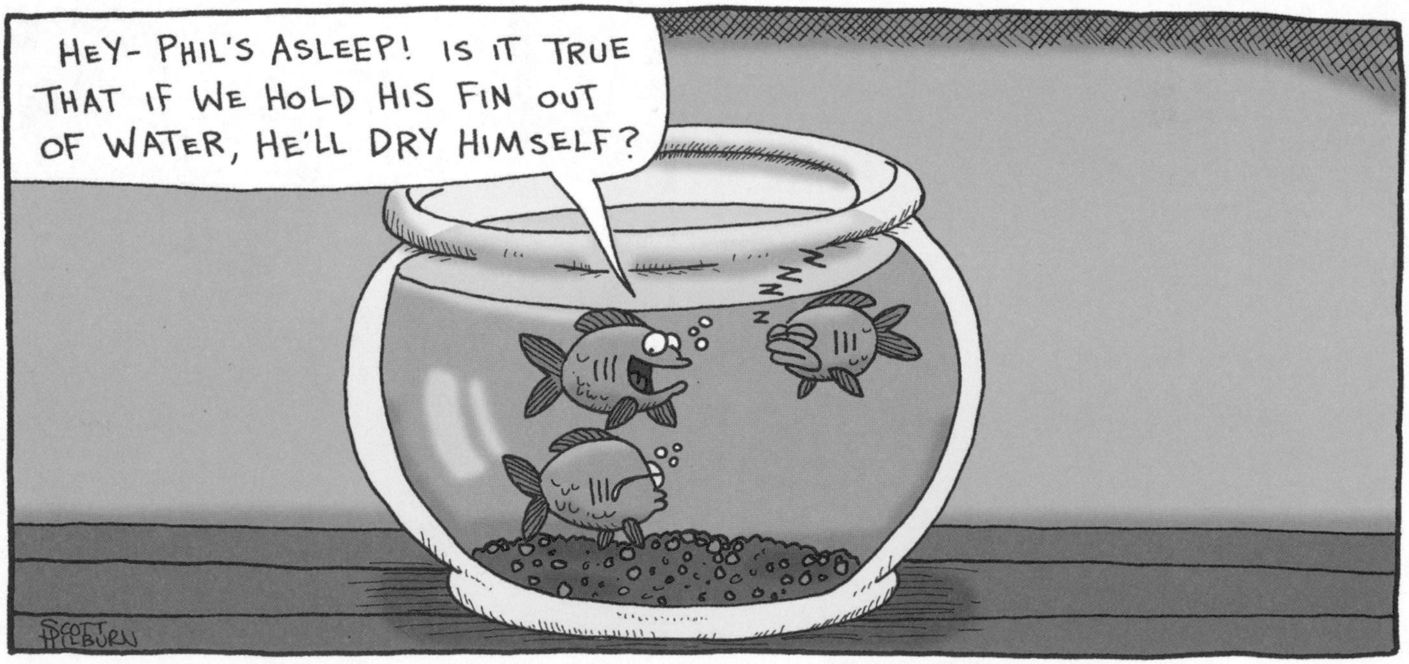
HEY- PHIL'S ASLEEP! IS IT TRUE THAT IF WE HOLD HIS FIN OUT OF WATER, HE'LL DRY HIMSELF?
ZZZZZ

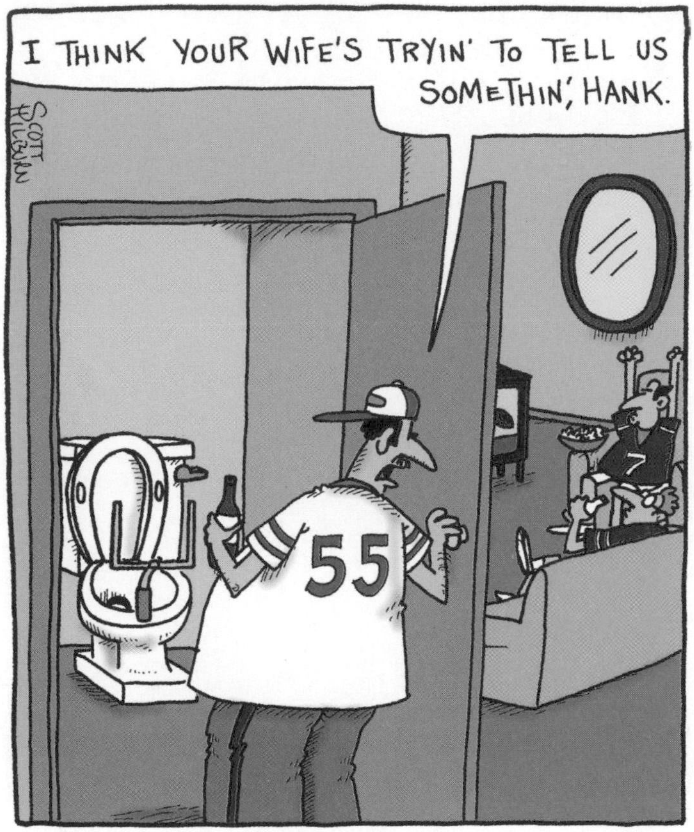
I THINK YOUR WIFE'S TRYIN' TO TELL US SOMETHIN', HANK.
SCOTT HILBURN
55
7

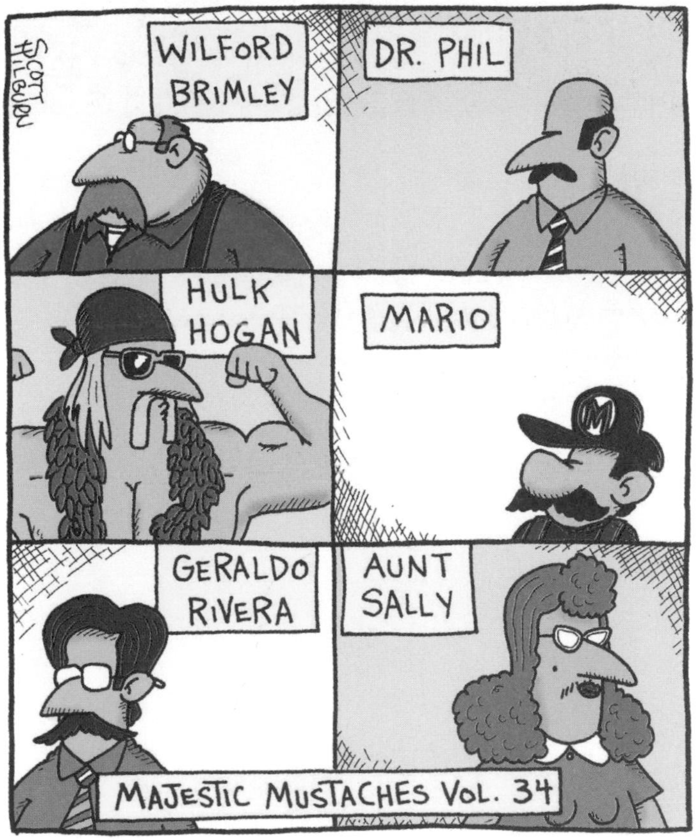
SCOTT HILBURN
WILFORD BRIMLEY
DR. PHIL
HULK HOGAN
MARIO
GERALDO RIVERA
AUNT SALLY
MAJESTIC MUSTACHES VOL. 34

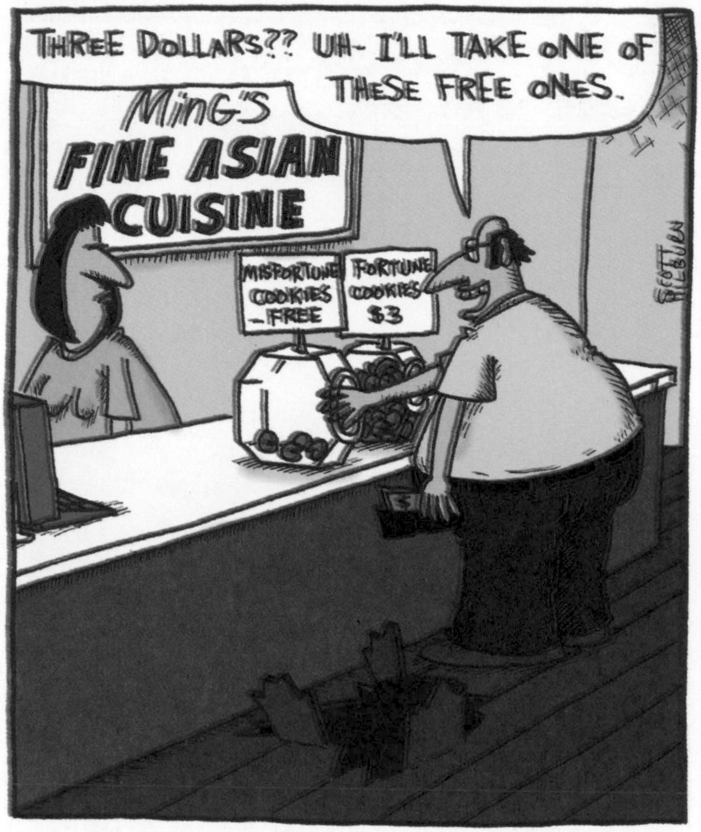
THREE DOLLARS?? UH- I'LL TAKE ONE OF THESE FREE ONES.
Ming's FINE ASIAN CUISINE
MISFORTUNE COOKIES -FREE
FORTUNE COOKIES $3

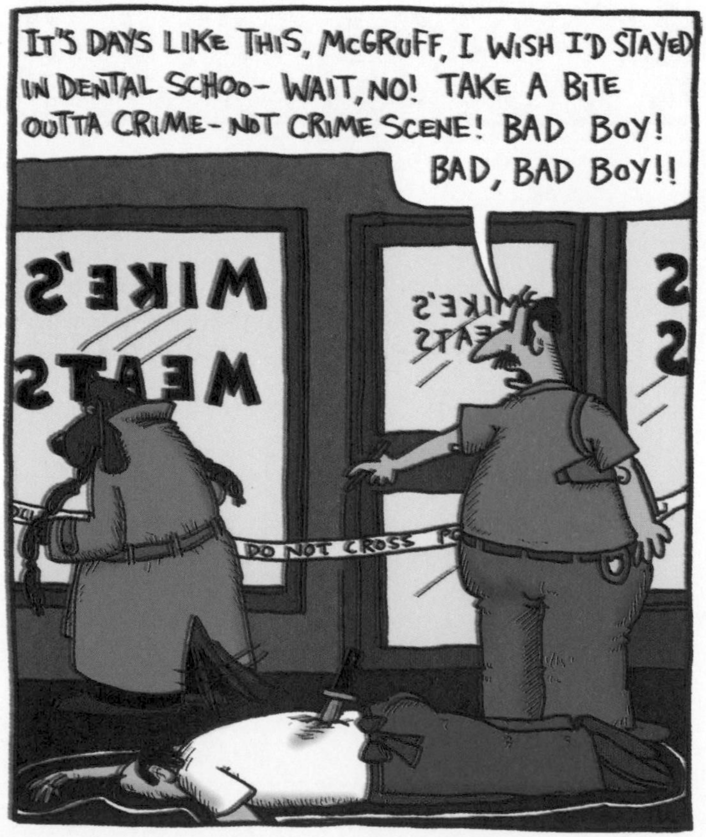
IT'S DAYS LIKE THIS, McGRUFF, I WISH I'D STAYED IN DENTAL SCHOO- WAIT, NO! TAKE A BITE OUTTA CRIME- NOT CRIME SCENE! BAD BOY! BAD, BAD BOY!!
DO NOT CROSS

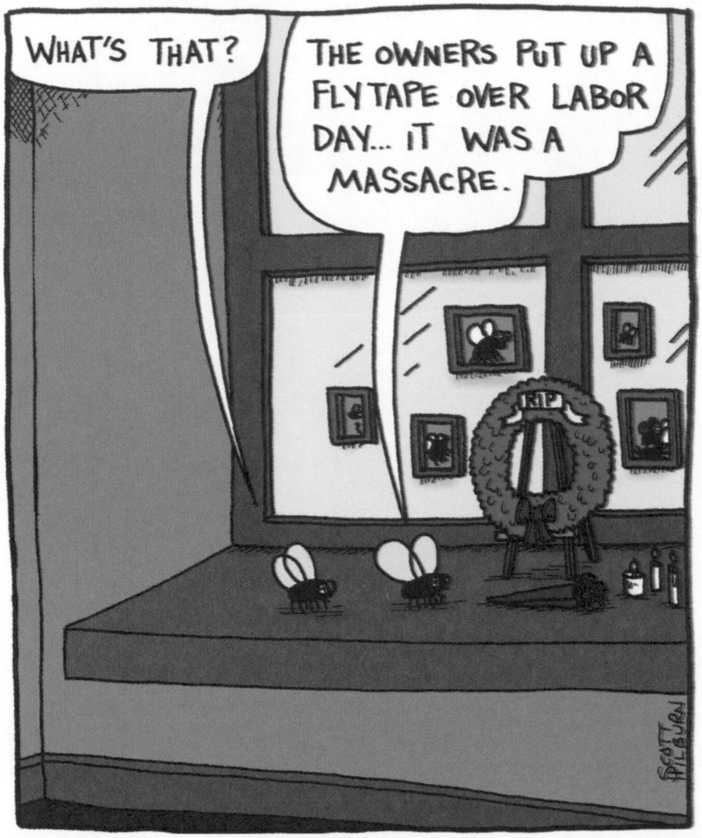
WHAT'S THAT?
THE OWNERS PUT UP A FLYTAPE OVER LABOR DAY... IT WAS A MASSACRE.
RIP

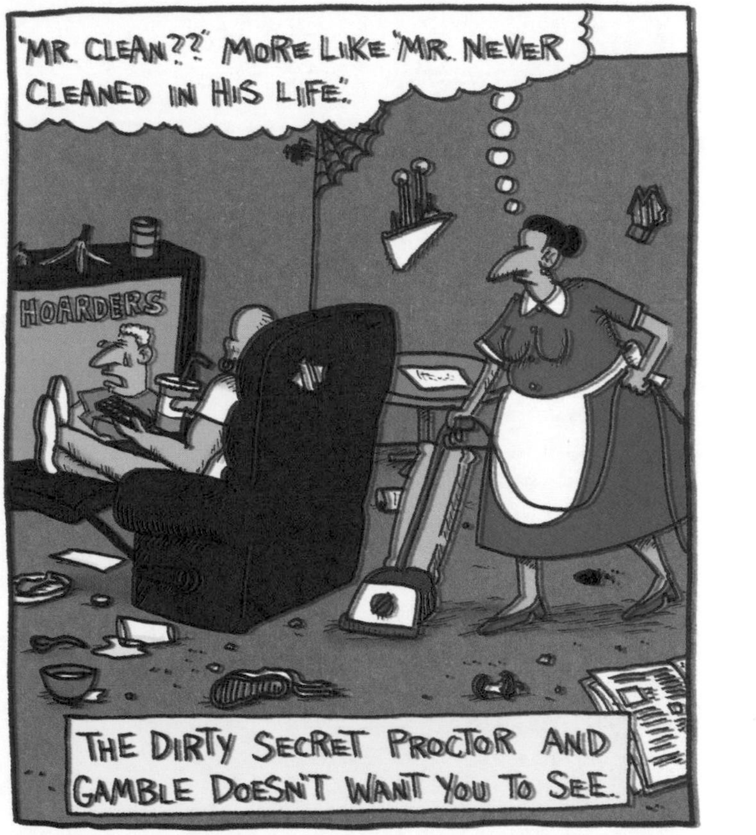
"MR. CLEAN??" MORE LIKE "MR. NEVER CLEANED IN HIS LIFE."
HOARDERS
THE DIRTY SECRET PROCTOR AND GAMBLE DOESN'T WANT YOU TO SEE.

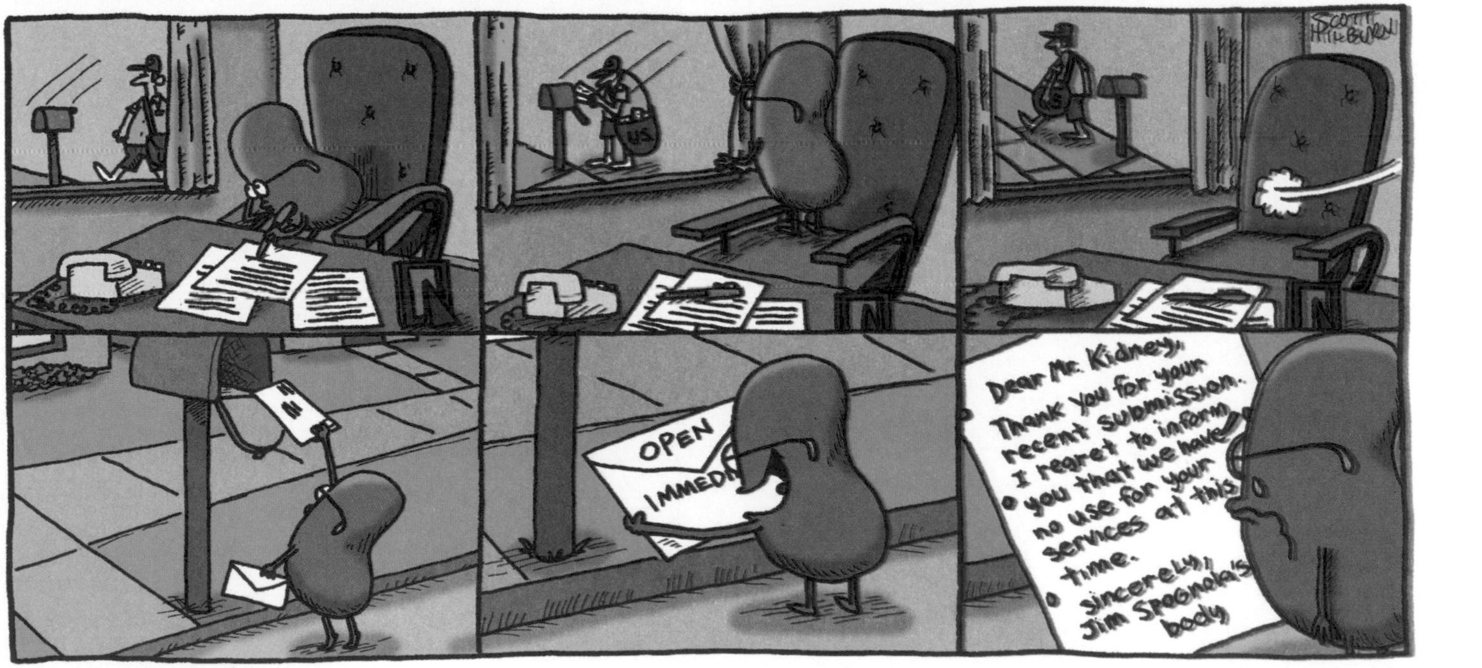
US
OPEN
IMMEDI
Dear Mr. Kidney,
Thank you for your recent submission. I regret to inform you that we have no use for your services at this time.
Sincerely,
Jim Spagnola's body

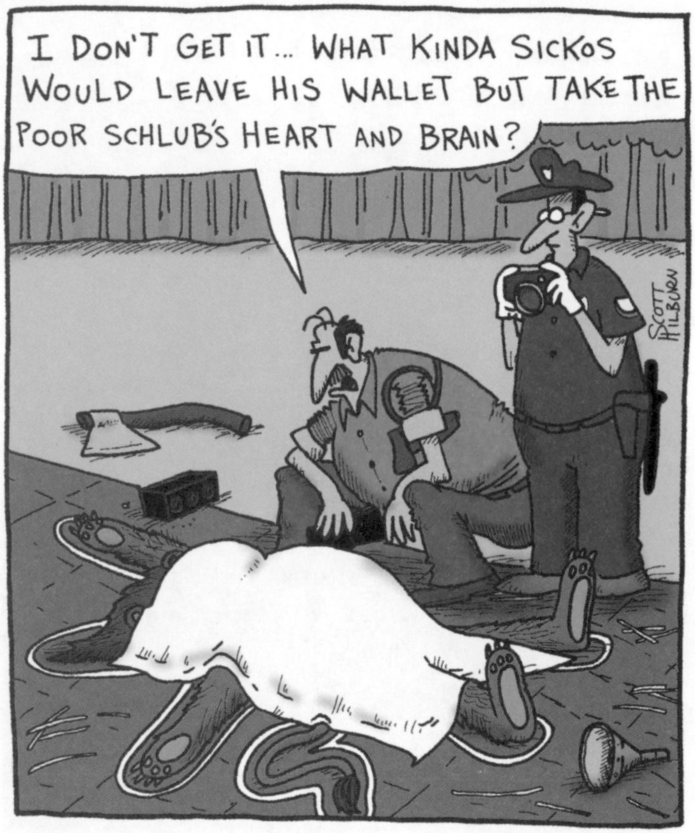
I DON'T GET IT... WHAT KINDA SICKOS WOULD LEAVE HIS WALLET BUT TAKE THE POOR SCHLUB'S HEART AND BRAIN?
SCOTT HILBURN

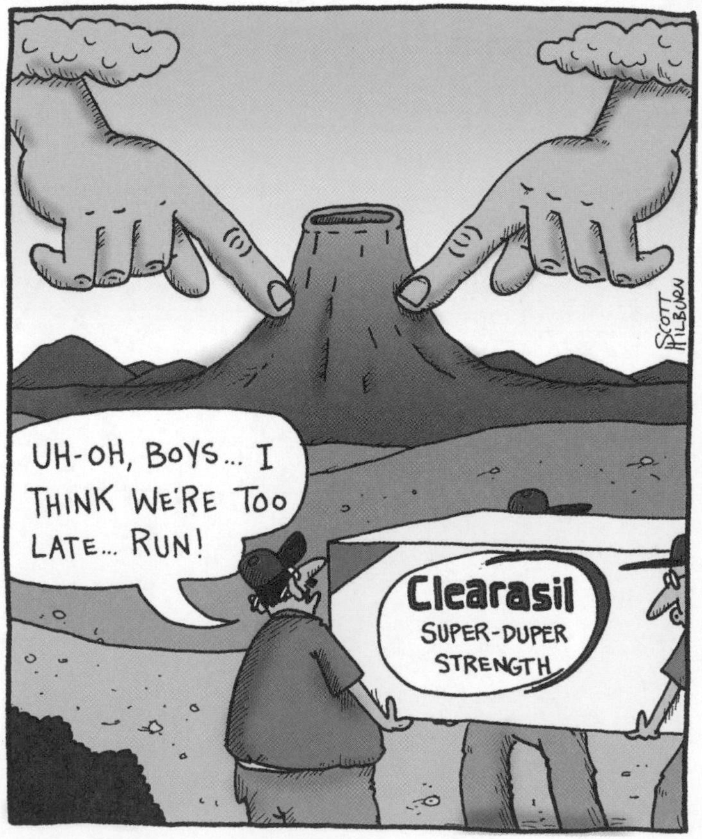
SCOTT HILBURN
UH-OH, BOYS... I THINK WE'RE TOO LATE... RUN!
Clearasil
SUPER-DUPER STRENGTH

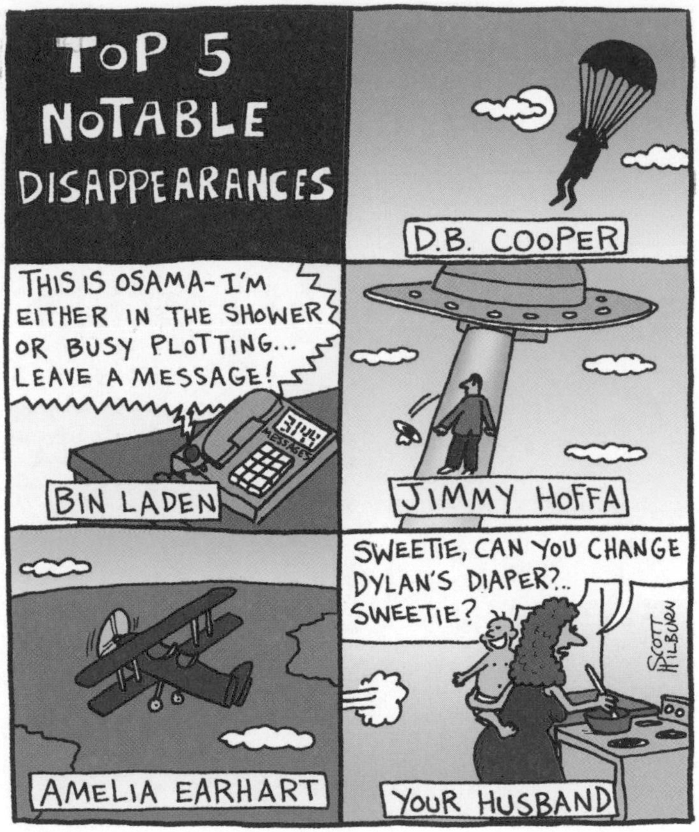
TOP 5 NOTABLE DISAPPEARANCES
D.B. COOPER
THIS IS OSAMA- I'M EITHER IN THE SHOWER OR BUSY PLOTTING... LEAVE A MESSAGE!
MESSAGES
BIN LADEN
JIMMY HOFFA
AMELIA EARHART
SWEETIE, CAN YOU CHANGE DYLAN'S DIAPER?.. SWEETIE?
YOUR HUSBAND
SCOTT HILBURN

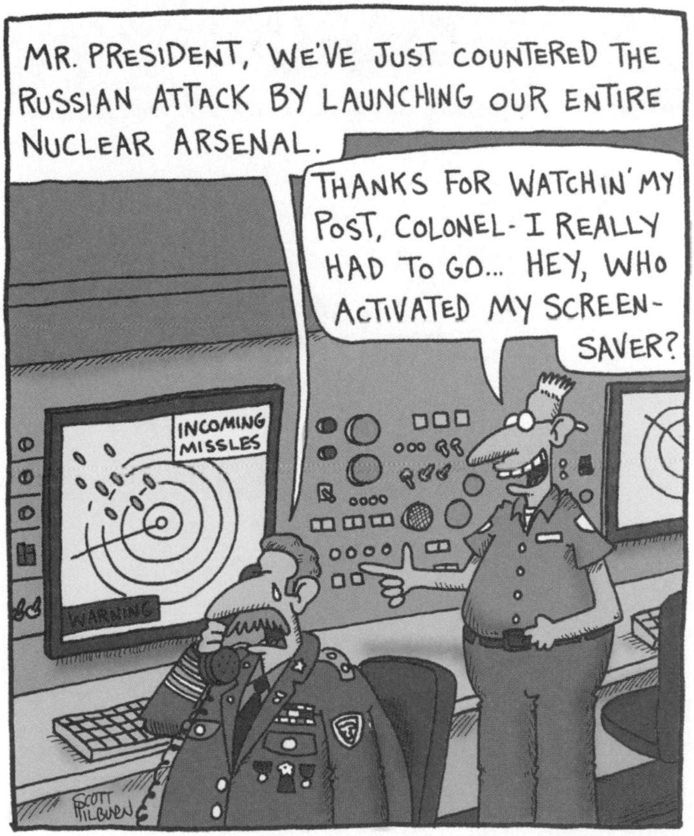
MR. PRESIDENT, WE'VE JUST COUNTERED THE RUSSIAN ATTACK BY LAUNCHING OUR ENTIRE NUCLEAR ARSENAL.
THANKS FOR WATCHIN' MY POST, COLONEL- I REALLY HAD TO GO... HEY, WHO ACTIVATED MY SCREEN-SAVER?
INCOMING MISSLES
WARNING
SCOTT HILBURN

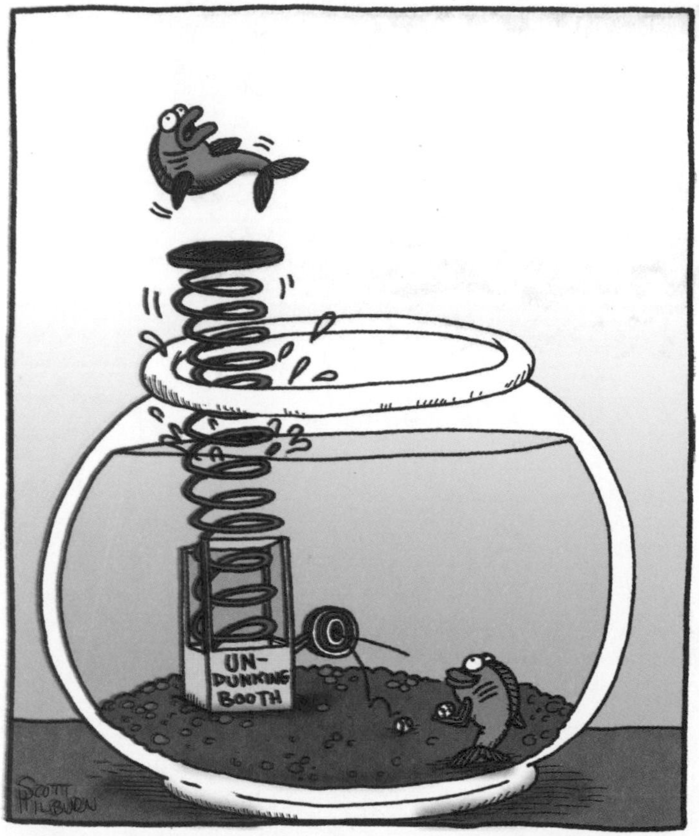
UN-DUNKING BOOTH
SCOTT HILBURN

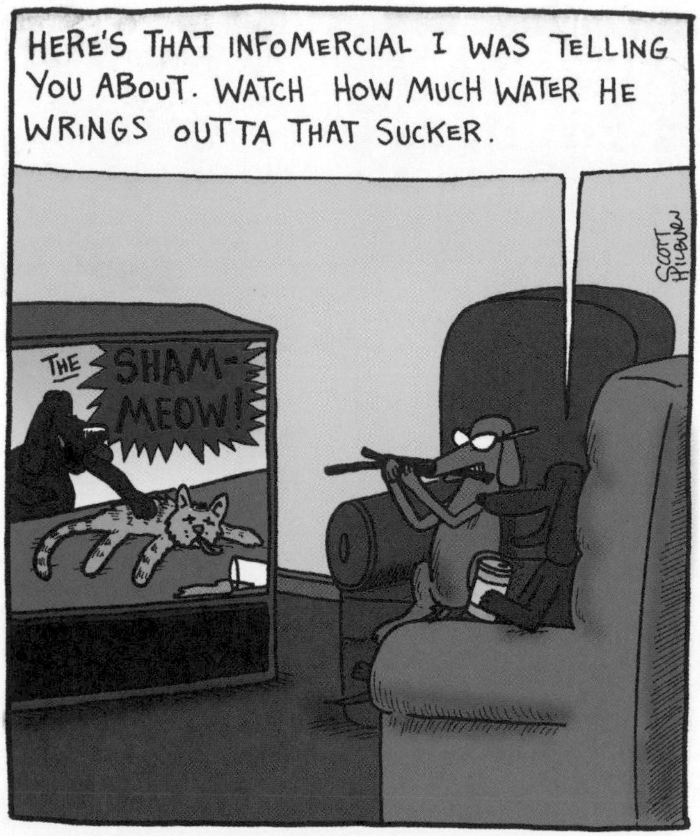
HERE'S THAT INFOMERCIAL I WAS TELLING YOU ABOUT. WATCH HOW MUCH WATER HE WRINGS OUTTA THAT SUCKER.
THE SHAM-MEOW!
SCOTT HILBURN

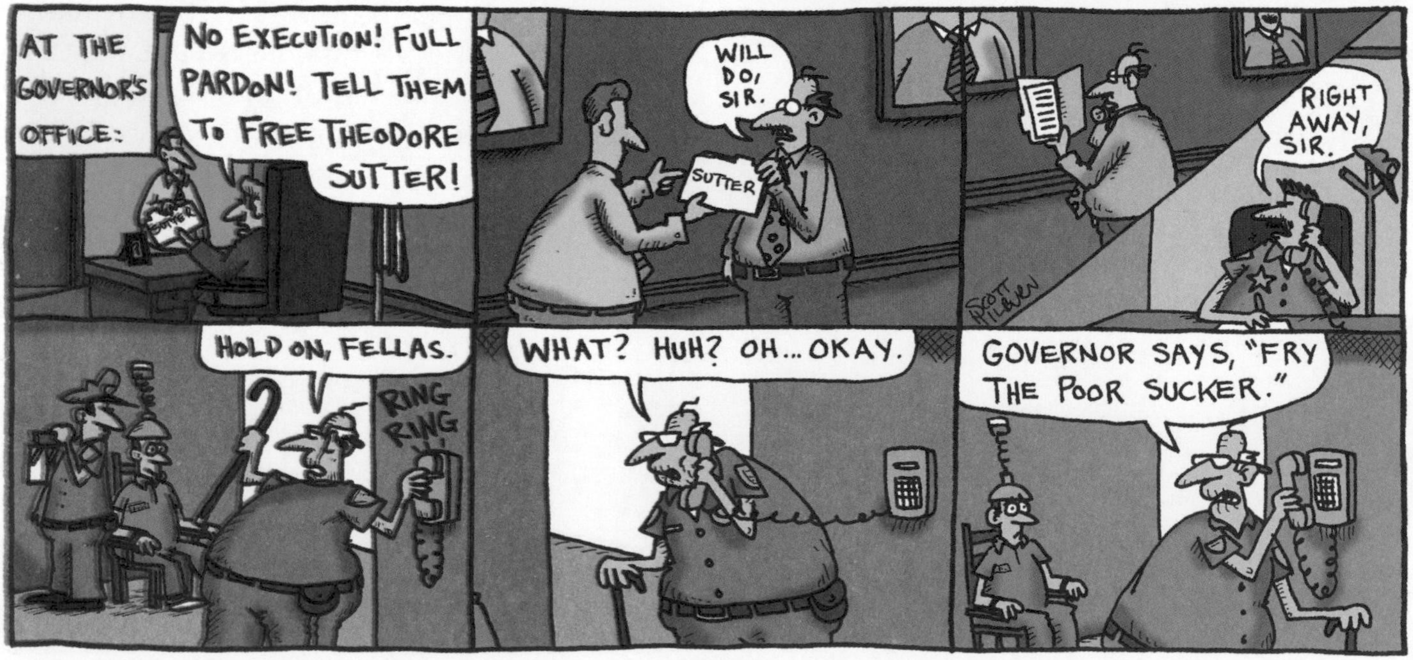
AT THE GOVERNOR'S OFFICE:
NO EXECUTION! FULL PARDON! TELL THEM TO FREE THEODORE SUTTER!
SUTTER
WILL DO, SIR.
RIGHT AWAY, SIR.
SCOTT HILBURN
HOLD ON, FELLAS.
RING RING
WHAT? HUH? OH... OKAY.
GOVERNOR SAYS, "FRY THE POOR SUCKER."

SORRY, MR. GORE, BUT THIS ROOT CANAL'S GONNA TAKE LONGER THAN I THOUGHT. THAT SUCKER'S WAAAY BACK THERE. JUST NOOO EASY WAY TO GET TO IT.
SCOTT HILBURN

AN INCONVENIENT TOOTH

YOU BLESS YOU.
SCOTT HILBURN

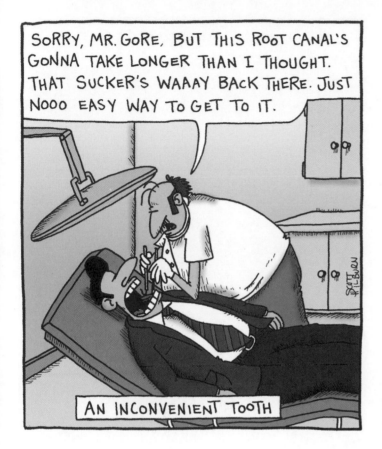

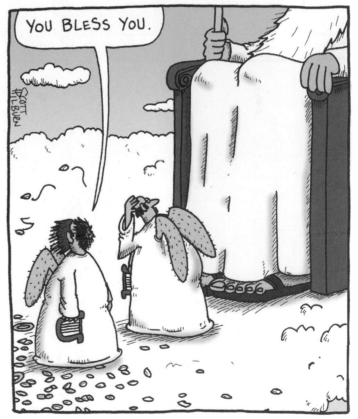

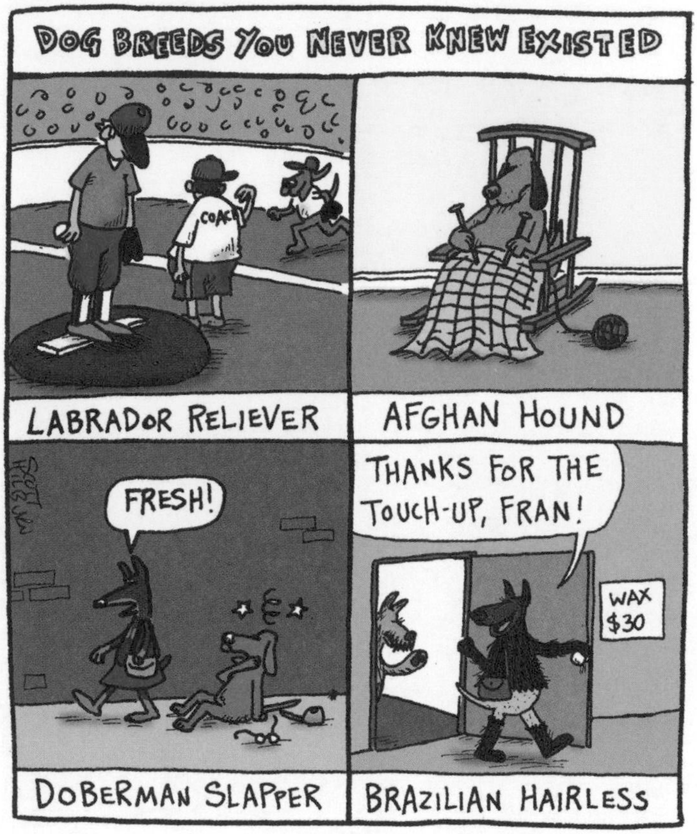
DOG BREEDS YOU NEVER KNEW EXISTED
COACH
LABRADOR RELIEVER
AFGHAN HOUND
SCOTT HILBURN
FRESH!
THANKS FOR THE TOUCH-UP, FRAN!
WAX $30
DOBERMAN SLAPPER
BRAZILIAN HAIRLESS

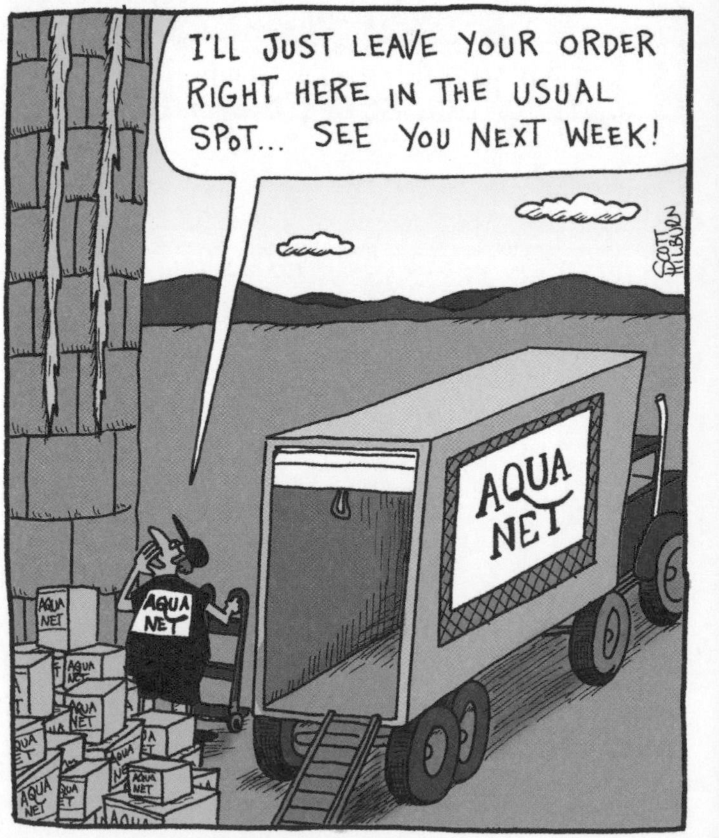
I'LL JUST LEAVE YOUR ORDER RIGHT HERE IN THE USUAL SPOT... SEE YOU NEXT WEEK!
SCOTT HILBURN
AQUA NET
AQUA NET
AQUA NET

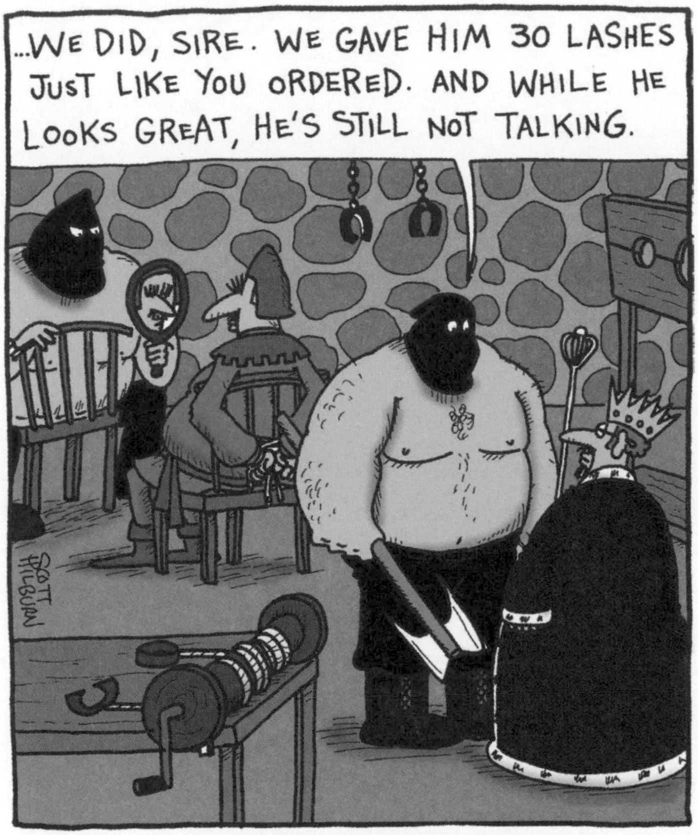
...WE DID, SIRE. WE GAVE HIM 30 LASHES JUST LIKE YOU ORDERED. AND WHILE HE LOOKS GREAT, HE'S STILL NOT TALKING.
SCOTT HILBURN

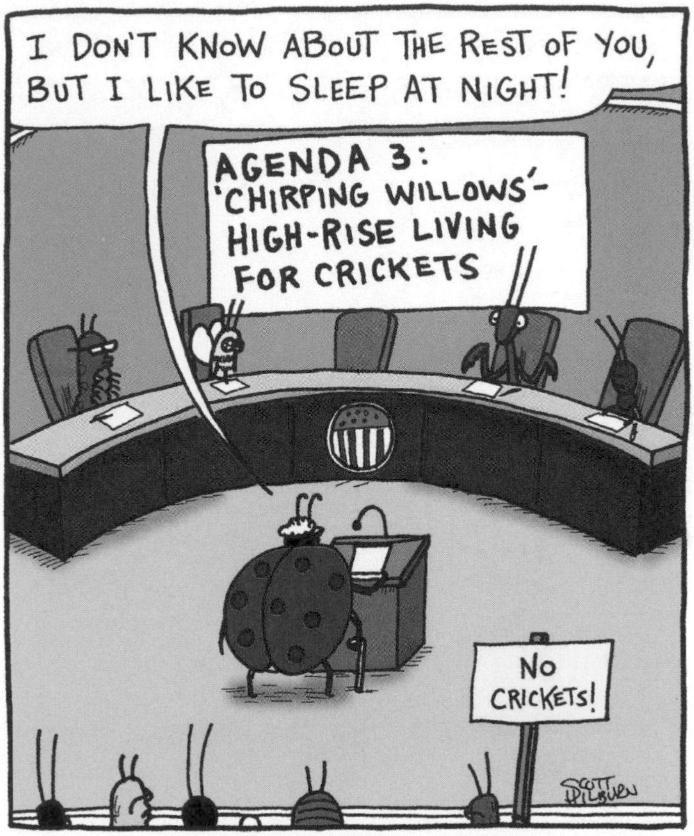
I DON'T KNOW ABOUT THE REST OF YOU, BUT I LIKE TO SLEEP AT NIGHT!
AGENDA 3: 'CHIRPING WILLOWS'- HIGH-RISE LIVING FOR CRICKETS
NO CRICKETS!
SCOTT HILBURN

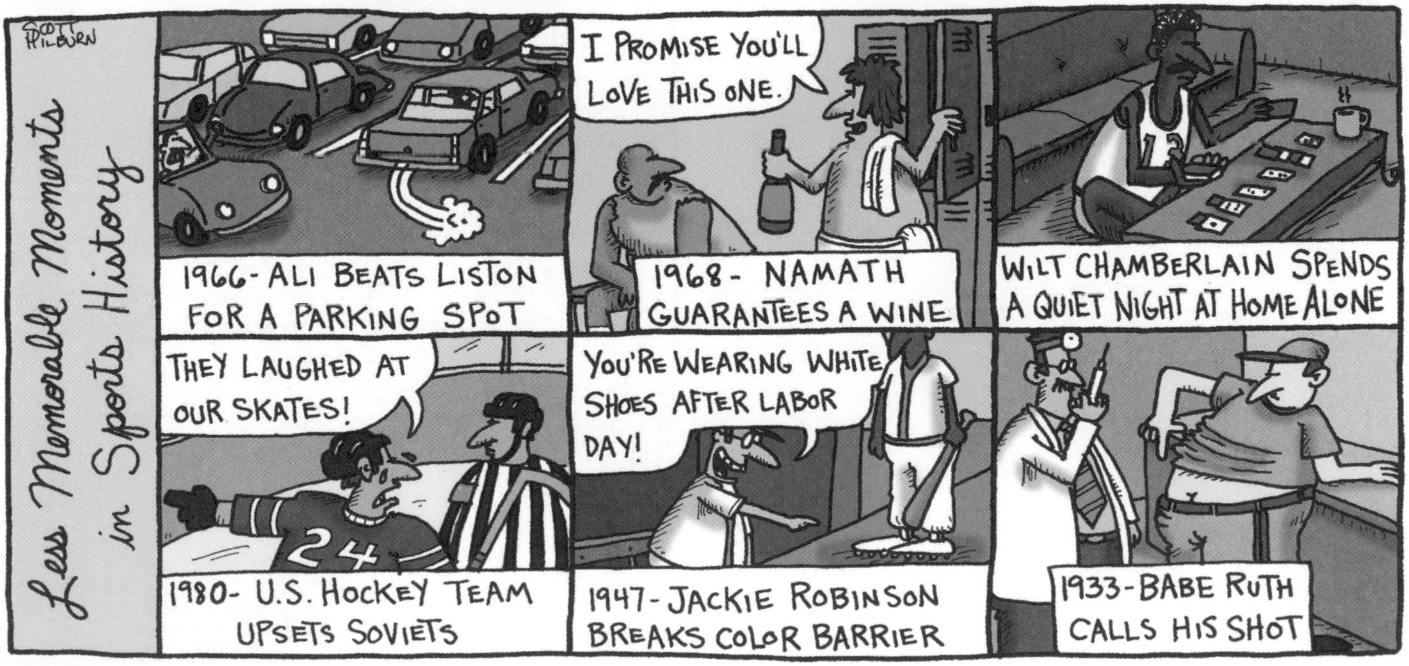
SCOTT HILBURN
Less Memorable Moments in Sports History
1966- ALI BEATS LISTON FOR A PARKING SPOT
I PROMISE YOU'LL LOVE THIS ONE.
1968- NAMATH GUARANTEES A WINE
WILT CHAMBERLAIN SPENDS A QUIET NIGHT AT HOME ALONE
THEY LAUGHED AT OUR SKATES!
24
1980- U.S. HOCKEY TEAM UPSETS SOVIETS
YOU'RE WEARING WHITE SHOES AFTER LABOR DAY!
1947- JACKIE ROBINSON BREAKS COLOR BARRIER
1933- BABE RUTH CALLS HIS SHOT

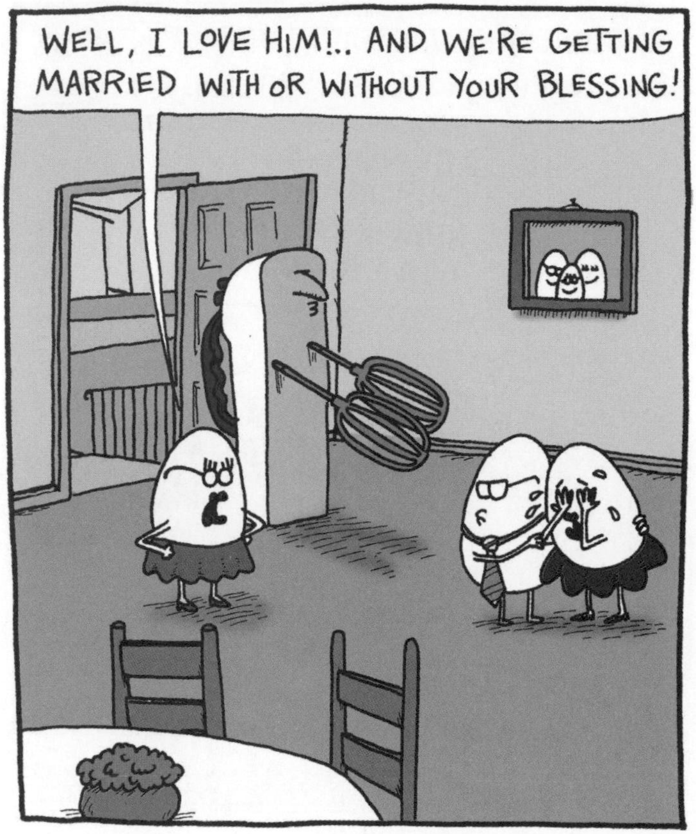
WELL, I LOVE HIM!.. AND WE'RE GETTING MARRIED WITH OR WITHOUT YOUR BLESSING!

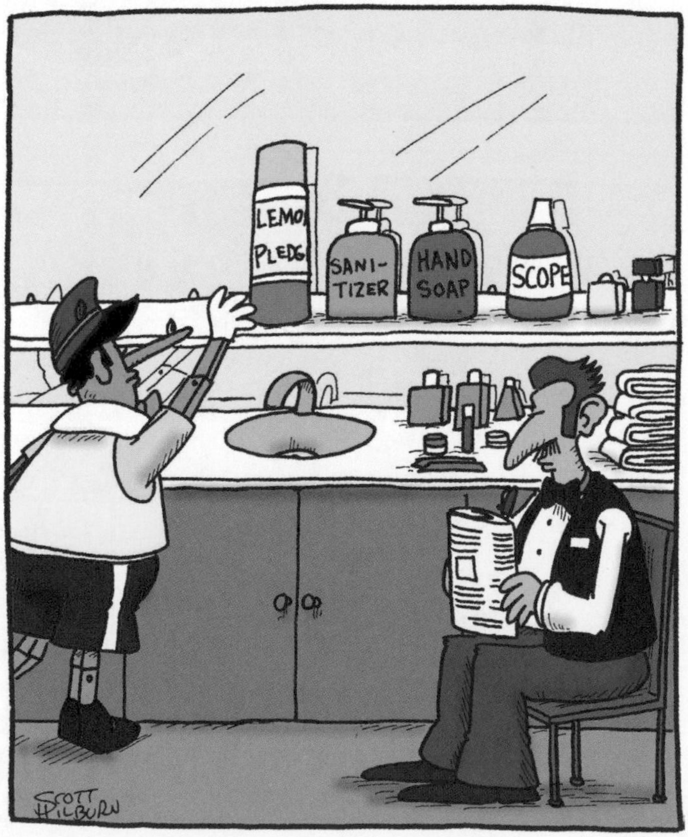
LEMO
PLEDG
SANI-TIZER
HAND SOAP
SCOPE
SCOTT HILBURN

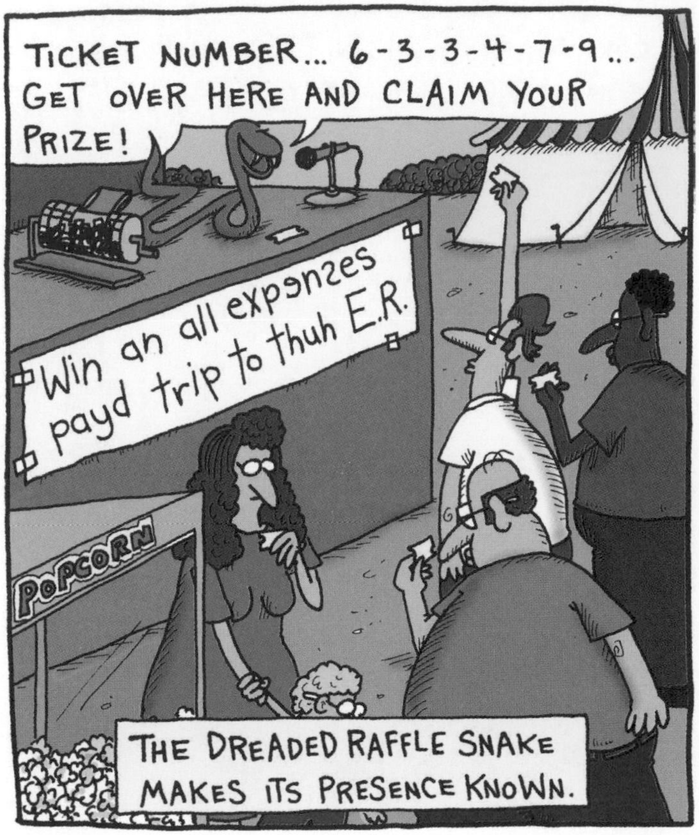
TICKET NUMBER... 6-3-3-4-7-9... GET OVER HERE AND CLAIM YOUR PRIZE!
Win an all expenzes payd trip to thuh E.R.
POPCORN
THE DREADED RAFFLE SNAKE MAKES ITS PRESENCE KNOWN.

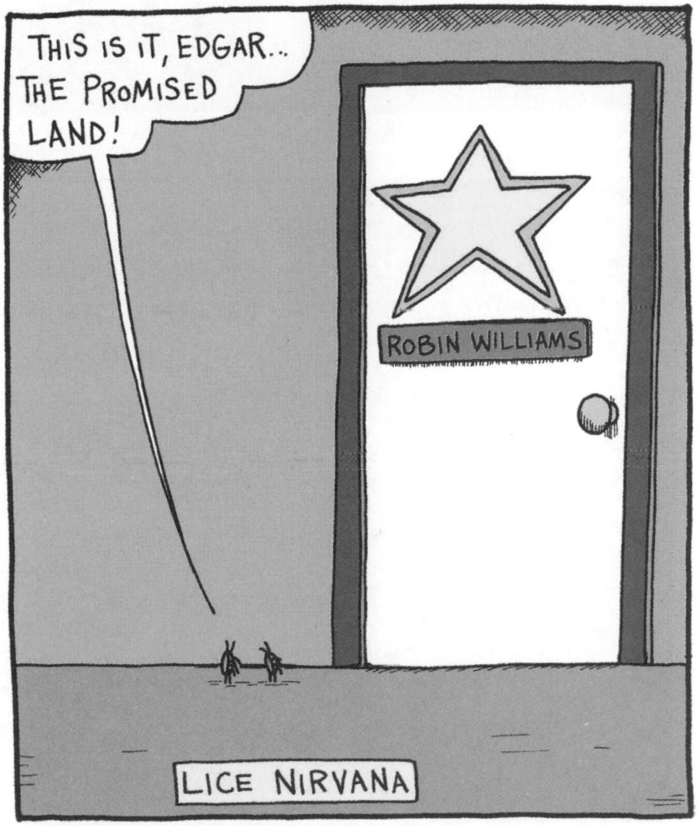
THIS IS IT, EDGAR... THE PROMISED LAND!
ROBIN WILLIAMS
LICE NIRVANA

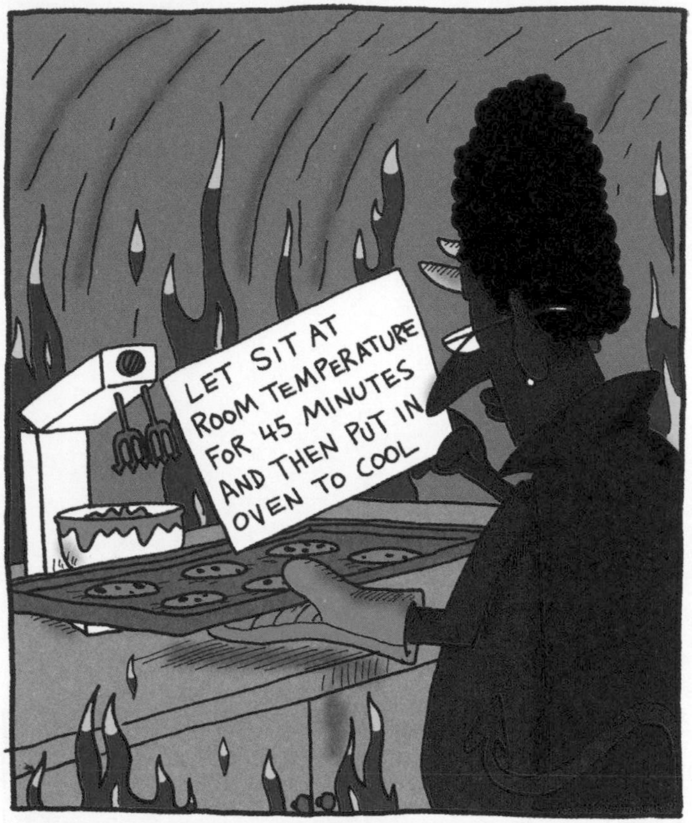
LET SIT AT ROOM TEMPERATURE FOR 45 MINUTES AND THEN PUT IN OVEN TO COOL

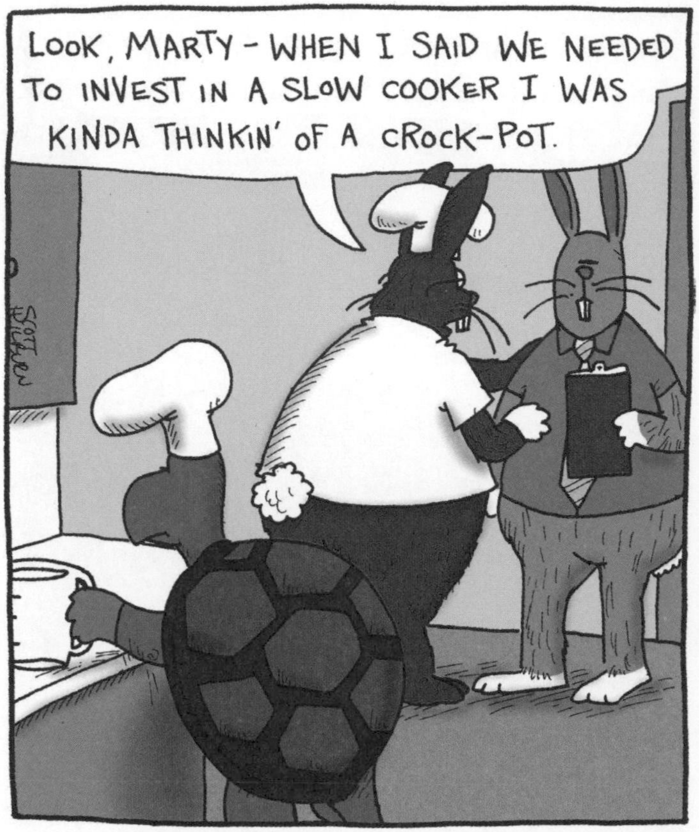
LOOK, MARTY - WHEN I SAID WE NEEDED TO INVEST IN A SLOW COOKER I WAS KINDA THINKIN' OF A CROCK-POT.

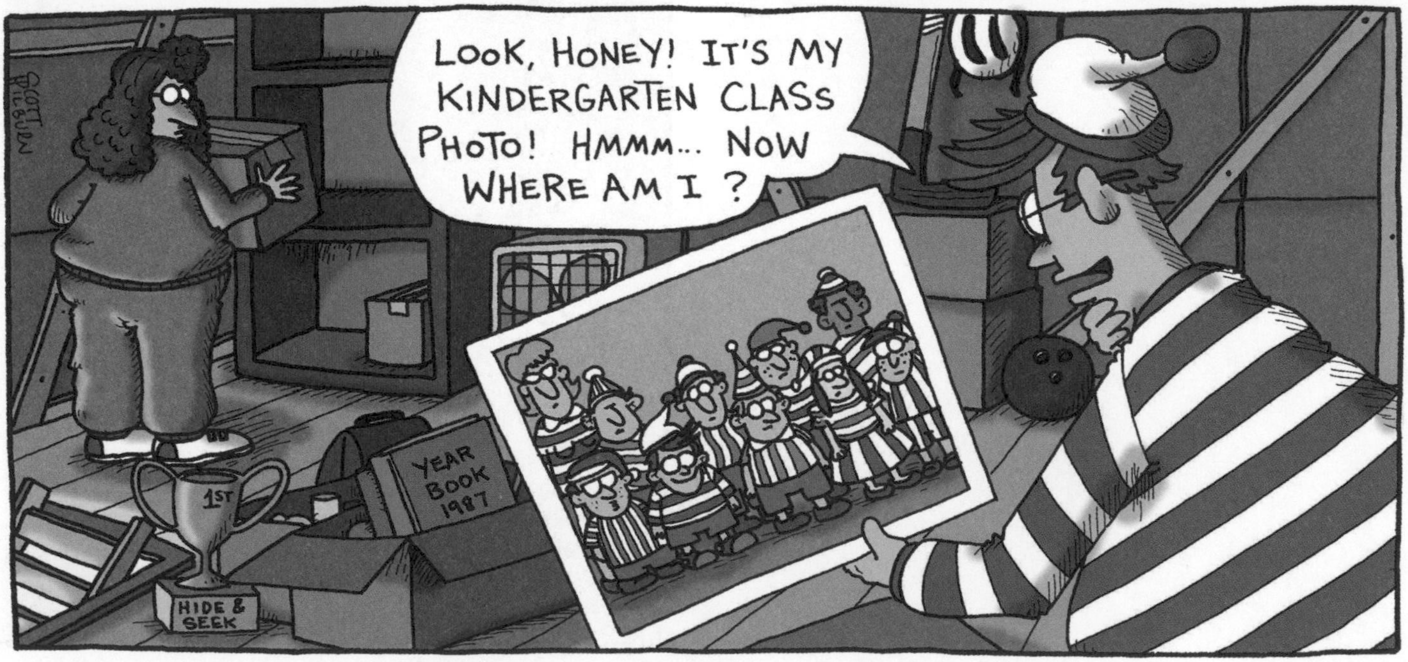
LOOK, HONEY! IT'S MY KINDERGARTEN CLASS PHOTO! HMMM... NOW WHERE AM I ?
YEAR BOOK 1987
1ST
HIDE & SEEK

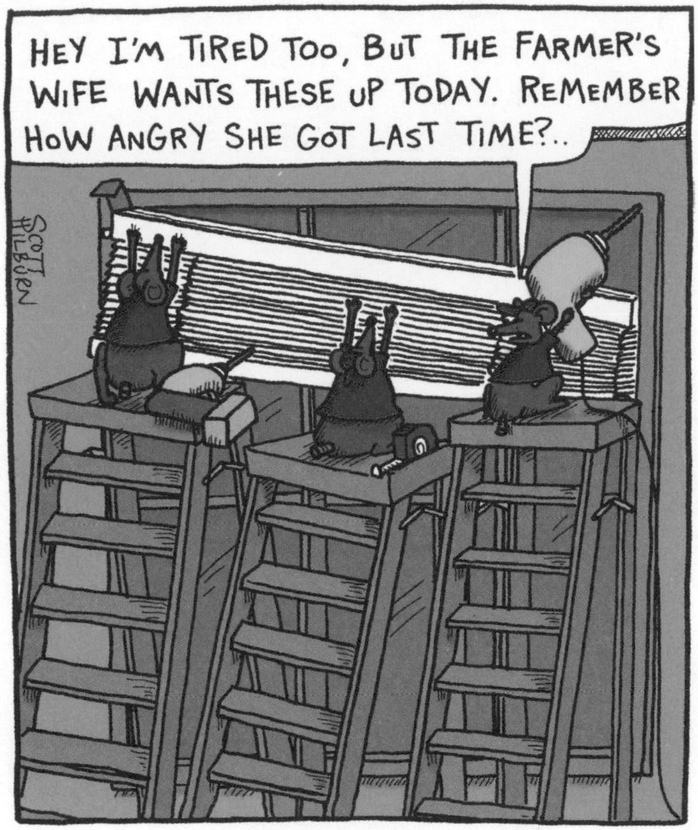
HEY I'M TIRED TOO, BUT THE FARMER'S WIFE WANTS THESE UP TODAY. REMEMBER HOW ANGRY SHE GOT LAST TIME?..
SCOTT HILBURN

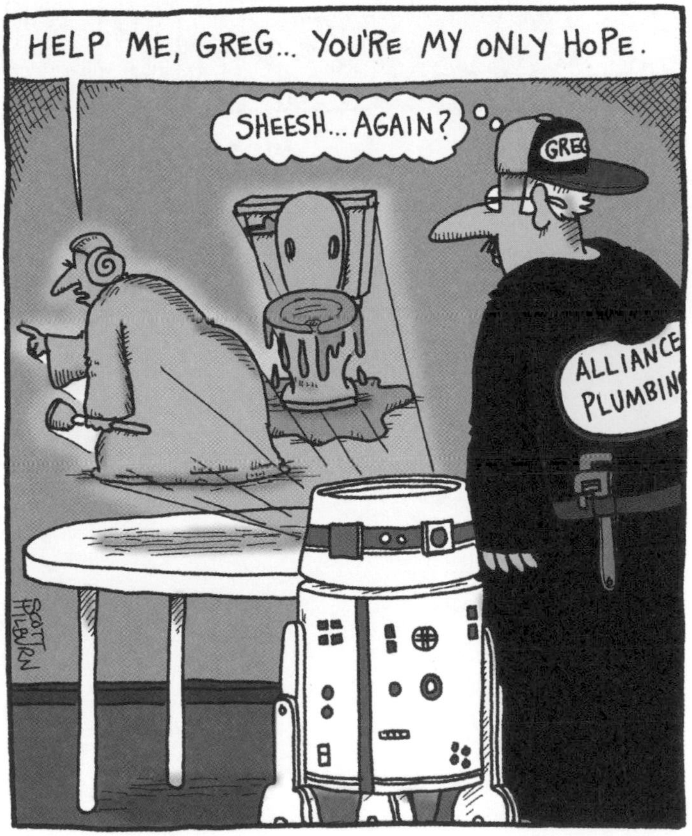
HELP ME, GREG... YOU'RE MY ONLY HOPE.
SHEESH... AGAIN?
GREG
ALLIANCE PLUMBIN
SCOTT HILBURN

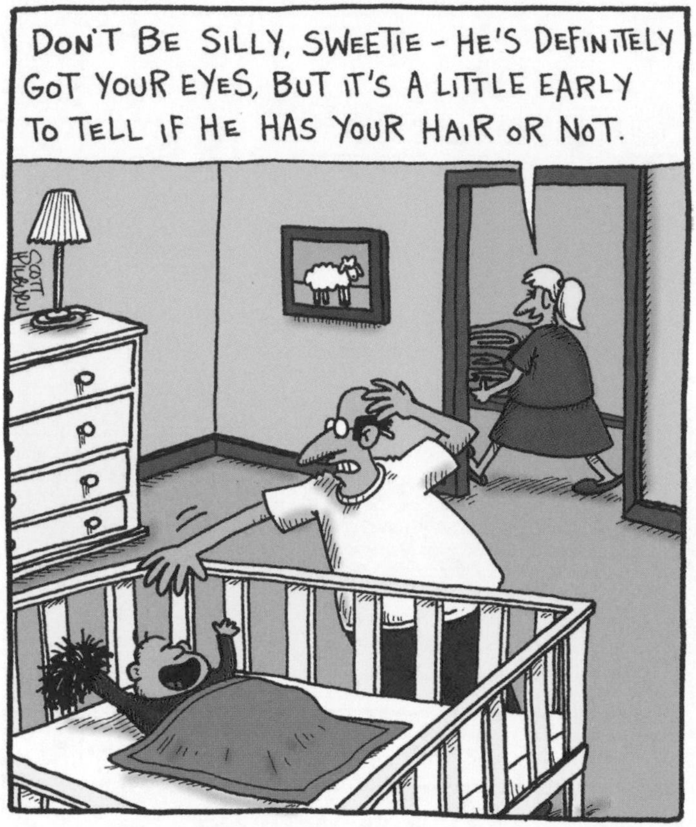
DON'T BE SILLY, SWEETIE - HE'S DEFINITELY GOT YOUR EYES, BUT IT'S A LITTLE EARLY TO TELL IF HE HAS YOUR HAIR OR NOT.

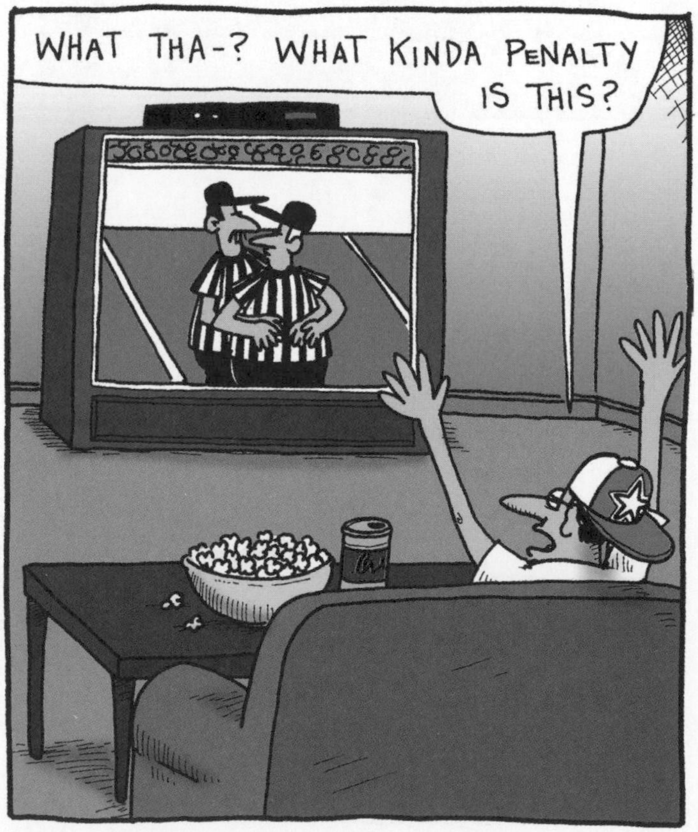
WHAT THA-? WHAT KINDA PENALTY IS THIS?

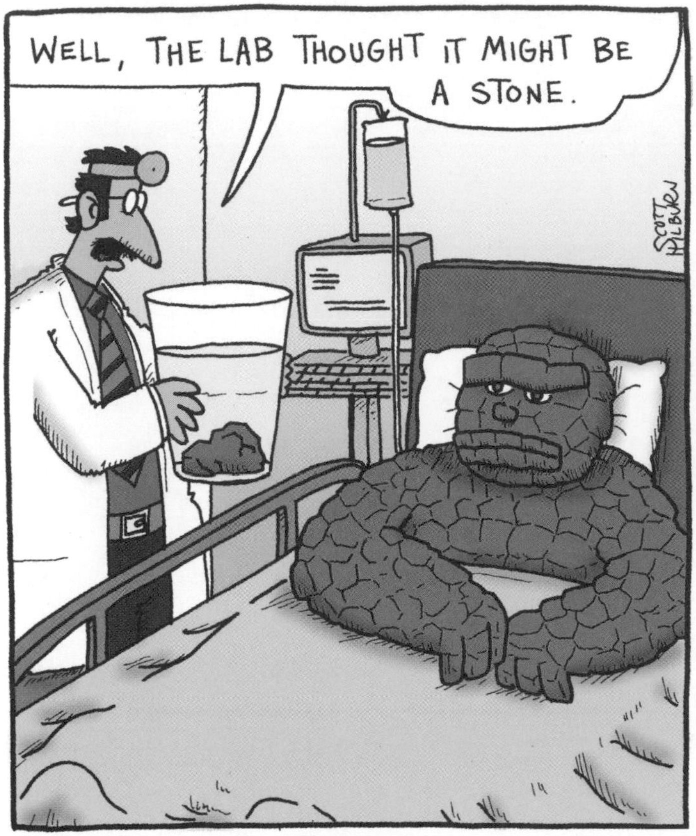
WELL, THE LAB THOUGHT IT MIGHT BE A STONE.
SCOTT HILBURN

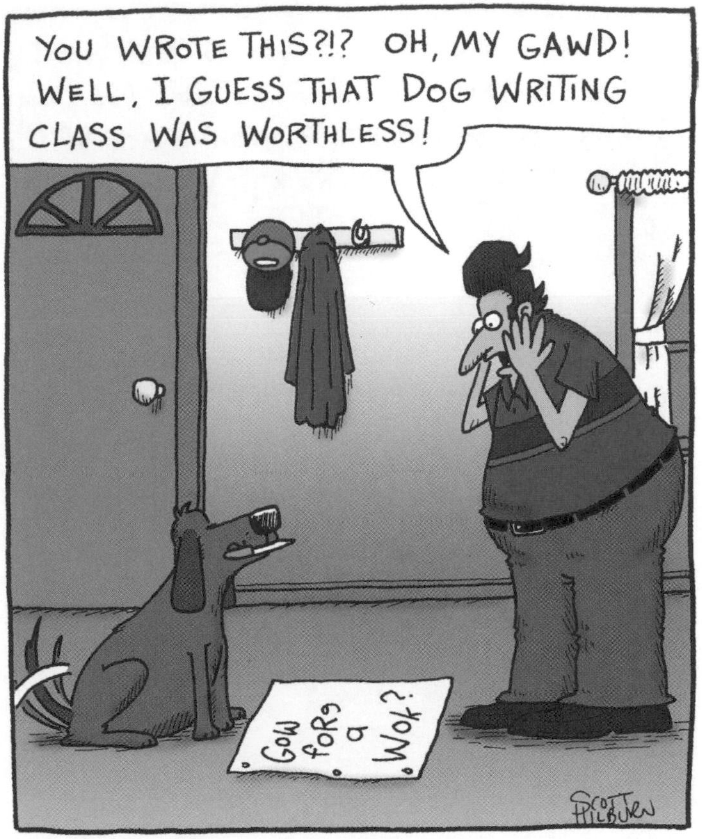
YOU WROTE THIS?!? OH, MY GAWD! WELL, I GUESS THAT DOG WRITING CLASS WAS WORTHLESS!
Gow foRg a Wok?
SCOTT HILBURN

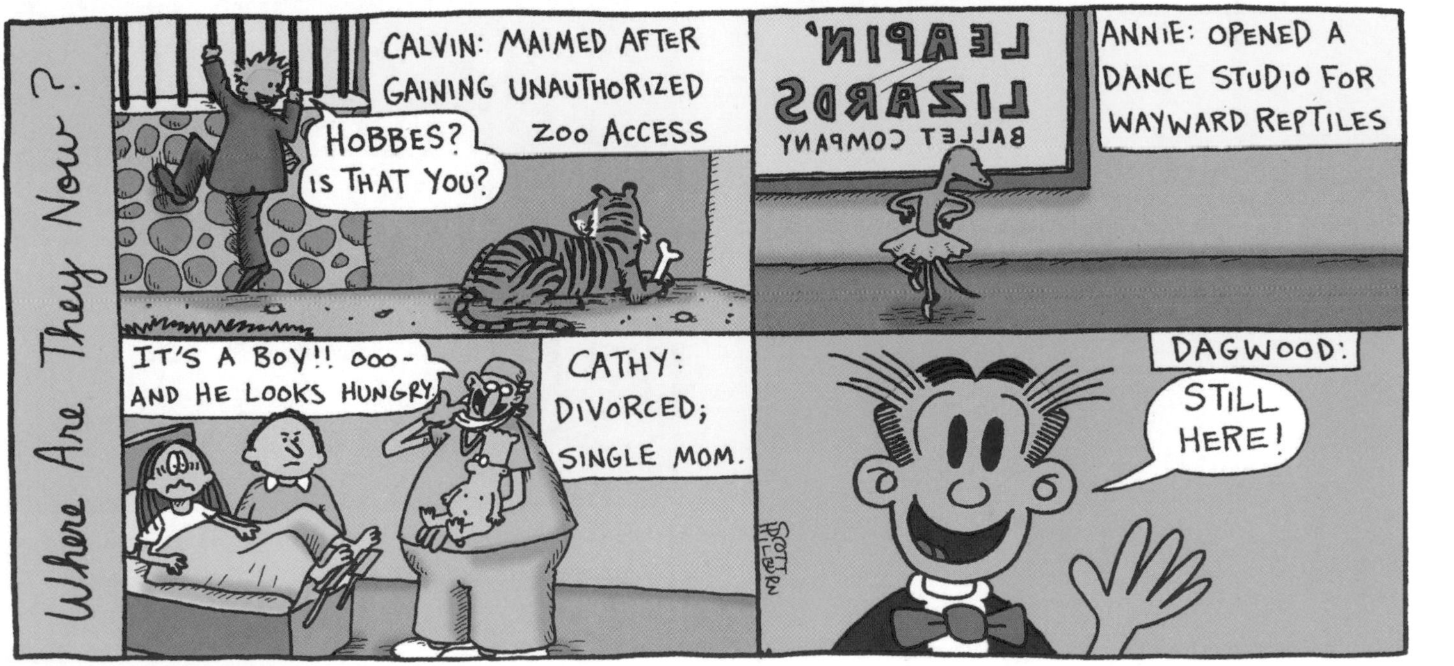
Where Are They Now?
CALVIN: MAIMED AFTER GAINING UNAUTHORIZED ZOO ACCESS
HOBBES? IS THAT YOU?
LEAPIN' LIZARDS BALLET COMPANY
ANNIE: OPENED A DANCE STUDIO FOR WAYWARD REPTILES
IT'S A BOY!! OOO- AND HE LOOKS HUNGRY.
CATHY: DIVORCED; SINGLE MOM.
SCOTT HILBURN
DAGWOOD:
STILL HERE!

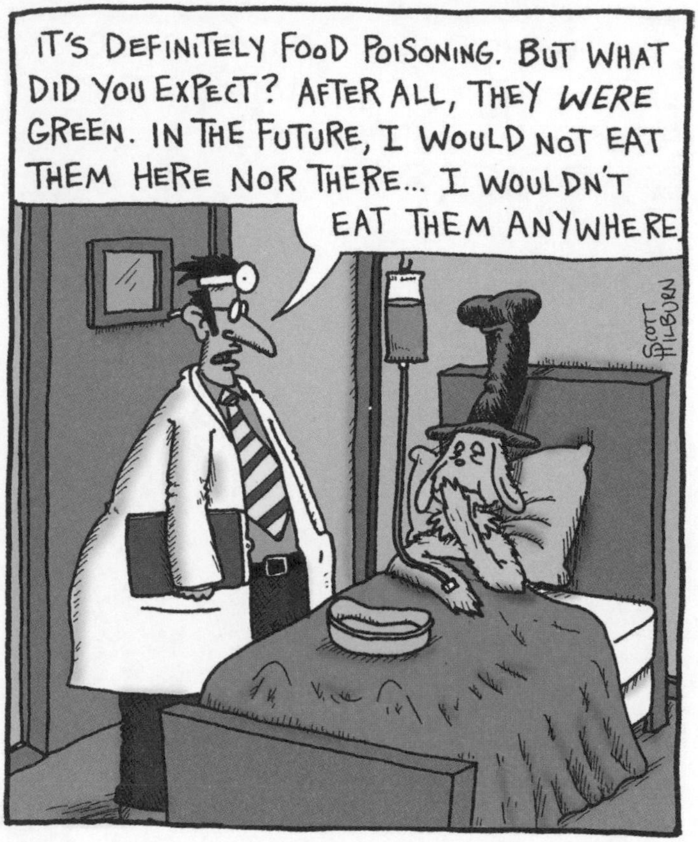
IT'S DEFINITELY FOOD POISONING. BUT WHAT DID YOU EXPECT? AFTER ALL, THEY *WERE* GREEN. IN THE FUTURE, I WOULD NOT EAT THEM HERE NOR THERE... I WOULDN'T EAT THEM ANYWHERE.
SCOTT HILBURN

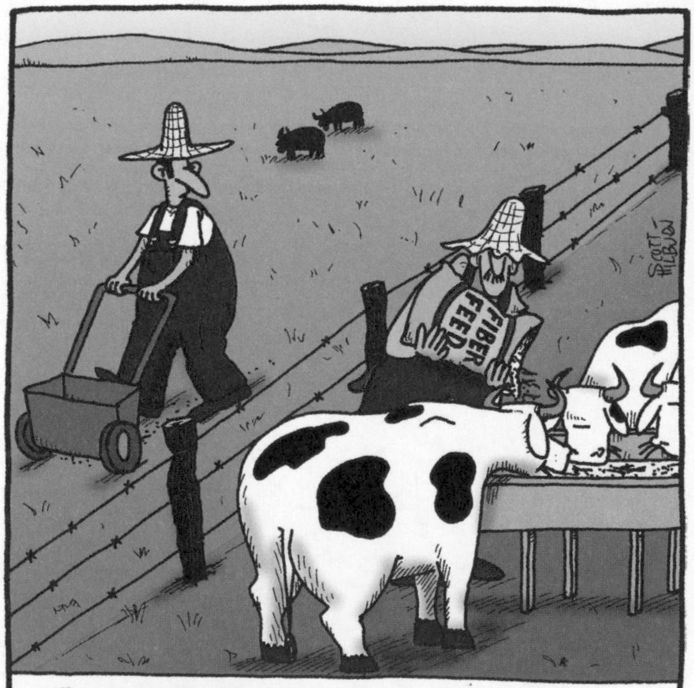
FIBER FEED
SCOTT HILBURN

FOR ERNEST, THE GRASS WAS ALWAYS GREENER ON THE OTHER SIDE. TODAY HE INADVERTENTLY DISCOVERED WHY.

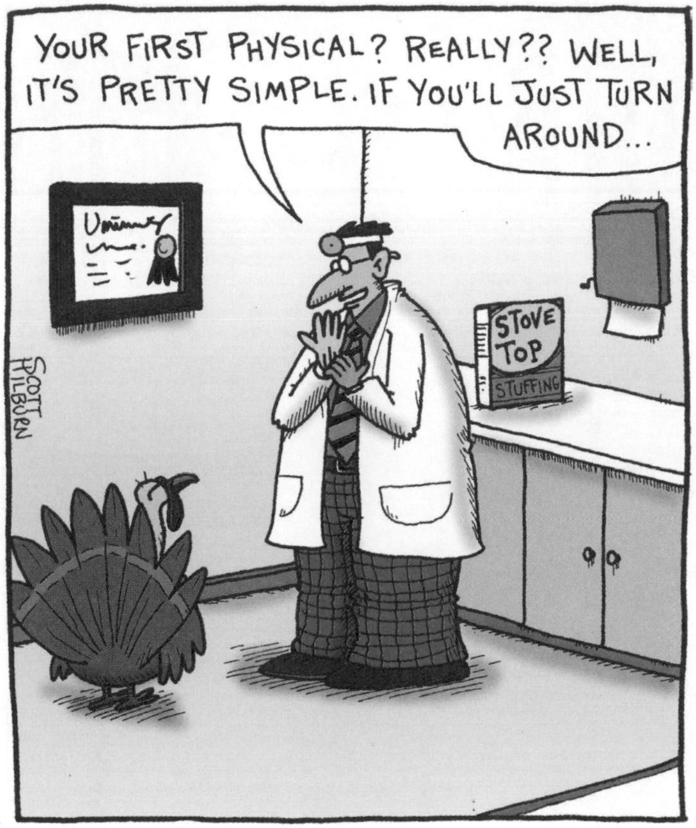
YOUR FIRST PHYSICAL? REALLY?? WELL, IT'S PRETTY SIMPLE. IF YOU'LL JUST TURN AROUND...
STOVE TOP
STUFFING
SCOTT HILBURN

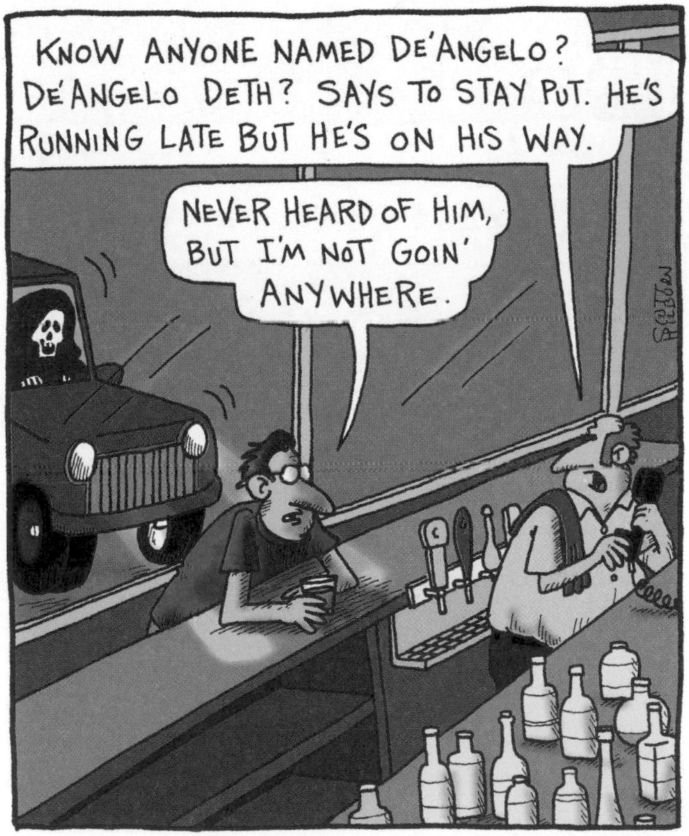
KNOW ANYONE NAMED DE'ANGELO? DE'ANGELO DETH? SAYS TO STAY PUT. HE'S RUNNING LATE BUT HE'S ON HIS WAY.
NEVER HEARD OF HIM, BUT I'M NOT GOIN' ANYWHERE.

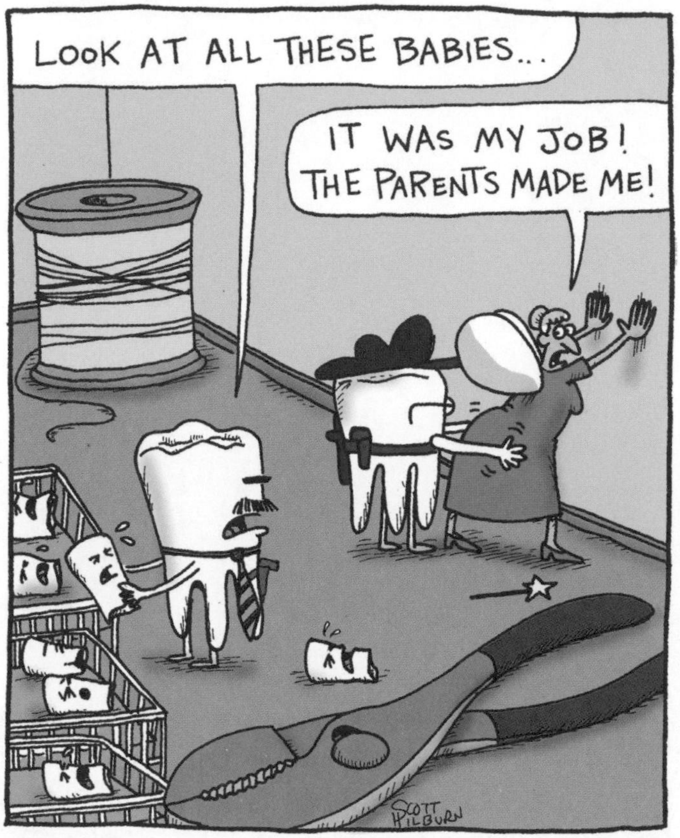
LOOK AT ALL THESE BABIES...
IT WAS MY JOB! THE PARENTS MADE ME!
SCOTT HILBURN

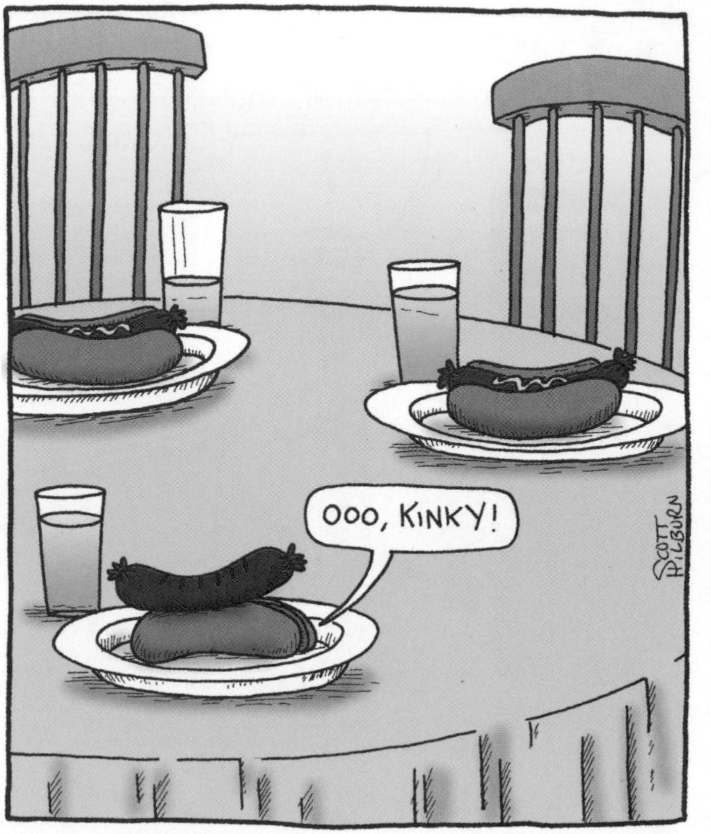
OOO, KINKY!
SCOTT HILBURN

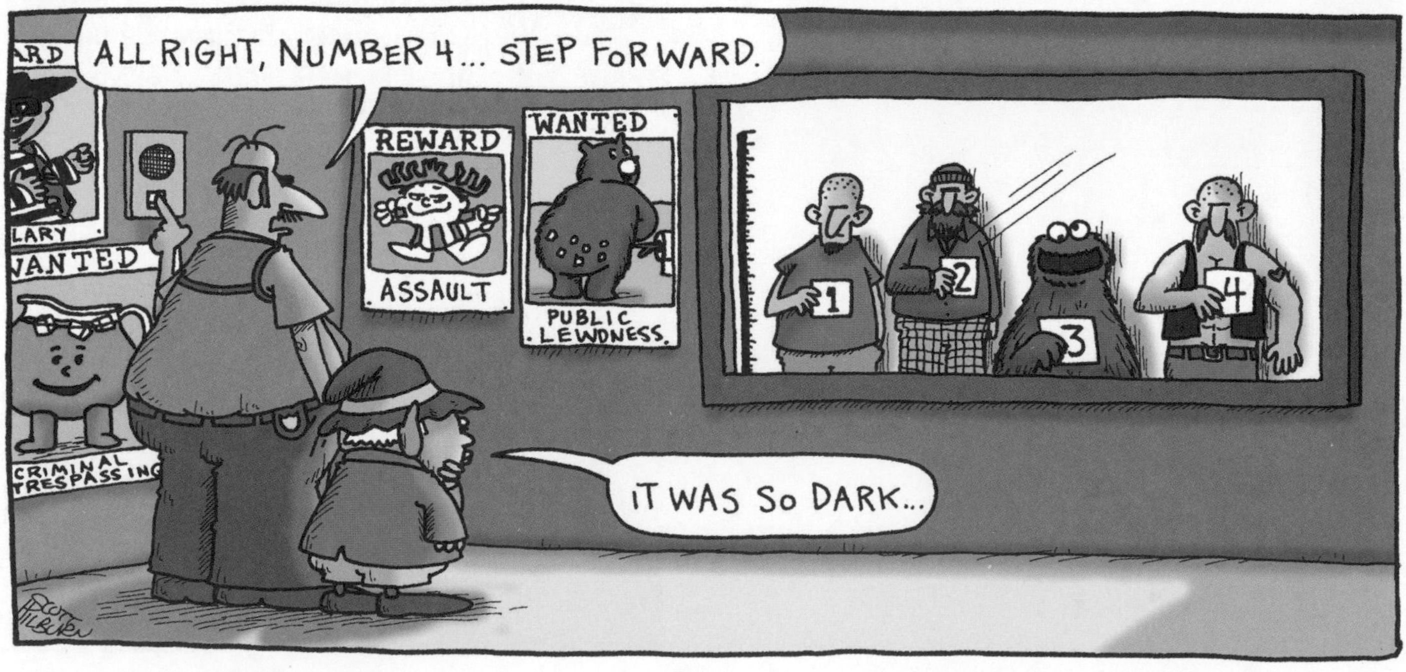
ALL RIGHT, NUMBER 4... STEP FORWARD.
REWARD
ASSAULT
WANTED
PUBLIC LEWDNESS.
1
2
3
4
IT WAS SO DARK...
SCOTT HILBURN

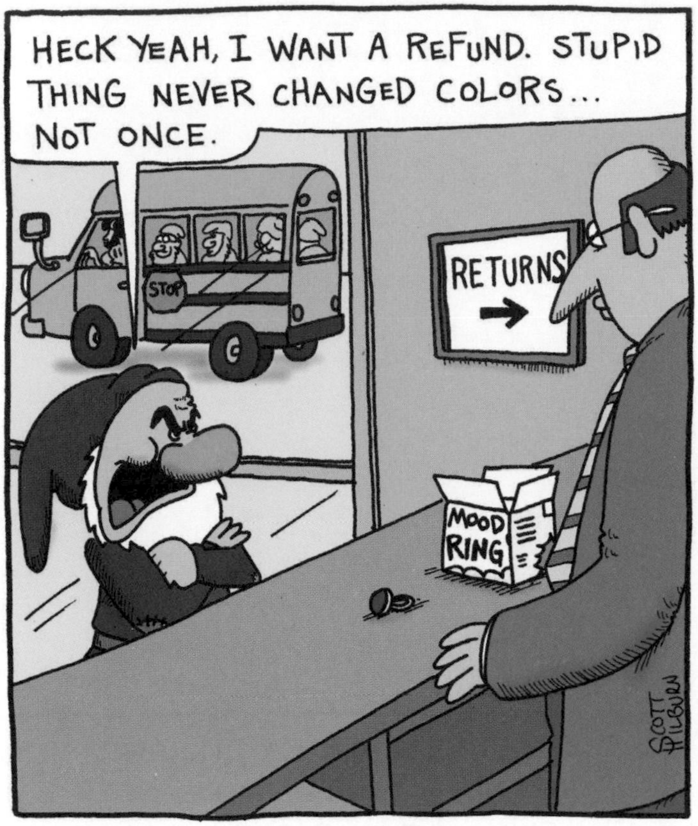
HECK YEAH, I WANT A REFUND. STUPID THING NEVER CHANGED COLORS... NOT ONCE.
RETURNS
STOP
MOOD RING
SCOTT HILBURN

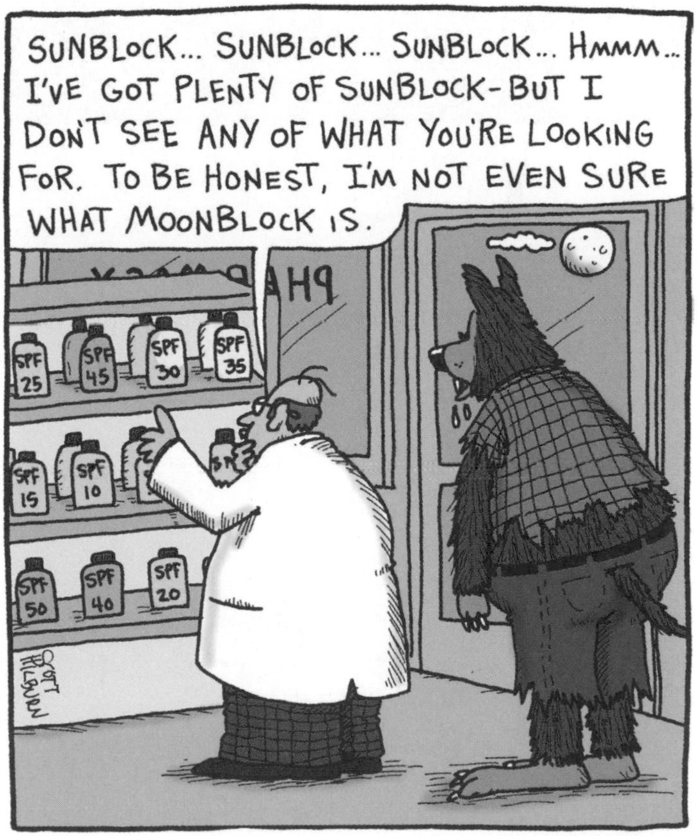
SUNBLOCK... SUNBLOCK... SUNBLOCK... HMMM... I'VE GOT PLENTY OF SUNBLOCK- BUT I DON'T SEE ANY OF WHAT YOU'RE LOOKING FOR. TO BE HONEST, I'M NOT EVEN SURE WHAT MOONBLOCK IS.
SPF 25
SPF 45
SPF 30
SPF 35
SPF 15
SPF 10
SPF 50
SPF 40
SPF 20
SCOTT HILBURN

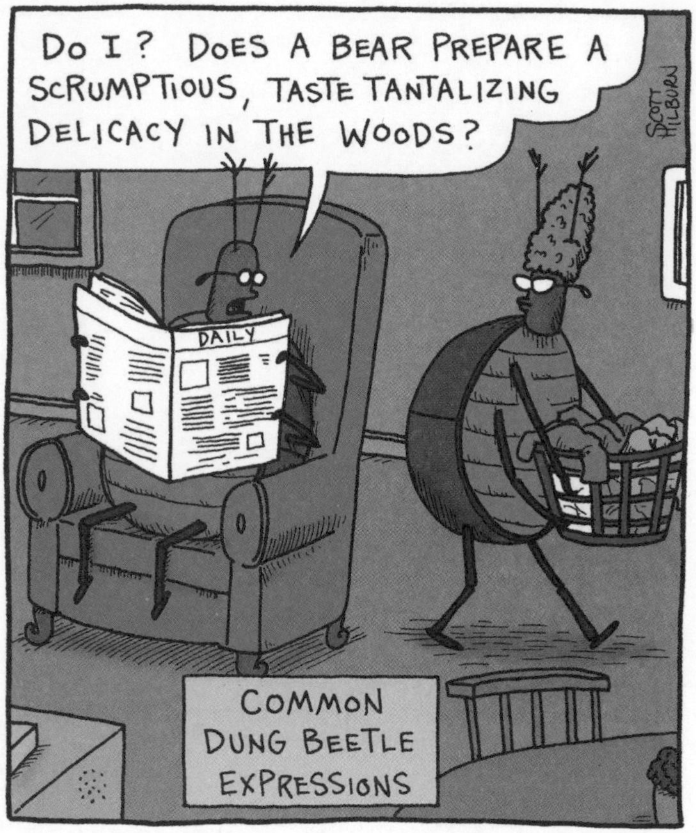

DO I? DOES A BEAR PREPARE A SCRUMPTIOUS, TASTE TANTALIZING DELICACY IN THE WOODS?
DAILY
SCOTT HILBURN
COMMON DUNG BEETLE EXPRESSIONS

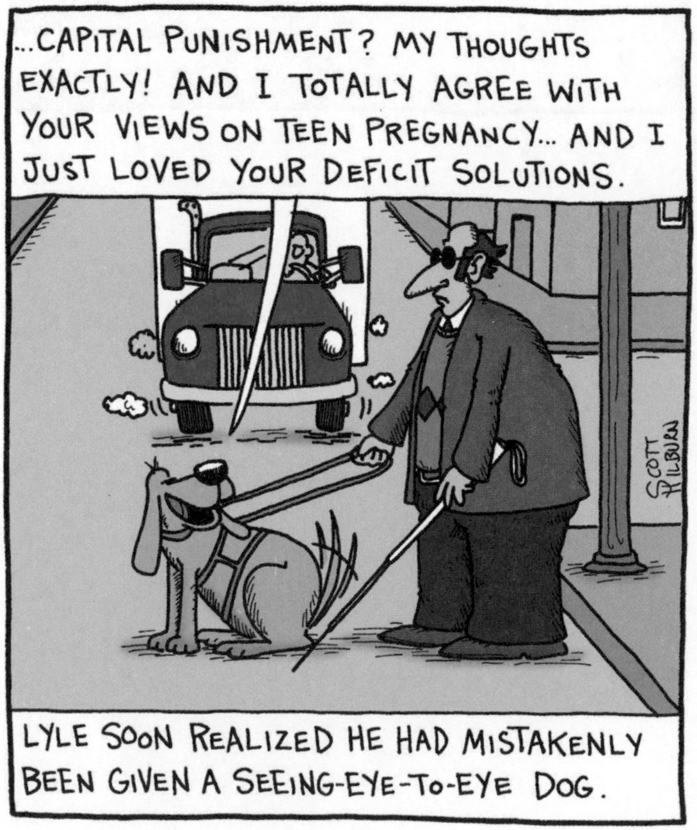

...CAPITAL PUNISHMENT? MY THOUGHTS EXACTLY! AND I TOTALLY AGREE WITH YOUR VIEWS ON TEEN PREGNANCY... AND I JUST LOVED YOUR DEFICIT SOLUTIONS.
SCOTT HILBURN
LYLE SOON REALIZED HE HAD MISTAKENLY BEEN GIVEN A SEEING-EYE-TO-EYE DOG.

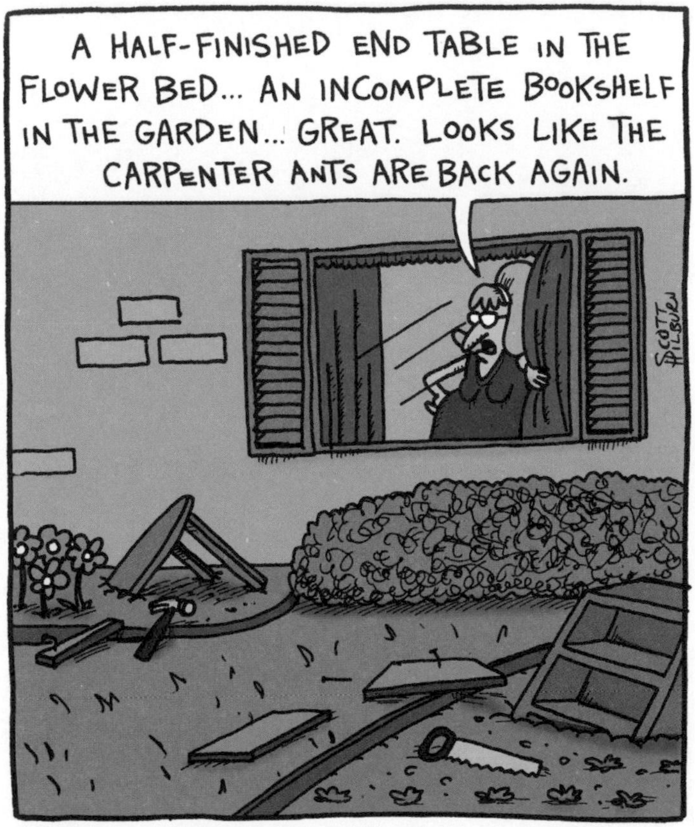
A HALF-FINISHED END TABLE IN THE FLOWER BED... AN INCOMPLETE BOOKSHELF IN THE GARDEN... GREAT. LOOKS LIKE THE CARPENTER ANTS ARE BACK AGAIN.
SCOTT HILBURN

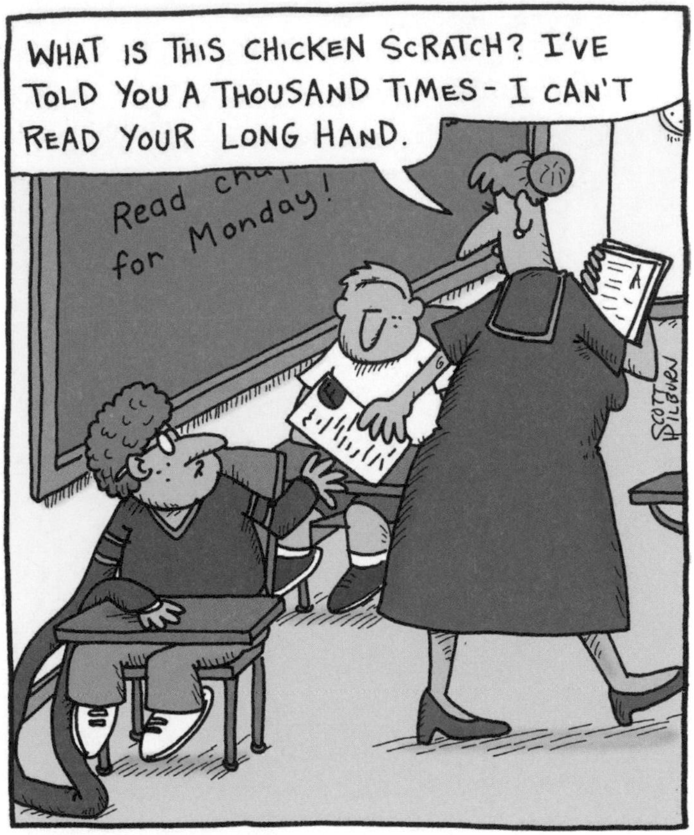
WHAT IS THIS CHICKEN SCRATCH? I'VE TOLD YOU A THOUSAND TIMES - I CAN'T READ YOUR LONG HAND.
Read
for Monday!
SCOTT HILBURN

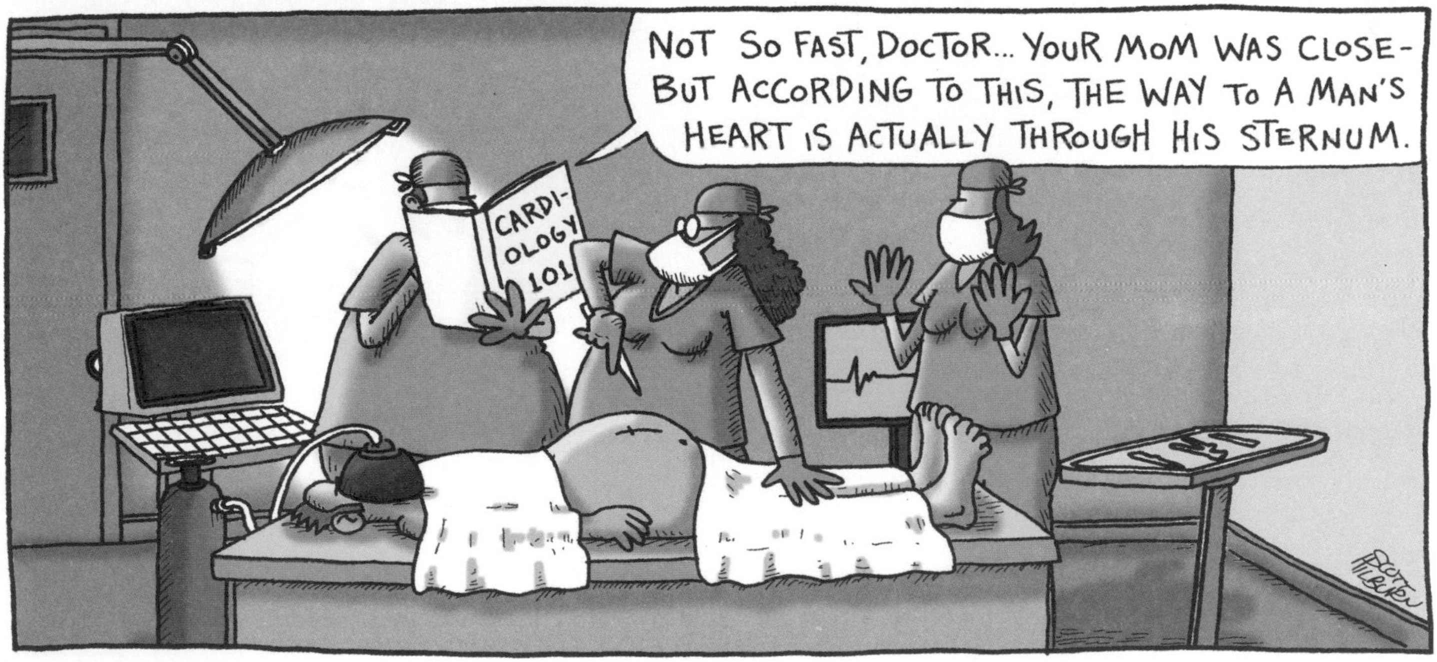
NOT SO FAST, DOCTOR... YOUR MOM WAS CLOSE- BUT ACCORDING TO THIS, THE WAY TO A MAN'S HEART IS ACTUALLY THROUGH HIS STERNUM.
CARDI-OLOGY 101
SCOTT HILBURN

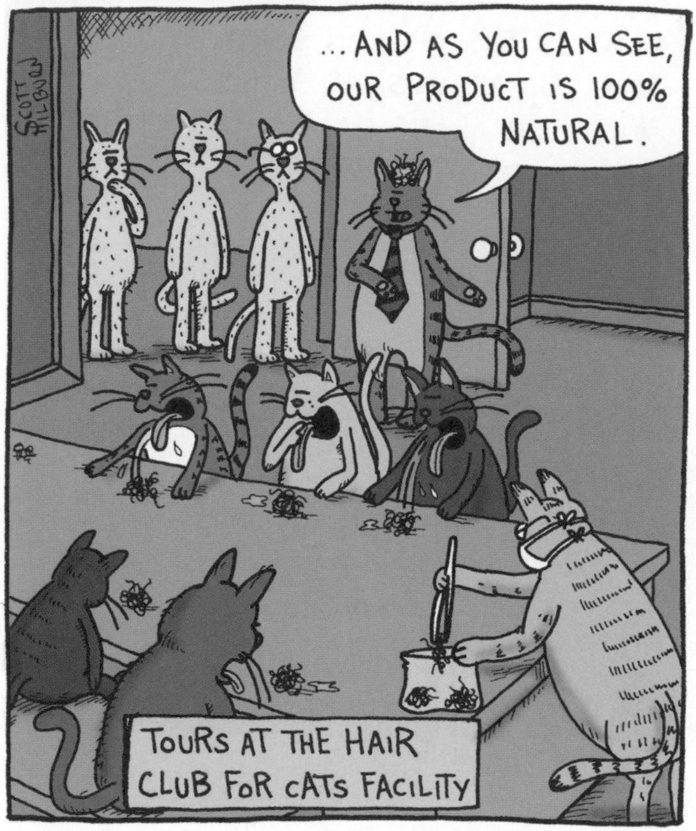
...AND AS YOU CAN SEE, OUR PRODUCT IS 100% NATURAL.
SCOTT HILBURN
TOURS AT THE HAIR CLUB FOR CATS FACILITY

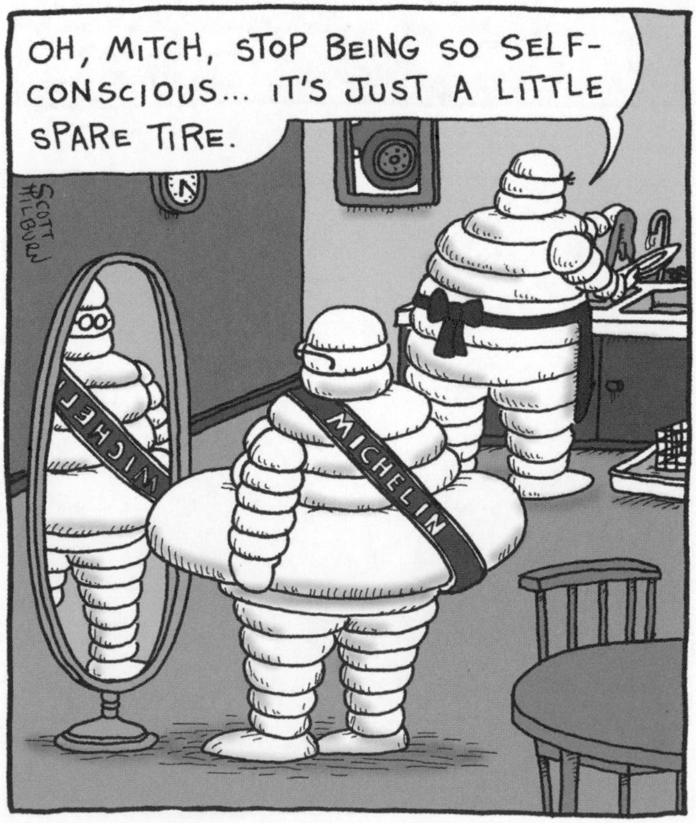
OH, MITCH, STOP BEING SO SELF-CONSCIOUS... IT'S JUST A LITTLE SPARE TIRE.
SCOTT HILBURN
MICHELIN

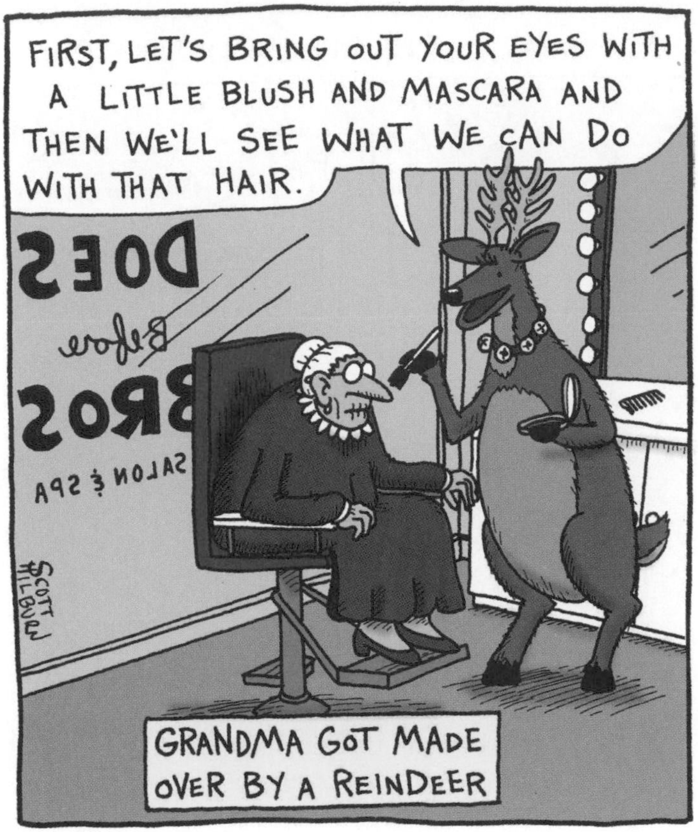
FIRST, LET'S BRING OUT YOUR EYES WITH A LITTLE BLUSH AND MASCARA AND THEN WE'LL SEE WHAT WE CAN DO WITH THAT HAIR.
SCOTT HILBURN

GRANDMA GOT MADE OVER BY A REINDEER

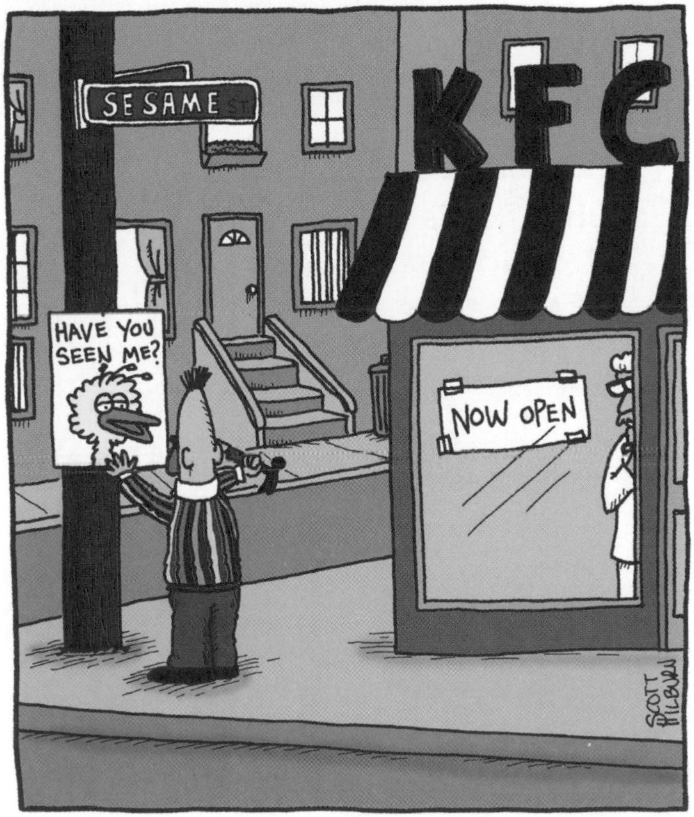
SESAME ST
KFC
HAVE YOU SEEN ME?
NOW OPEN
SCOTT HILBURN

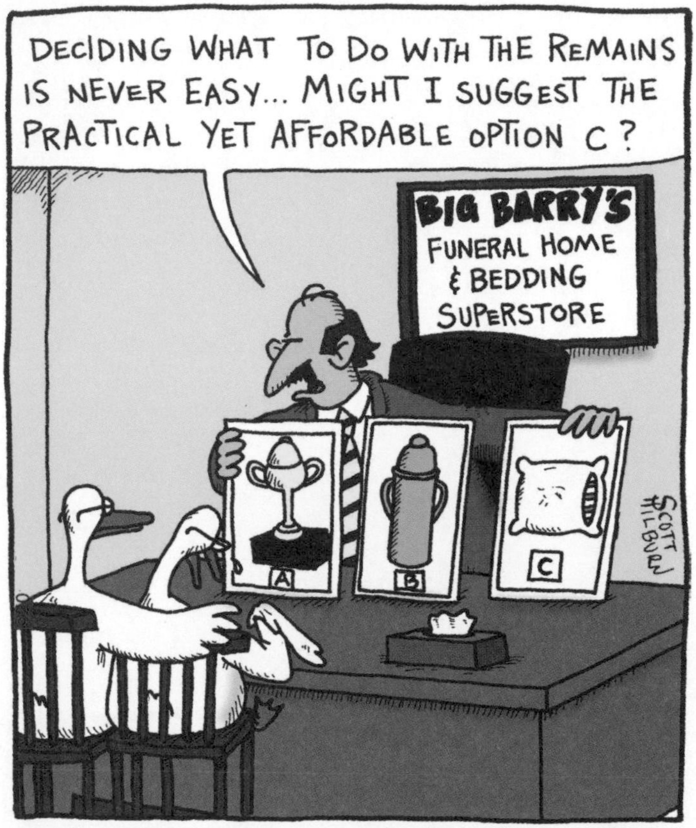
DECIDING WHAT TO DO WITH THE REMAINS IS NEVER EASY... MIGHT I SUGGEST THE PRACTICAL YET AFFORDABLE OPTION C?
BIG BARRY'S
FUNERAL HOME & BEDDING SUPERSTORE
A
B
C
SCOTT HILBURN

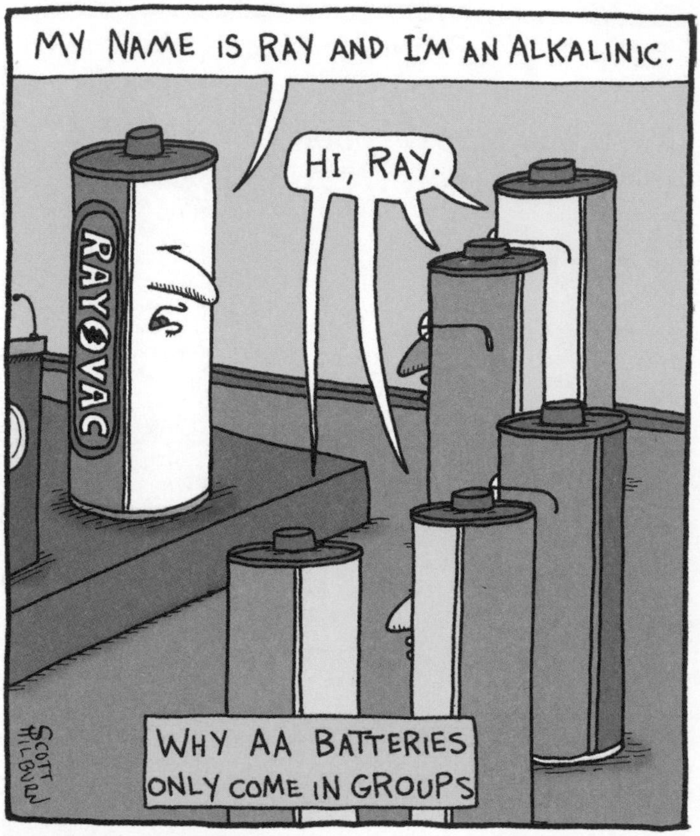
MY NAME IS RAY AND I'M AN ALKALINIC.
HI, RAY.
RAYOVAC
WHY AA BATTERIES ONLY COME IN GROUPS
SCOTT HILBURN

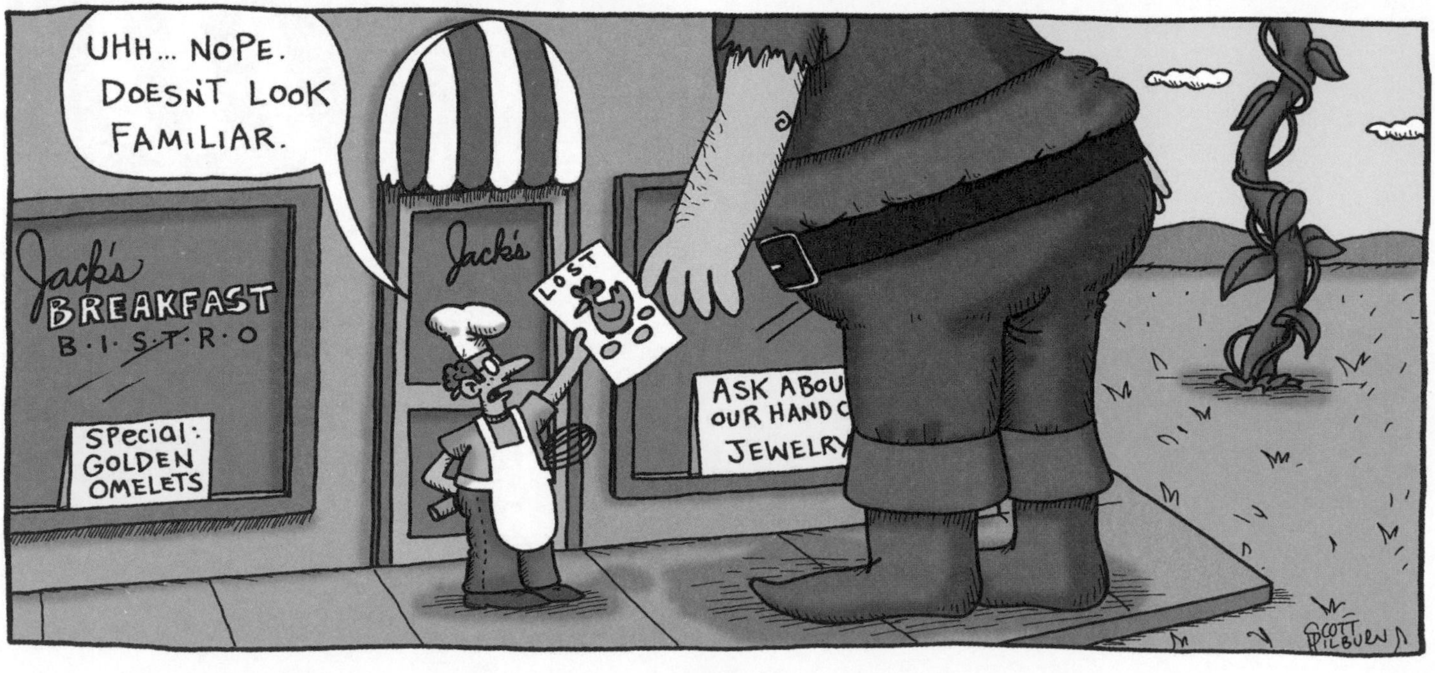
UHH... NOPE. DOESN'T LOOK FAMILIAR.
Jack's BREAKFAST B·I·S·T·R·O
Jack's
LOST
Special: GOLDEN OMELETS
ASK ABOU
OUR HAND C
JEWELRY
SCOTT HILBURN

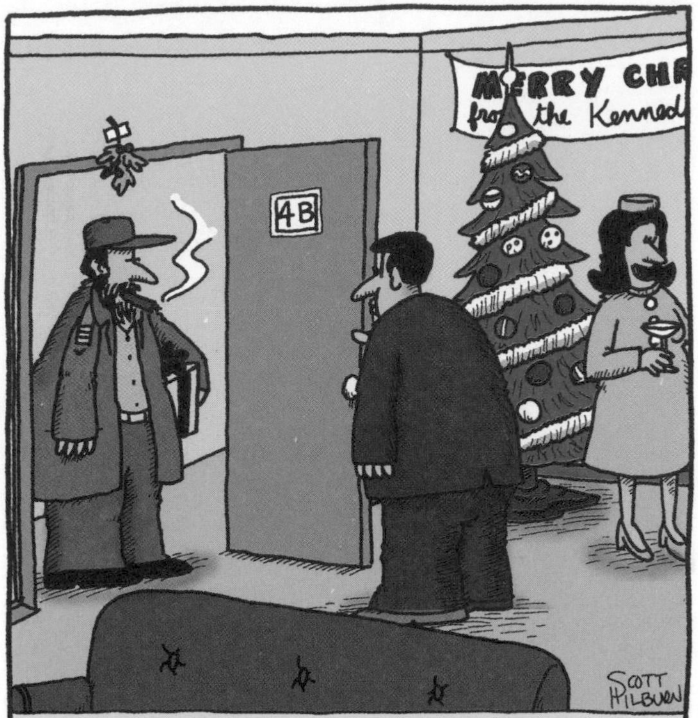
4B
SCOTT HILBURN

ONE OF HISTORY'S LESS-TALKED ABOUT INCIDENTS: THE CUBAN MISTLETOE CRISIS.

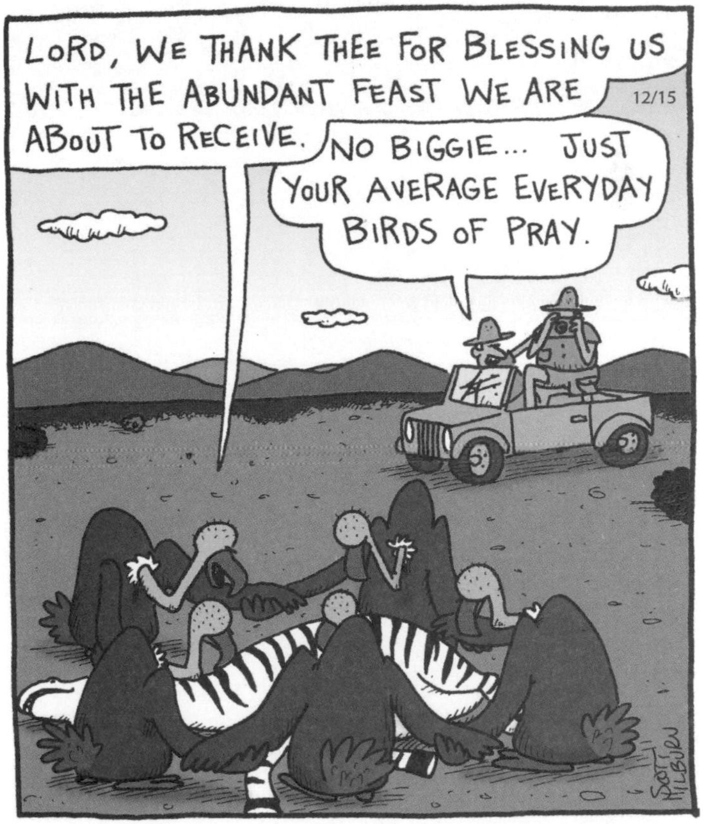
LORD, WE THANK THEE FOR BLESSING US WITH THE ABUNDANT FEAST WE ARE ABOUT TO RECEIVE.
12/15
NO BIGGIE... JUST YOUR AVERAGE EVERYDAY BIRDS OF PRAY.
SCOTT HILBURN

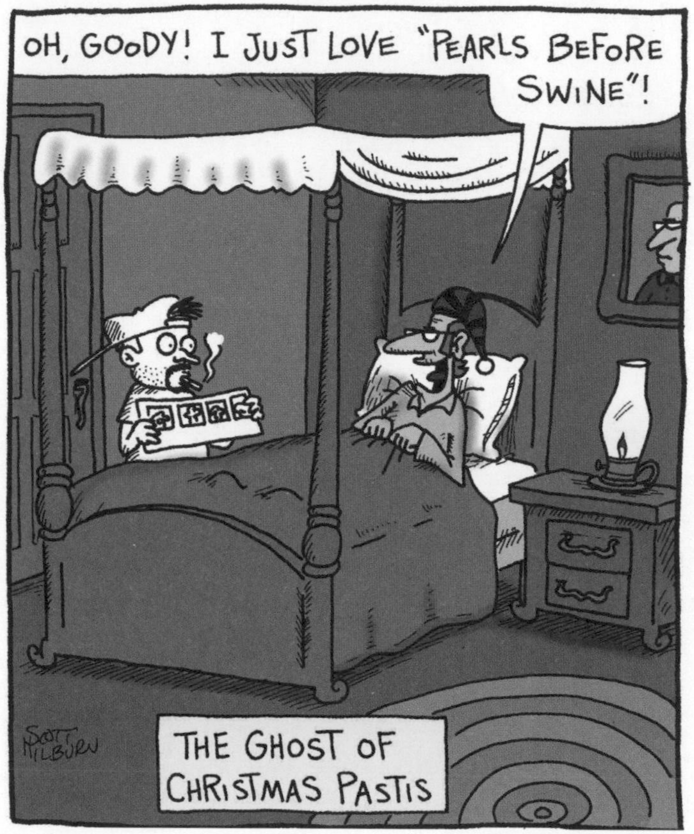
OH, GOODY! I JUST LOVE "PEARLS BEFORE SWINE"!
SCOTT HILBURN
THE GHOST OF CHRISTMAS PASTIS

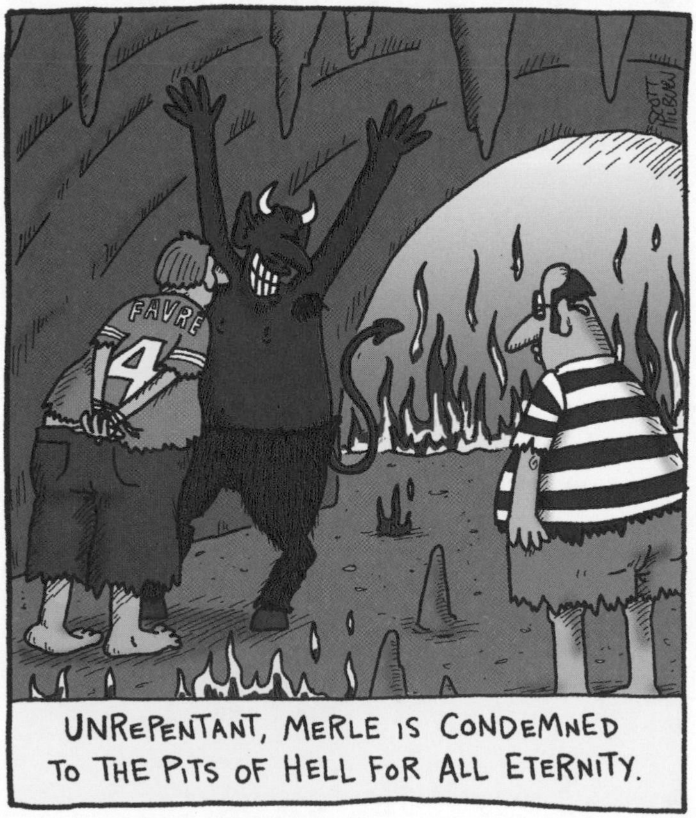
SCOTT HILBURN
FAVRE
4
UNREPENTANT, MERLE IS CONDEMNED TO THE PITS OF HELL FOR ALL ETERNITY.

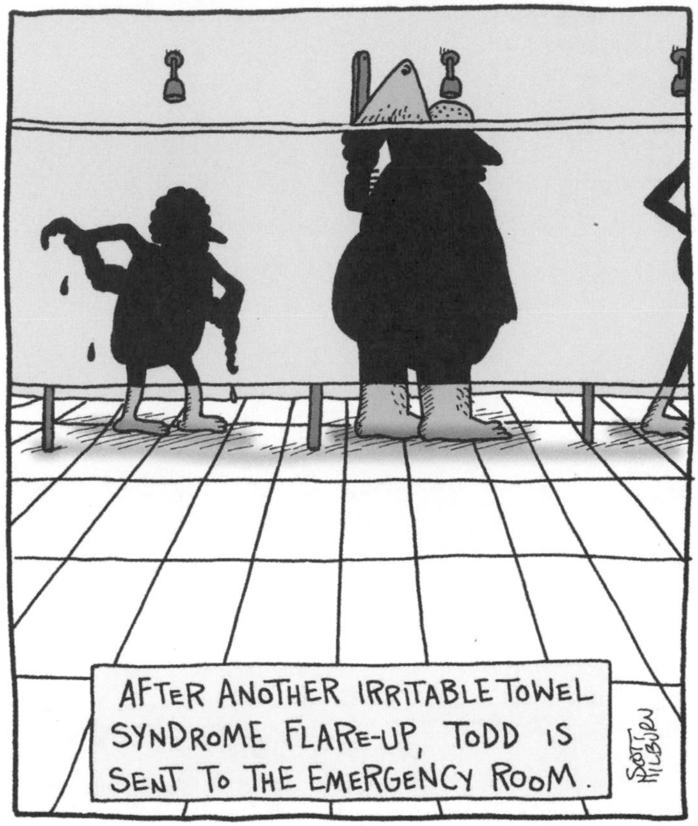
SCOTT HILBURN

AFTER ANOTHER IRRITABLE TOWEL SYNDROME FLARE-UP, TODD IS SENT TO THE EMERGENCY ROOM.

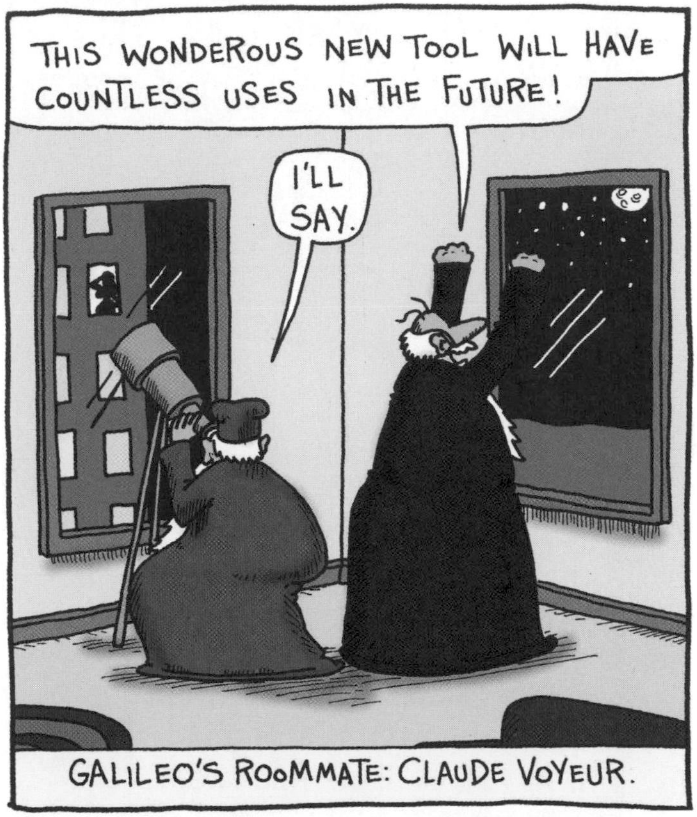
THIS WONDEROUS NEW TOOL WILL HAVE COUNTLESS USES IN THE FUTURE!
I'LL SAY.

GALILEO'S ROOMMATE: CLAUDE VOYEUR.

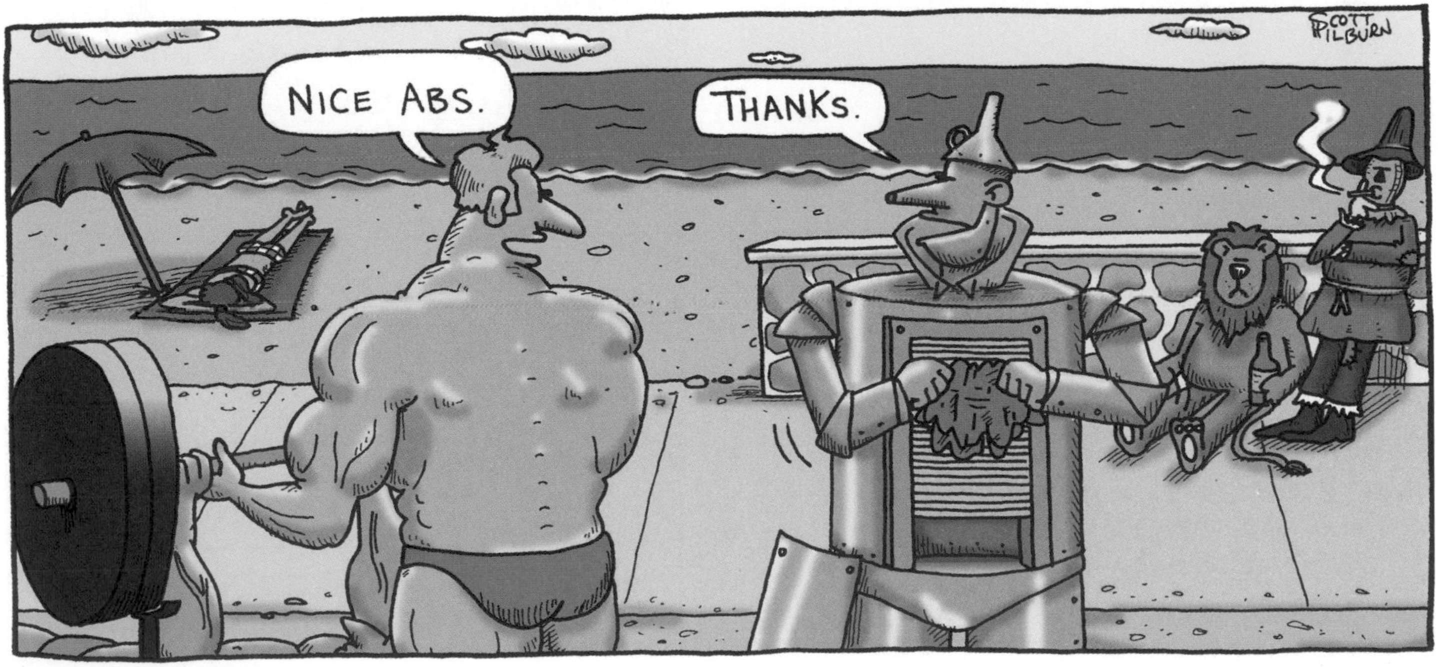
SCOTT HILBURN
NICE ABS.
THANKS.

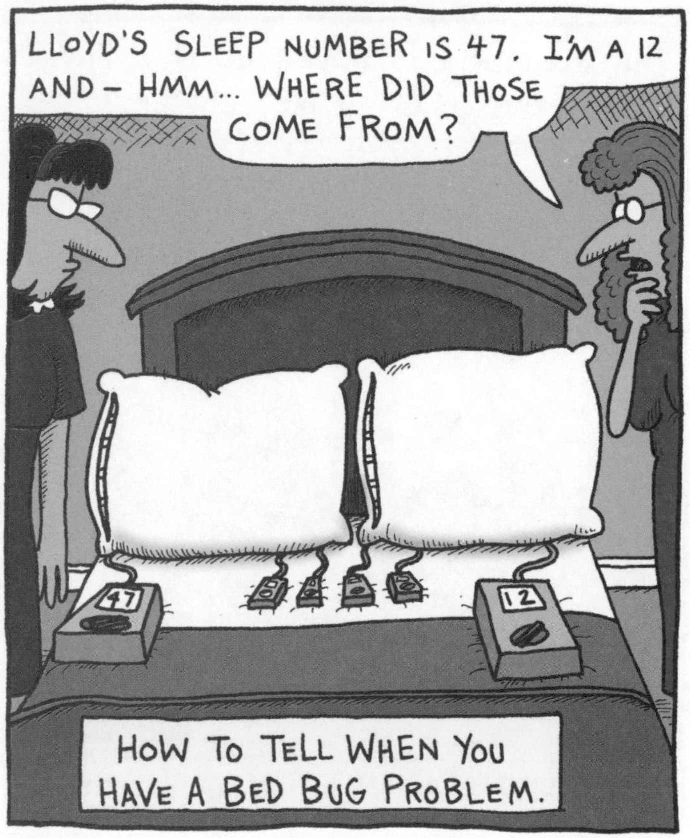
LLOYD'S SLEEP NUMBER IS 47. I'M A 12 AND – HMM... WHERE DID THOSE COME FROM?
47
12
HOW TO TELL WHEN YOU HAVE A BED BUG PROBLEM.

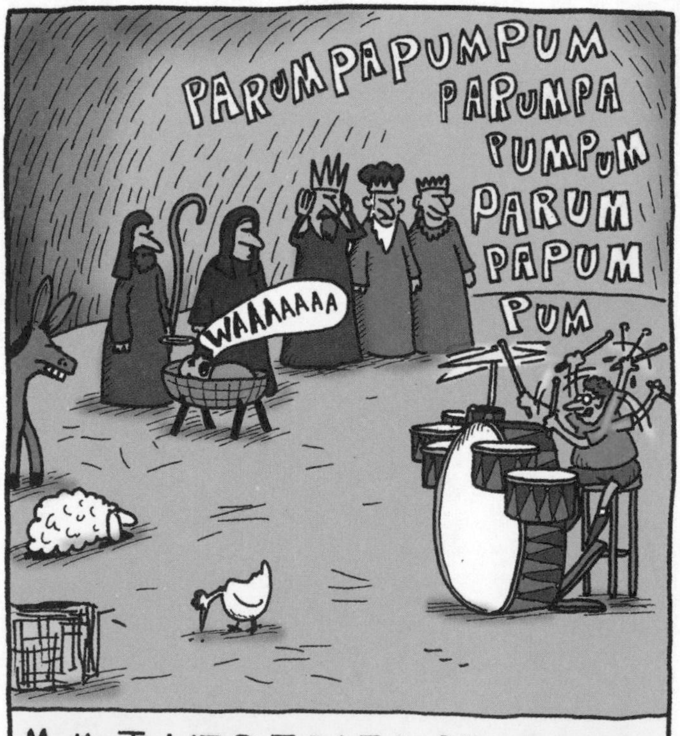
PARUMPAPUMPUM
PARUMPA
PUMPUM
PARUM
PAPUM
PUM
WAAAAAAA
MOMENTS LATER, THE LITTLE DRUMMER BOY WAS FORCIBLY REMOVED FROM THE MANGER.

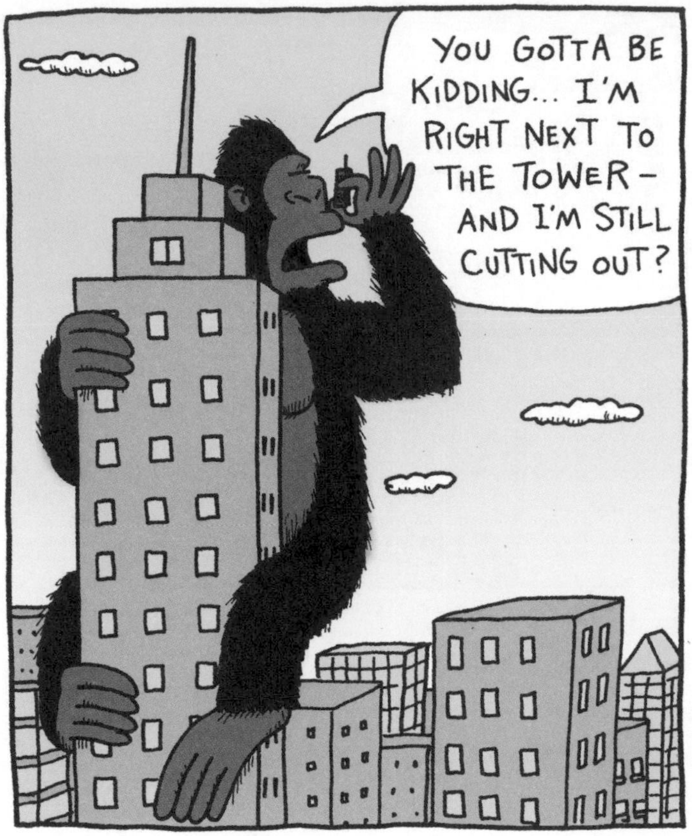
YOU GOTTA BE KIDDING... I'M RIGHT NEXT TO THE TOWER— AND I'M STILL CUTTING OUT?

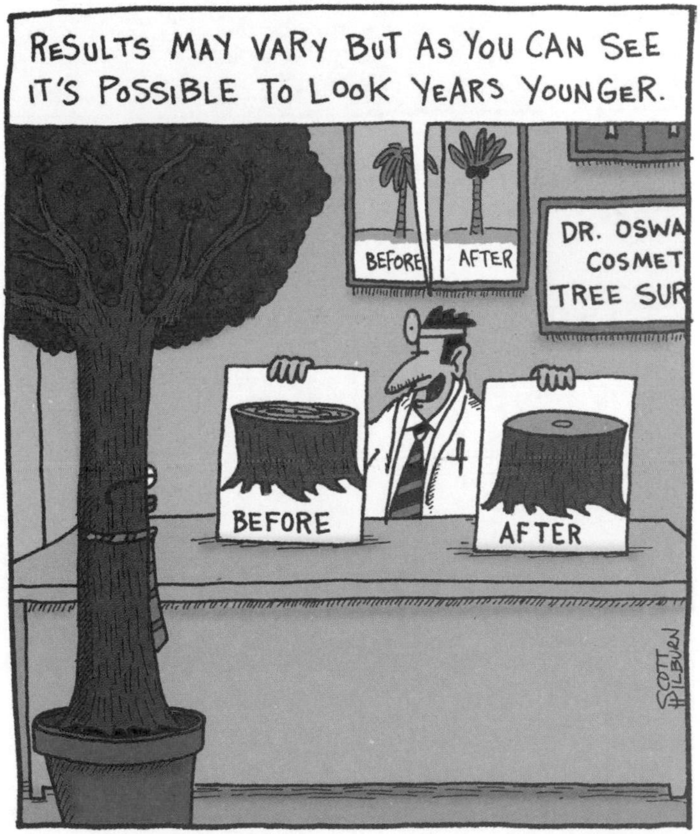
RESULTS MAY VARY BUT AS YOU CAN SEE IT'S POSSIBLE TO LOOK YEARS YOUNGER.
BEFORE
AFTER
DR. OSWA
COSMET
TREE SUR
BEFORE
AFTER
SCOTT HILBURN

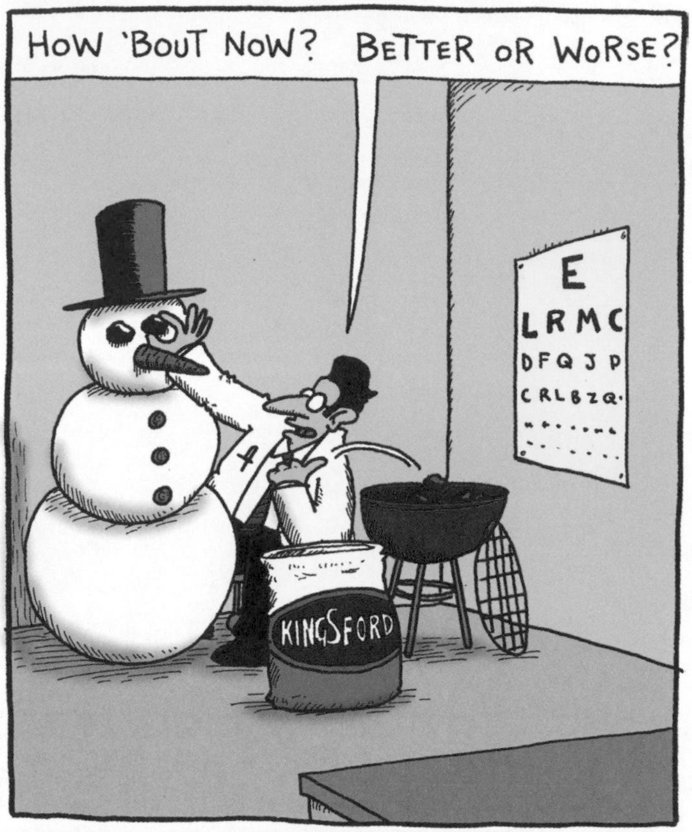
HOW 'BOUT NOW? BETTER OR WORSE?
E
LRMC
DFQJP
CRLBZQ
KINGSFORD

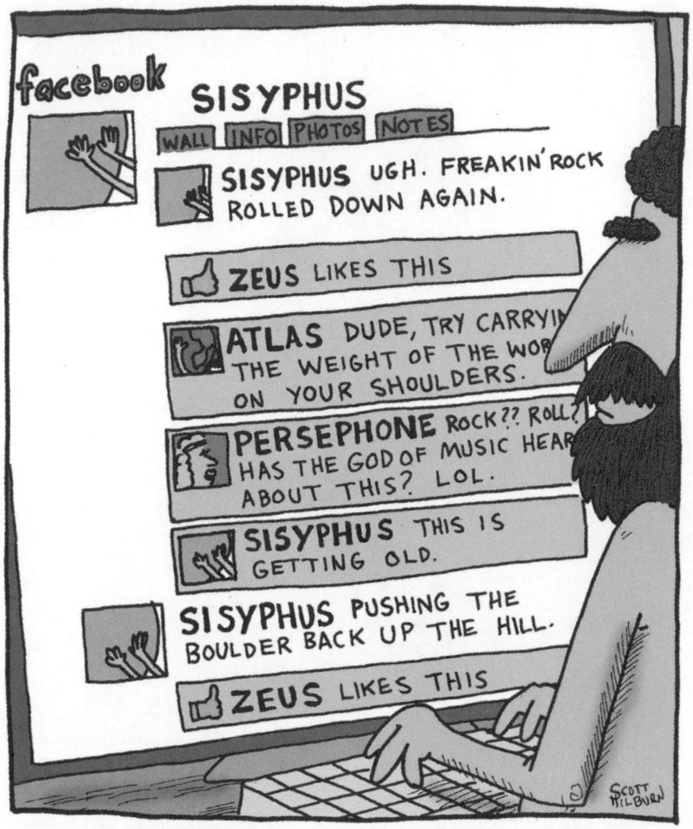
facebook
SISYPHUS
WALL
INFO
PHOTOS
NOTES
SISYPHUS UGH. FREAKIN' ROCK ROLLED DOWN AGAIN.
ZEUS LIKES THIS
ATLAS DUDE, TRY CARRYIN THE WEIGHT OF THE WOR ON YOUR SHOULDERS.
PERSEPHONE ROCK?? ROLL? HAS THE GOD OF MUSIC HEAR ABOUT THIS? LOL.
SISYPHUS THIS IS GETTING OLD.
SISYPHUS PUSHING THE BOULDER BACK UP THE HILL.
ZEUS LIKES THIS
SCOTT HILBURN

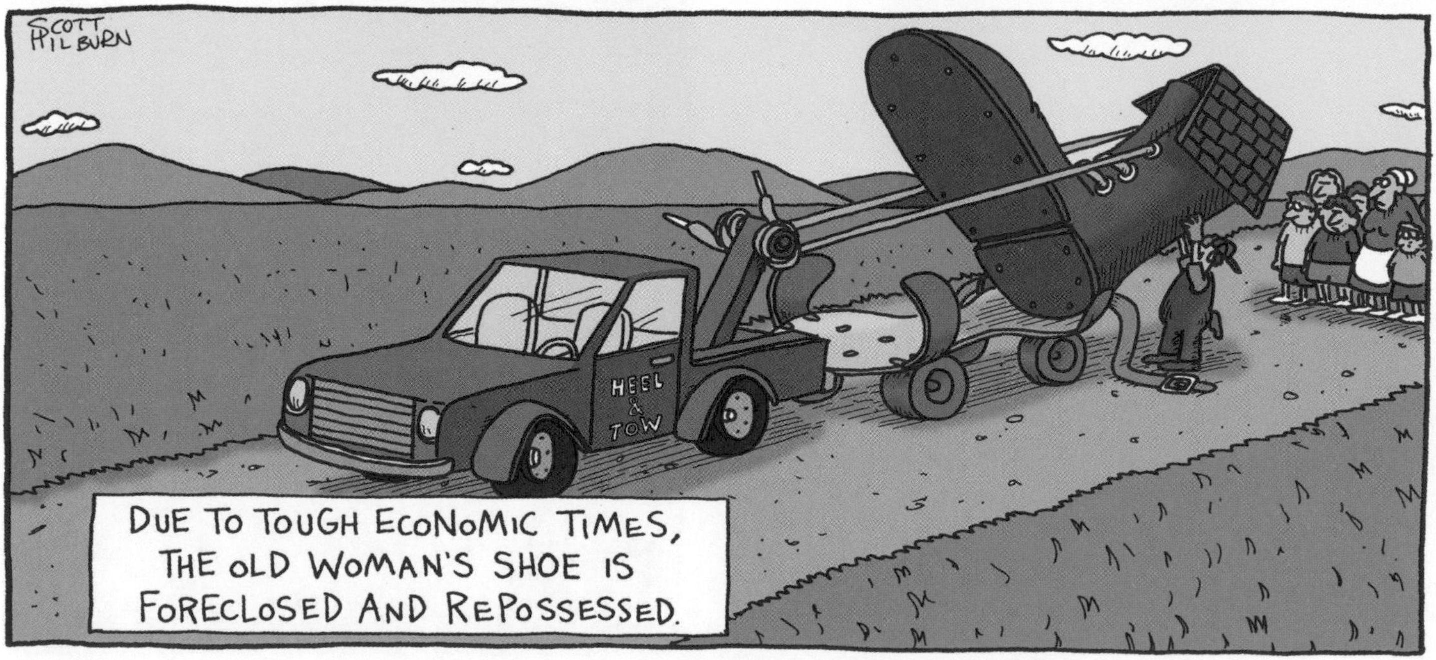
SCOTT HILBURN
HEEL & TOW
DUE TO TOUGH ECONOMIC TIMES, THE OLD WOMAN'S SHOE IS FORECLOSED AND REPOSSESSED.

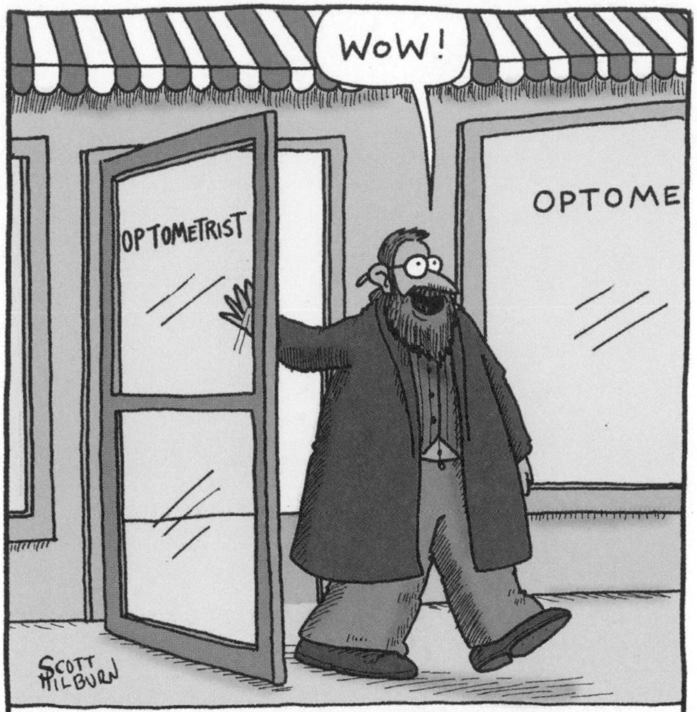
WOW!
OPTOMETRIST
OPTOME
SCOTT HILBURN

CLAUDE MONET'S ART CAREER WOULD SOON EXPERIENCE AN UNFORTUNATE DECLINE.

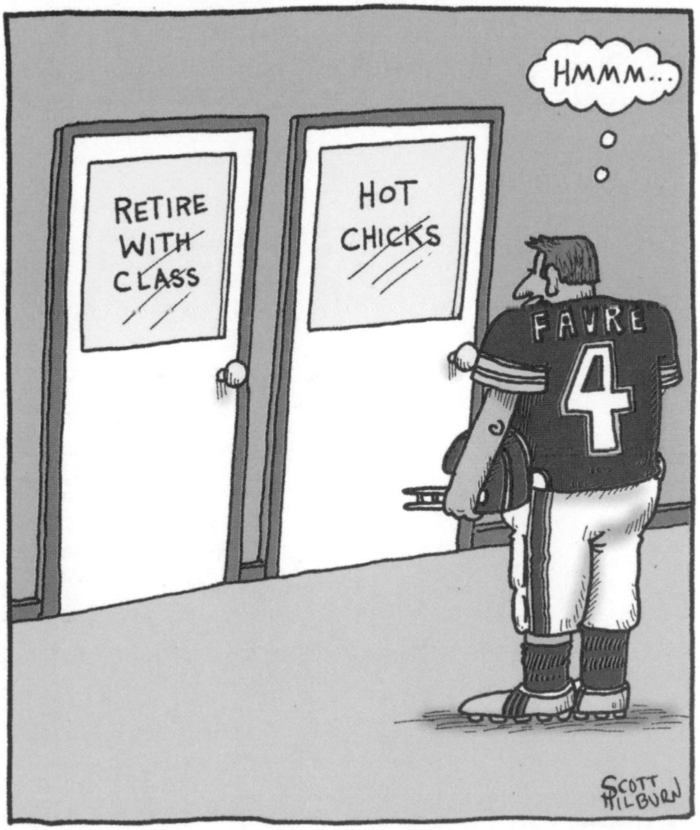
HMMM...
RETIRE WITH CLASS
HOT CHICKS
FAVRE
4
SCOTT HILBURN

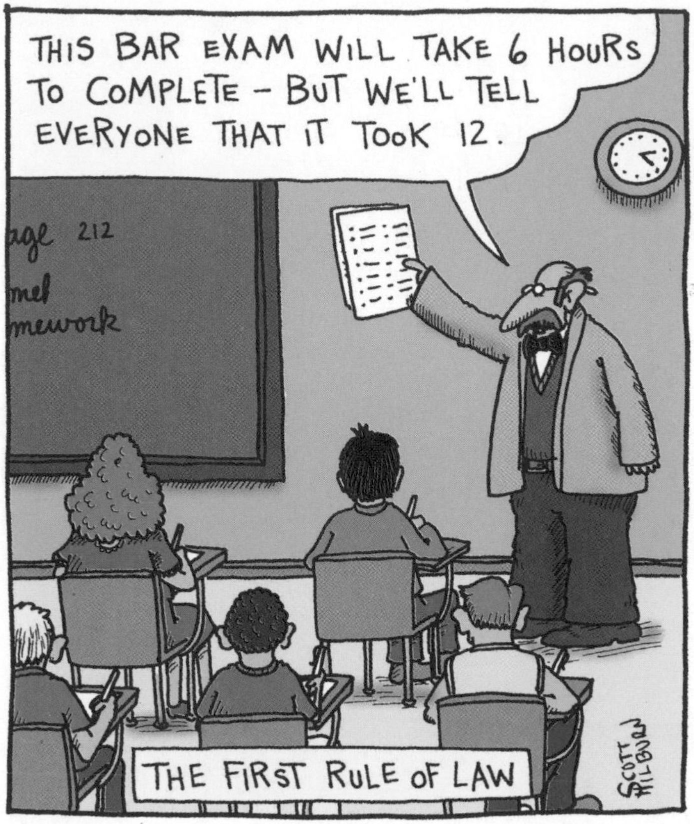
THIS BAR EXAM WILL TAKE 6 HOURS TO COMPLETE – BUT WE'LL TELL EVERYONE THAT IT TOOK 12.
SCOTT HILBURN

THE FIRST RULE OF LAW

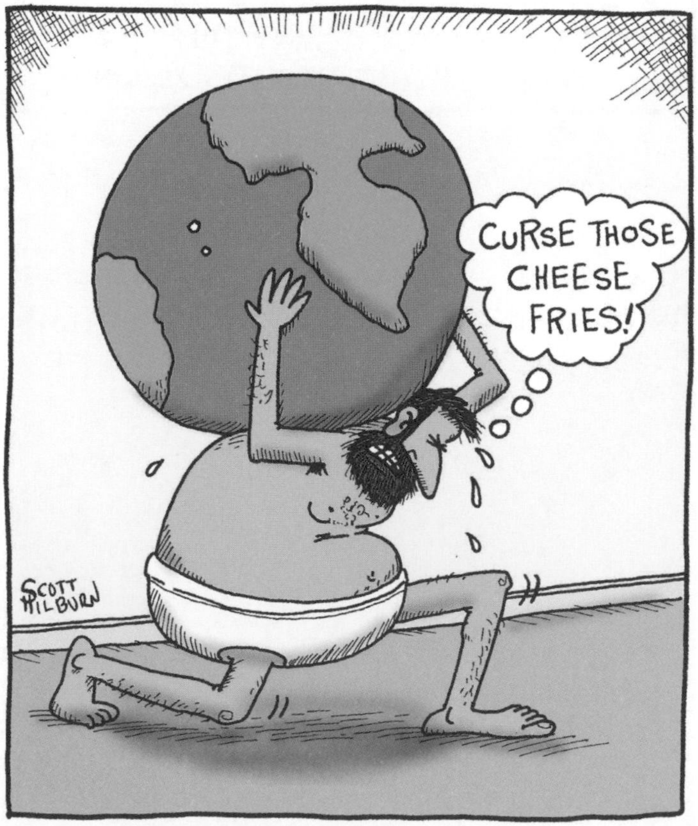
CURSE THOSE CHEESE FRIES!
SCOTT HILBURN

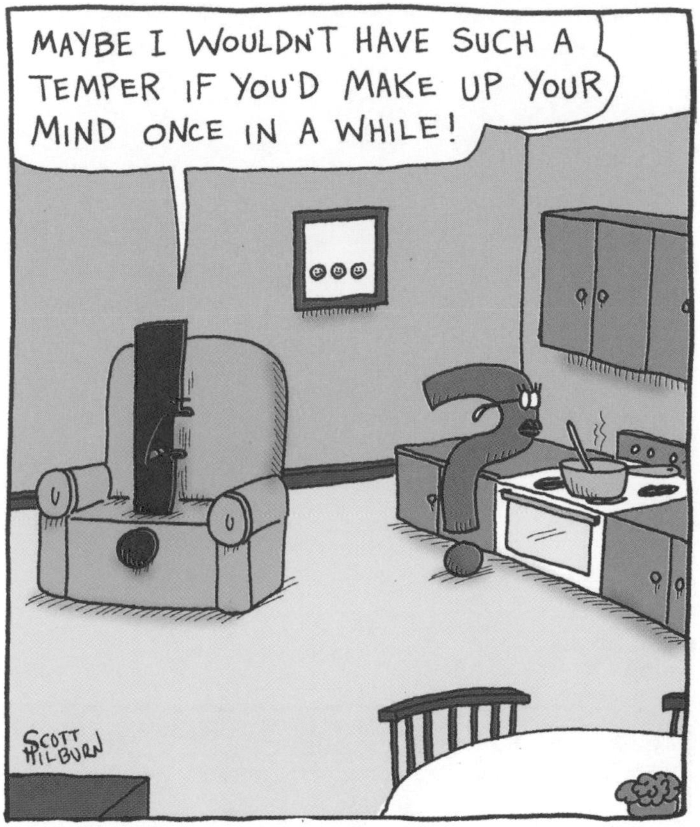
MAYBE I WOULDN'T HAVE SUCH A TEMPER IF YOU'D MAKE UP YOUR MIND ONCE IN A WHILE!
SCOTT HILBURN

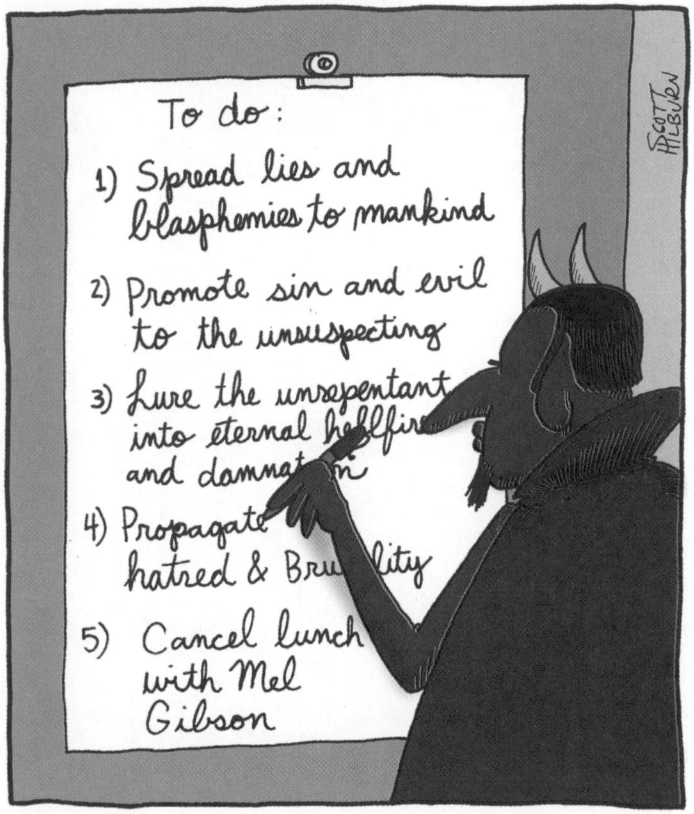
To do:
1) Spread lies and blasphemies to mankind
2) Promote sin and evil to the unsuspecting
3) Lure the unrepentant into eternal hellfire and damnation
4) Propagate hatred & Brutality
5) Cancel lunch with Mel Gibson
SCOTT HILBURN

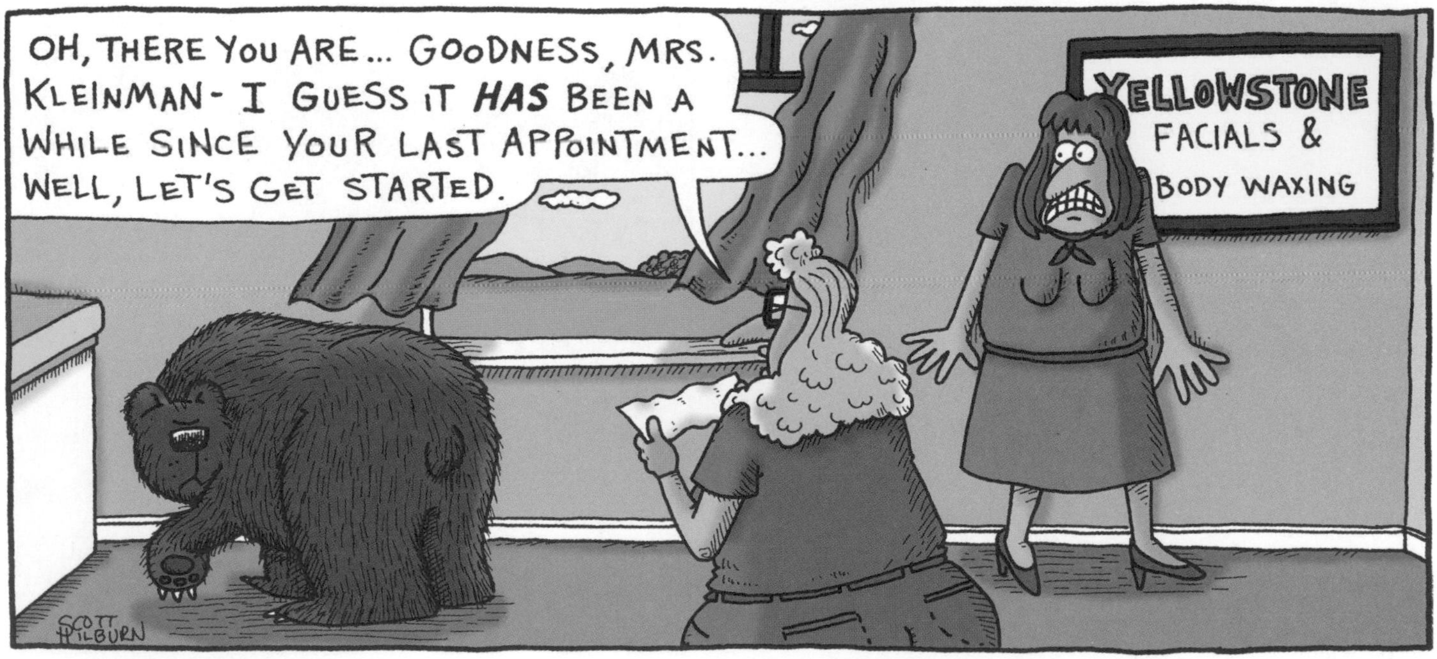
OH, THERE YOU ARE... GOODNESS, MRS. KLEINMAN- I GUESS IT HAS BEEN A WHILE SINCE YOUR LAST APPOINTMENT... WELL, LET'S GET STARTED.
YELLOWSTONE FACIALS & BODY WAXING
SCOTT HILBURN

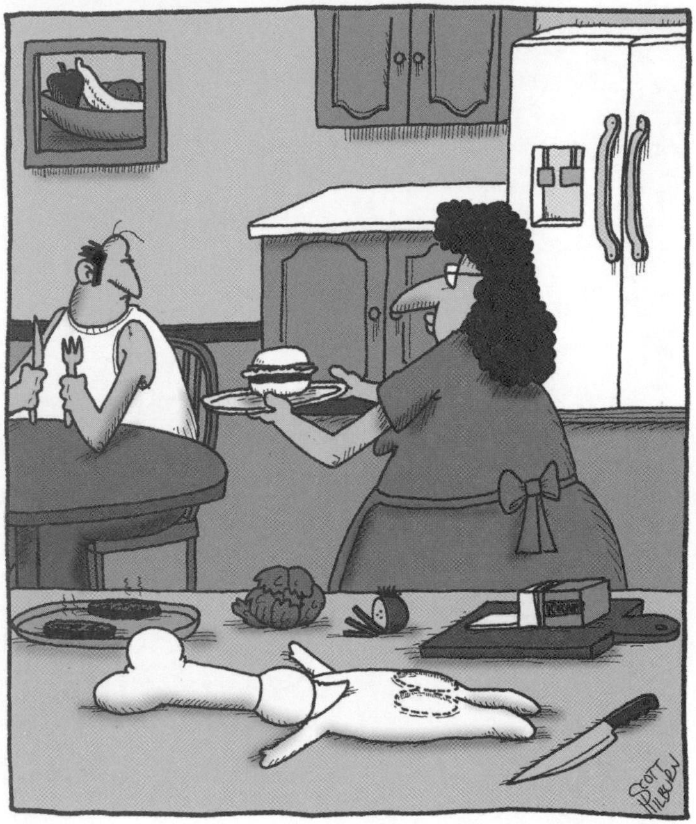

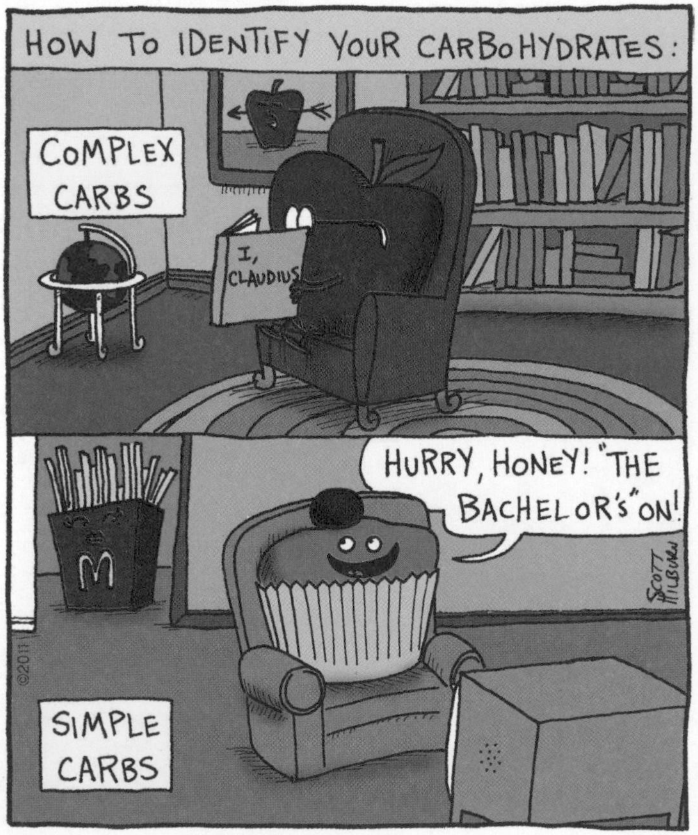
HOW TO IDENTIFY YOUR CARBOHYDRATES:
COMPLEX CARBS
I, CLAUDIUS
HURRY, HONEY! "THE BACHELOR'S" ON!
SIMPLE CARBS
©2011

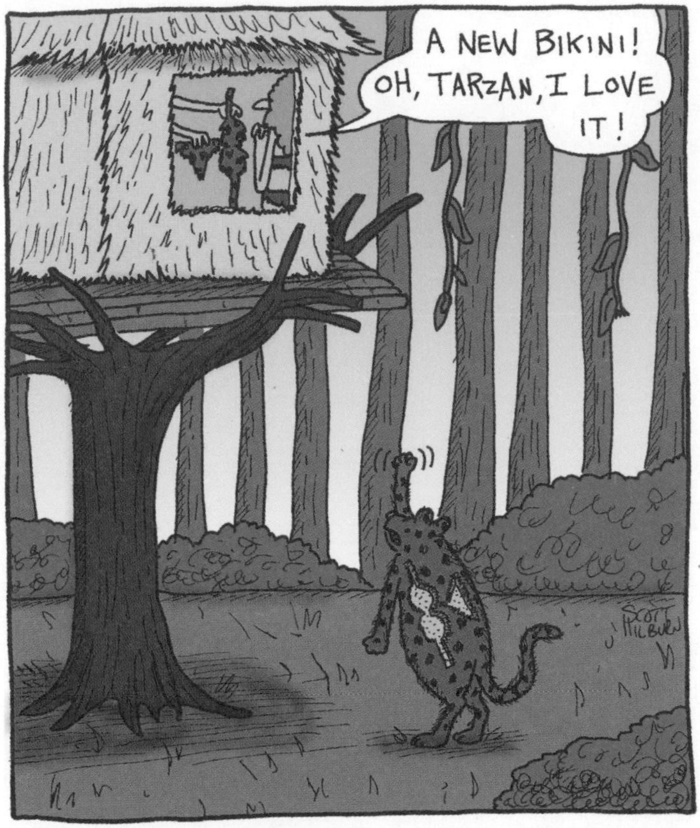
A NEW BIKINI! OH, TARZAN, I LOVE IT!
SCOTT HILBURN

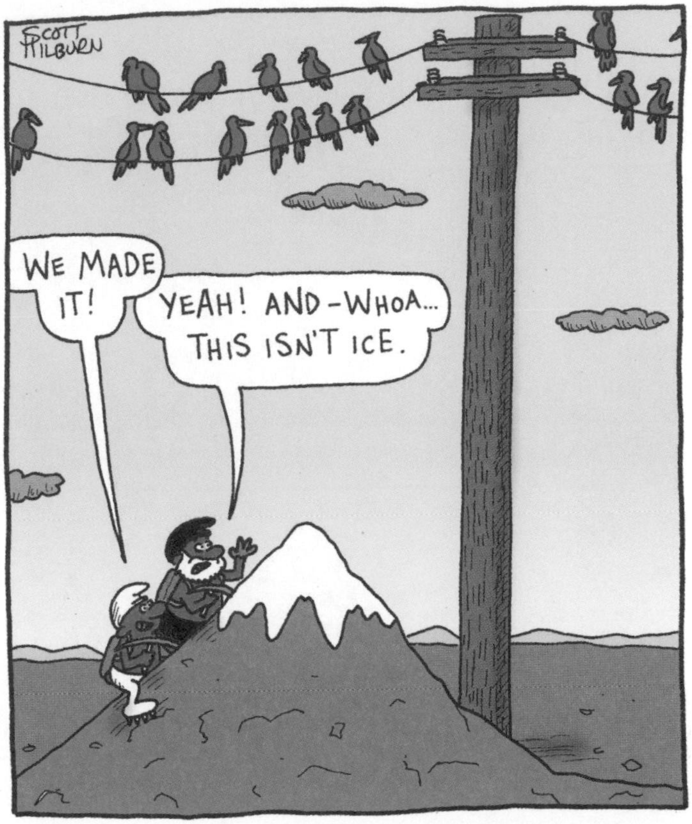
SCOTT HILBURN
WE MADE IT!
YEAH! AND-WHOA... THIS ISN'T ICE.

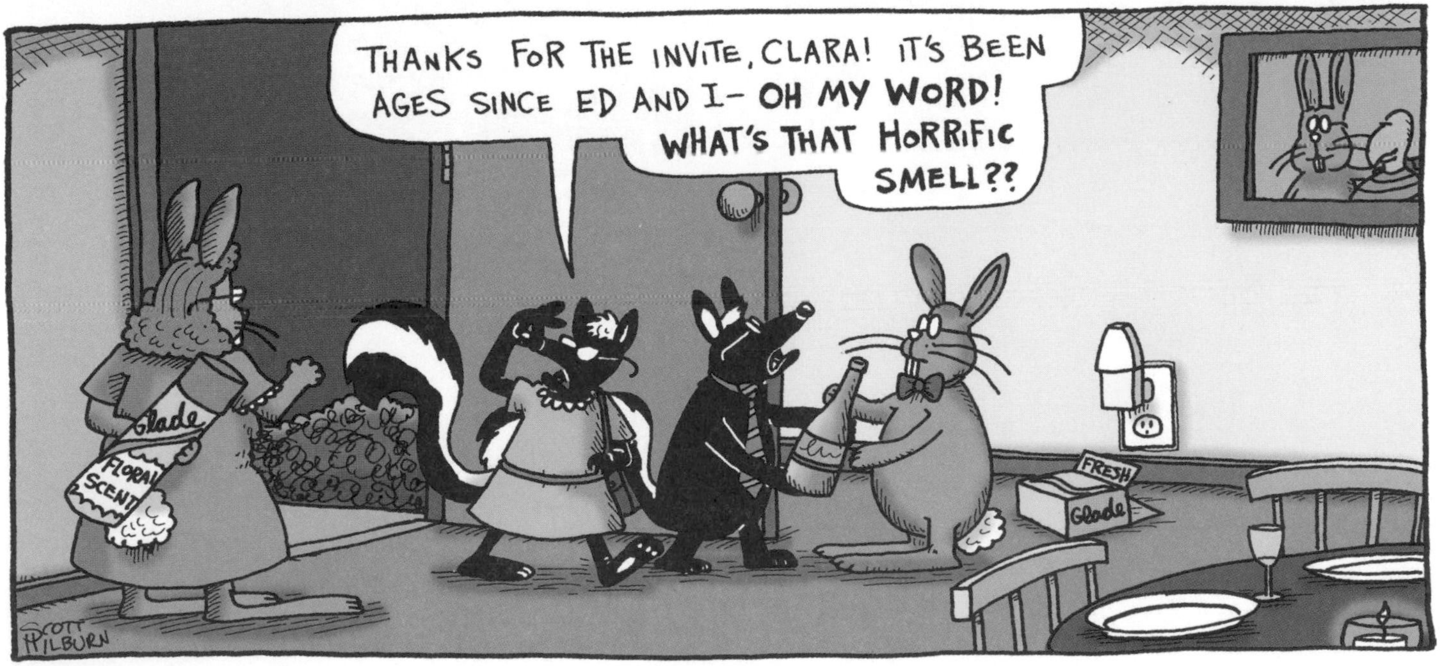
THANKS FOR THE INVITE, CLARA! IT'S BEEN AGES SINCE ED AND I- OH MY WORD! WHAT'S THAT HORRIFIC SMELL??
Glade
FLORAL SCENT
FRESH
Glade
SCOTT HILBURN

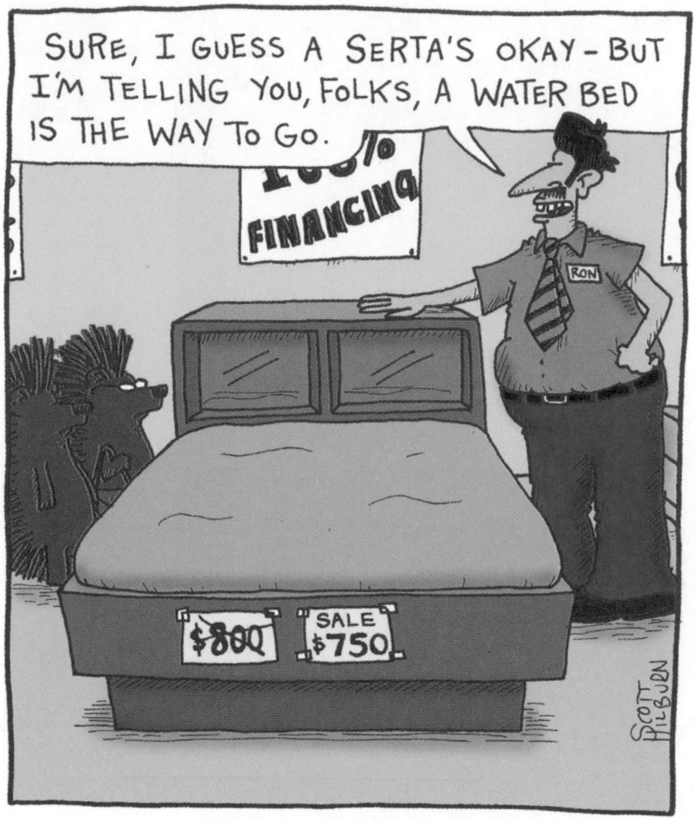
SURE, I GUESS A SERTA'S OKAY - BUT I'M TELLING YOU, FOLKS, A WATER BED IS THE WAY TO GO.
FINANCING
RON
$800
SALE $750
SCOTT HILBURN

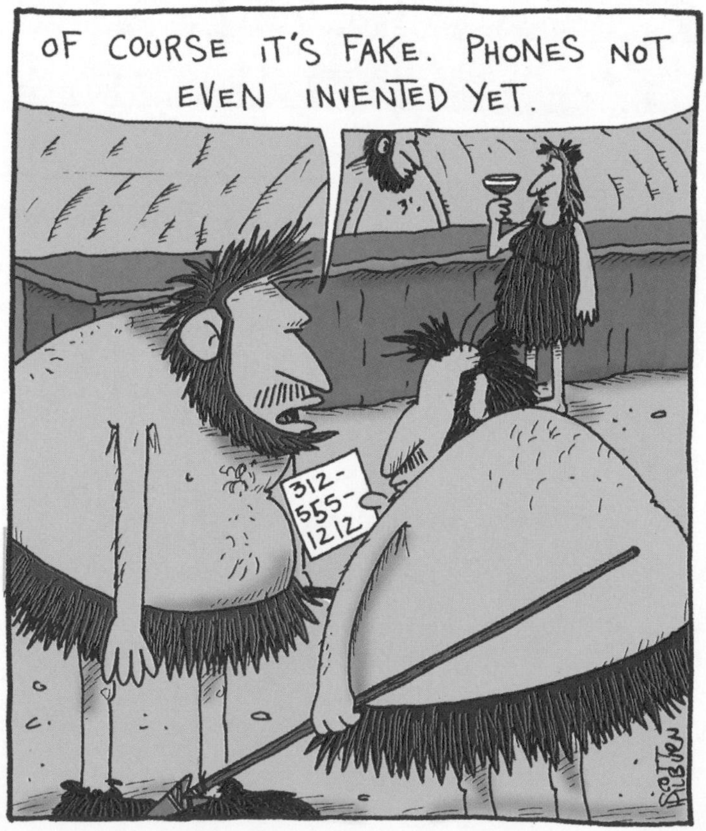
OF COURSE IT'S FAKE. PHONES NOT EVEN INVENTED YET.
312-555-1212
SCOTT HILBURN

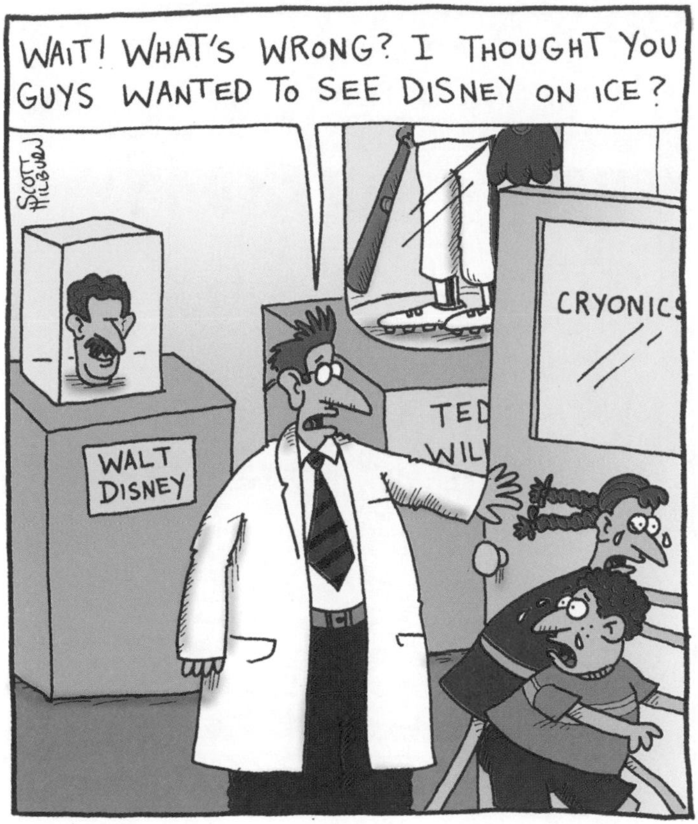
WAIT! WHAT'S WRONG? I THOUGHT YOU GUYS WANTED TO SEE DISNEY ON ICE?
SCOTT HILBURN
CRYONICS
WALT DISNEY
TED WIL

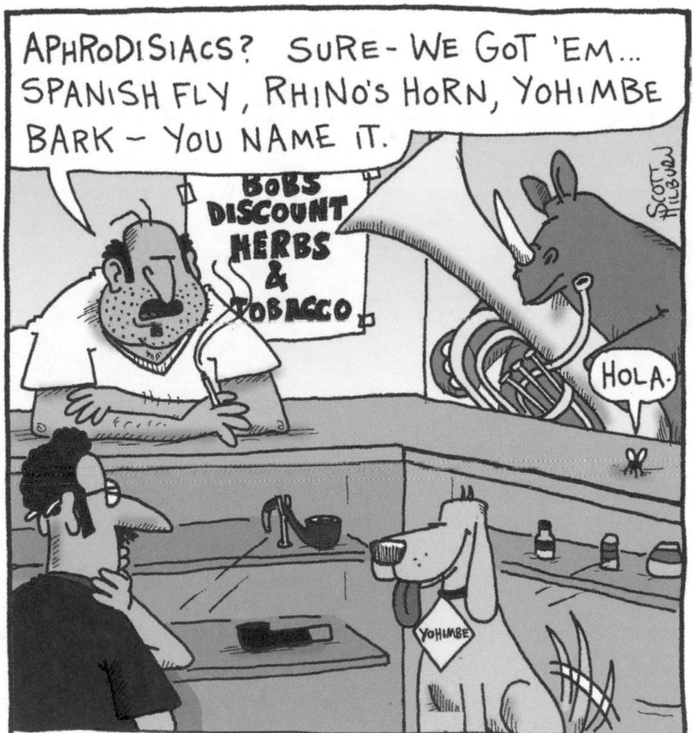
APHRODISIACS? SURE- WE GOT 'EM... SPANISH FLY, RHINO'S HORN, YOHIMBE BARK - YOU NAME IT.
BOBS DISCOUNT HERBS & TOBACCO
SCOTT HILBURN
HOLA.
YOHIMBE

ALAN BEGAN TO QUESTION THE POTENCY OF BOB'S PRODUCTS.

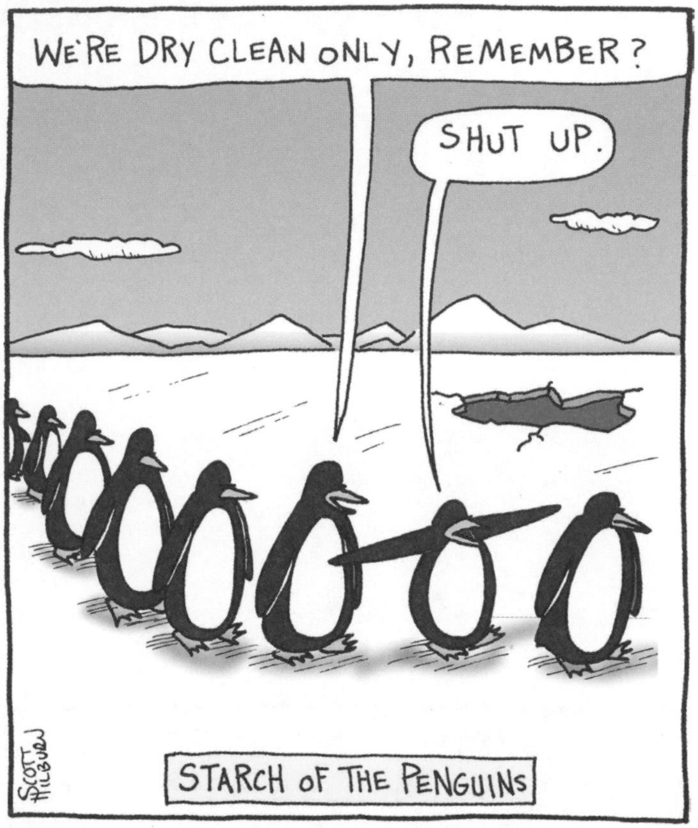
WE'RE DRY CLEAN ONLY, REMEMBER?
SHUT UP.
SCOTT HILBURN

STARCH OF THE PENGUINS

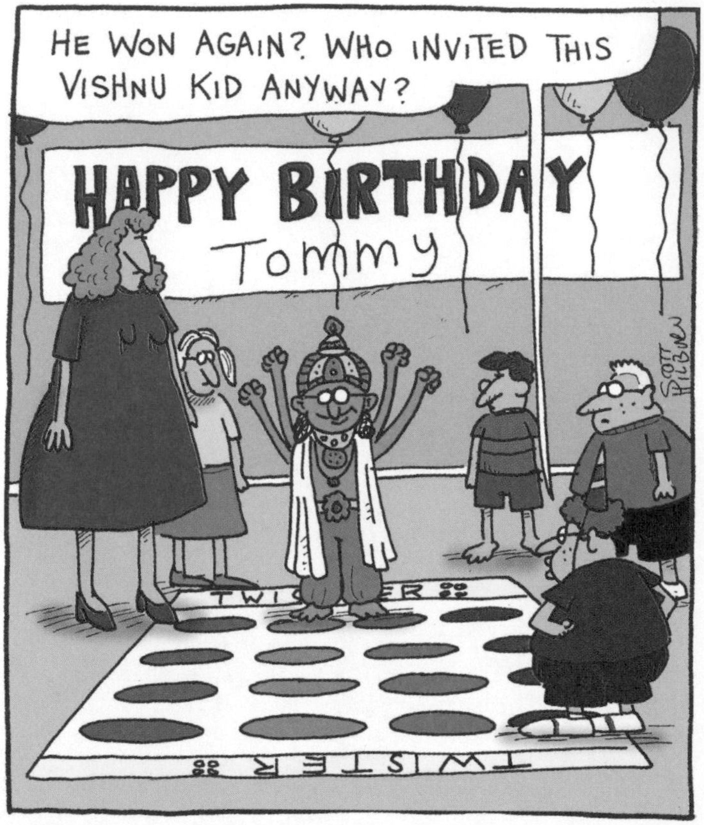
HE WON AGAIN? WHO INVITED THIS VISHNU KID ANYWAY?
HAPPY BIRTHDAY
Tommy
TWISTER
SCOTT HILBURN

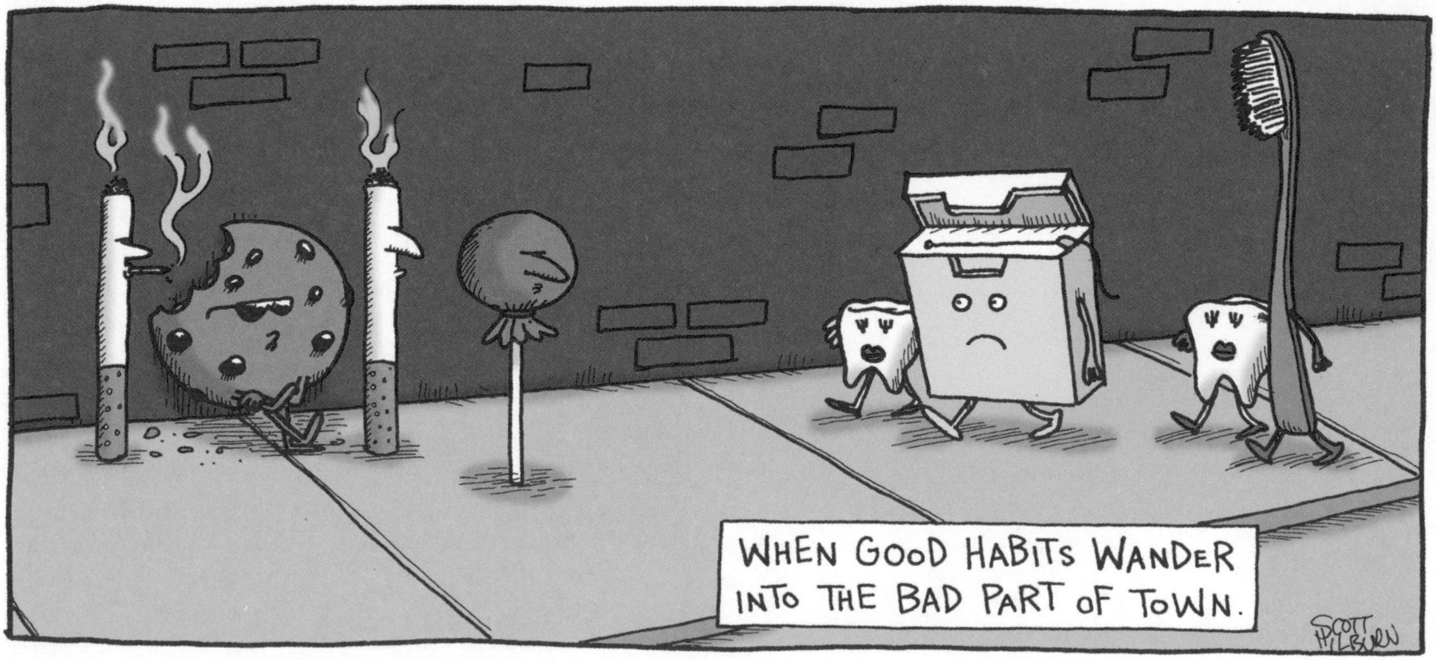
SCOTT HILBURN

WHEN GOOD HABITS WANDER INTO THE BAD PART OF TOWN.

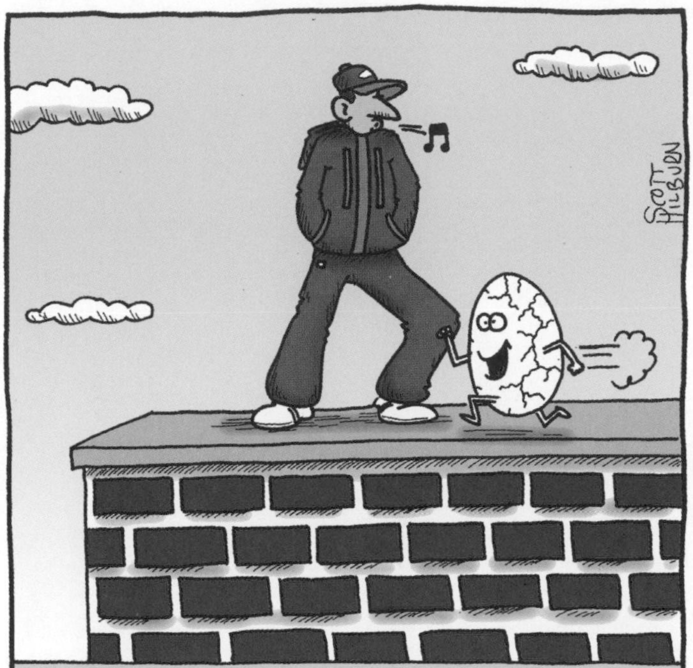
SCOTT HILBURN

JUST AS THE KING'S HORSES AND KING'S MEN FINISH PUTTING HIM BACK TOGETHER AGAIN, ALONG COMES THE JETS' STRENGTH & CONDITIONING COACH.

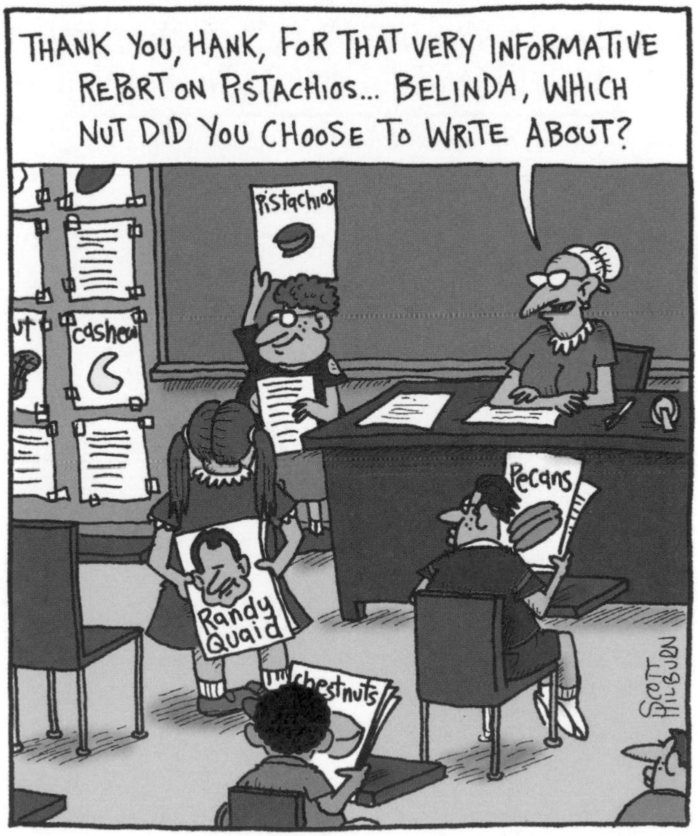
THANK YOU, HANK, FOR THAT VERY INFORMATIVE REPORT ON PISTACHIOS... BELINDA, WHICH NUT DID YOU CHOOSE TO WRITE ABOUT?
Pistachios
cashew
Pecans
Randy Quaid
chestnuts
SCOTT HILBURN

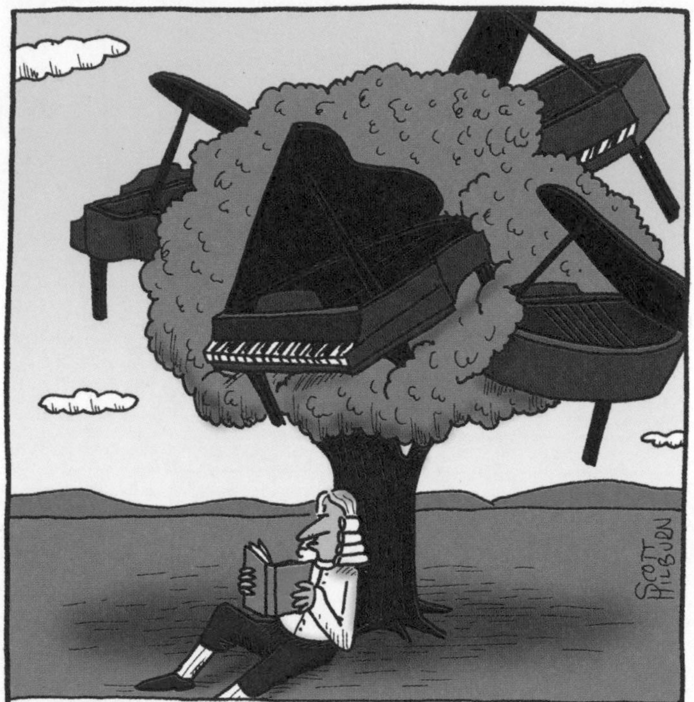
SCOTT HILBURN

IN FACT, IT WAS THE LATE SKIP NEWTON, NOT HIS BROTHER ISAAC, WHO FIRST DISCOVERED GRAVITY.

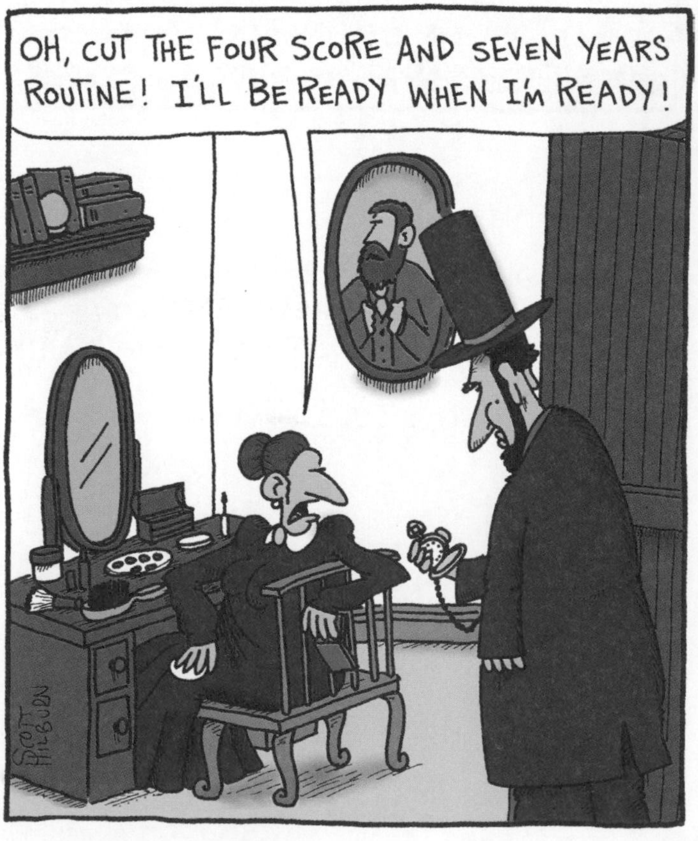
OH, CUT THE FOUR SCORE AND SEVEN YEARS ROUTINE! I'LL BE READY WHEN I'M READY!
SCOTT HILBURN

HEY, LOOK, SAL- I THINK IT'S WORKIN'!
41132
SCOTT HILBURN

WHAT? THE WORD WAS 'PORK CHOP'? WHAT THA-??
PORK CHOP
SCOTT HILBURN
ALTHOUGH AN ACCOMPLISHED ARTIST, JACKSON POLLOCK WAS NEVER INVITED BACK TO THE MAXWELL'S FOR PICTIONARY NIGHT.

MAYBE WE SHOULD SHOOT NOW.
NOT YET. HE SAID 'WHITES OF THEIR EYES.' I DON'T SEE 'EM YET.
REDCOATS SPONSORED BY Ray-Ban
SCOTT HILBURN
HOW THE BATTLE OF BUNKER HILL WAS LOST

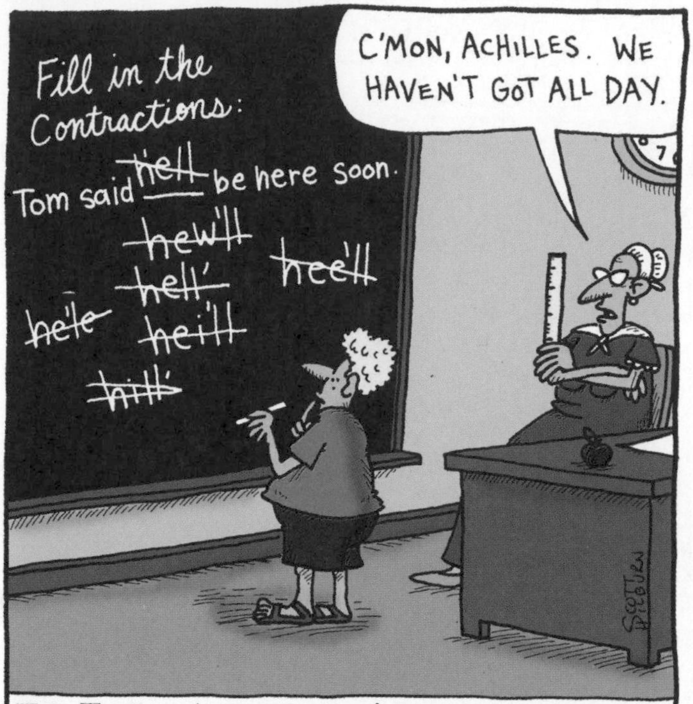
C'MON, ACHILLES. WE HAVEN'T GOT ALL DAY.
Fill in the Contractions:
Tom said he'll be here soon.
hew'll
hee'll
hell'
he'le
hei'll
hill'

THE STORY OF "ACHILLES' HE'LL" ACTUALLY BLOSSOMED FROM AN OTHERWISE ORDINARY ANECDOTE.

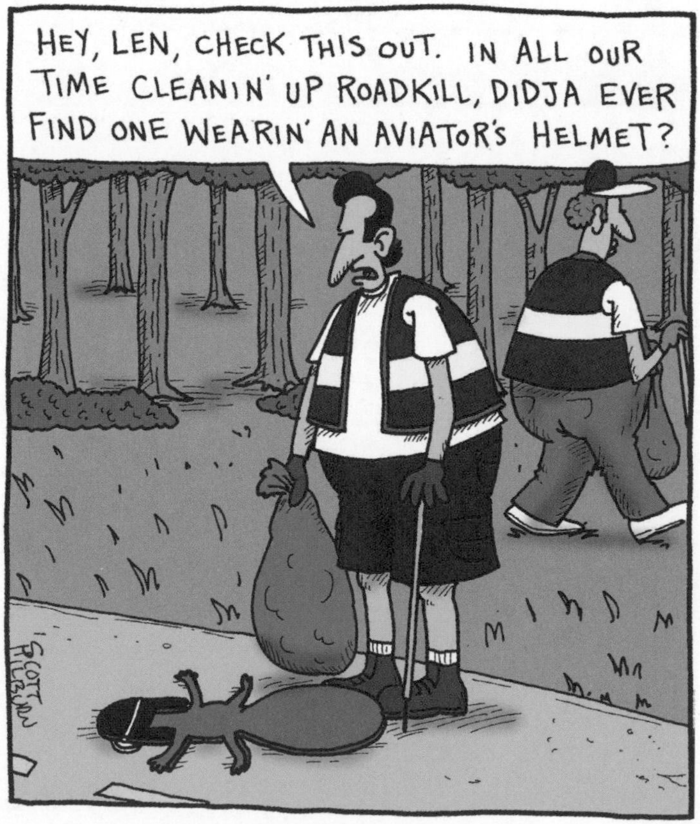
HEY, LEN, CHECK THIS OUT. IN ALL OUR TIME CLEANIN' UP ROADKILL, DIDJA EVER FIND ONE WEARIN' AN AVIATOR'S HELMET?

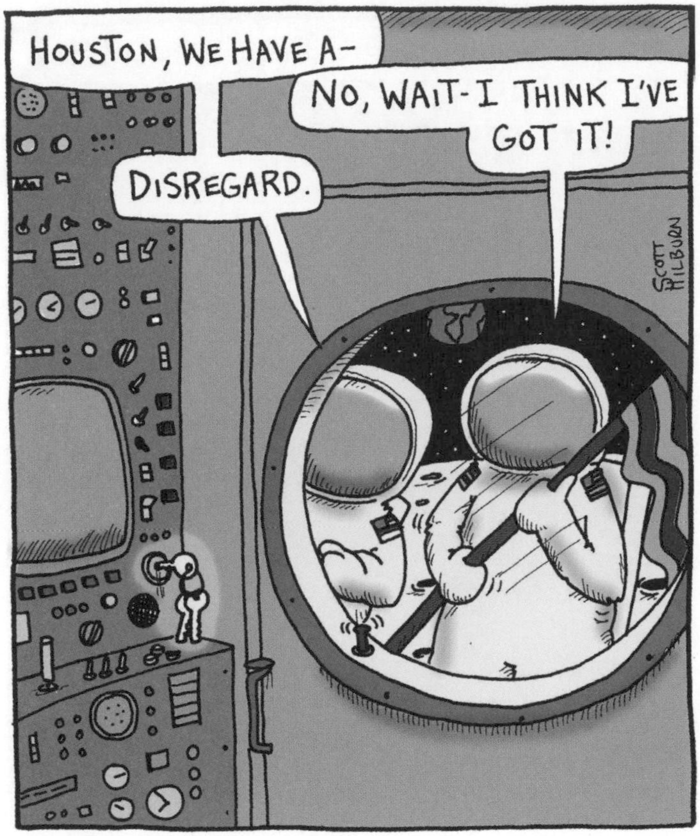
HOUSTON, WE HAVE A-
DISREGARD.
NO, WAIT- I THINK I'VE GOT IT!
SCOTT HILBURN

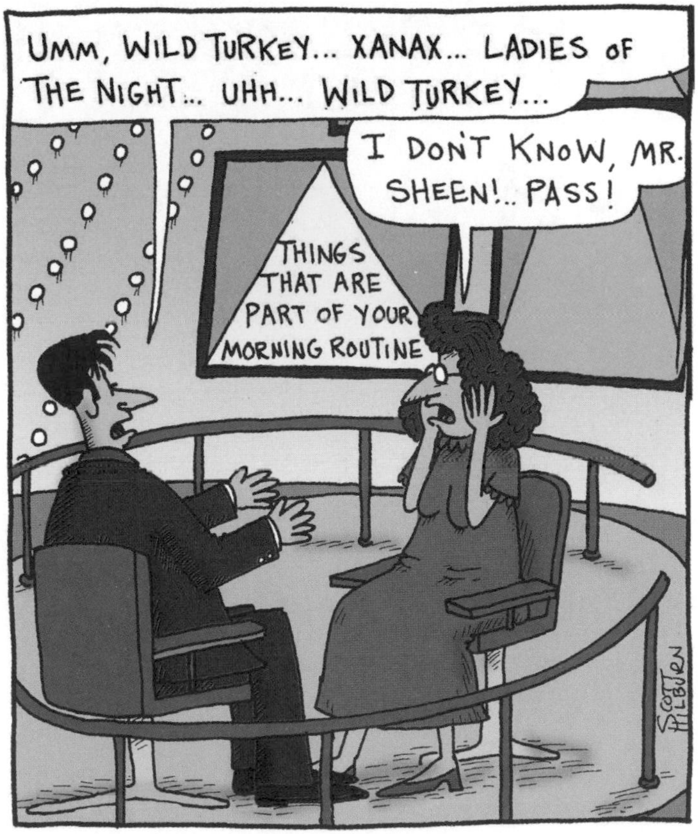
UMM, WILD TURKEY... XANAX... LADIES OF THE NIGHT... UHH... WILD TURKEY...
I DON'T KNOW, MR. SHEEN!.. PASS!
THINGS THAT ARE PART OF YOUR MORNING ROUTINE
SCOTT HILBURN

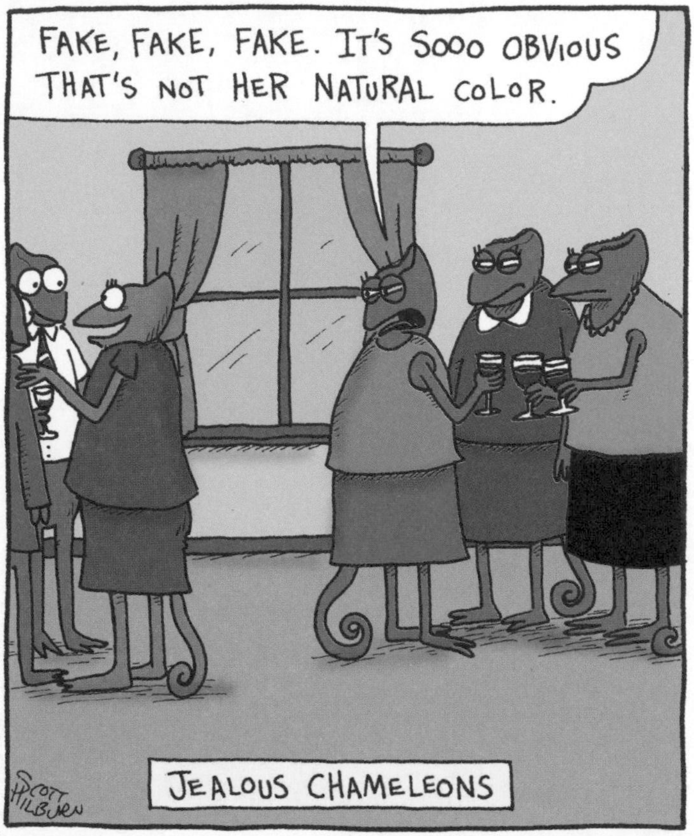
FAKE, FAKE, FAKE. IT'S SOOO OBVIOUS THAT'S NOT HER NATURAL COLOR.
SCOTT HILBURN

JEALOUS CHAMELEONS

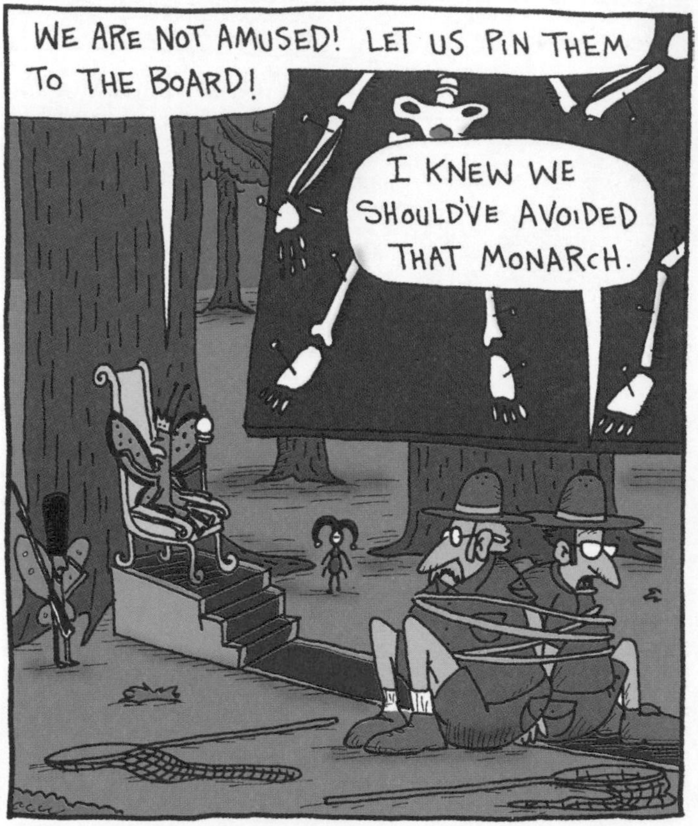
WE ARE NOT AMUSED! LET US PIN THEM TO THE BOARD!
I KNEW WE SHOULD'VE AVOIDED THAT MONARCH.

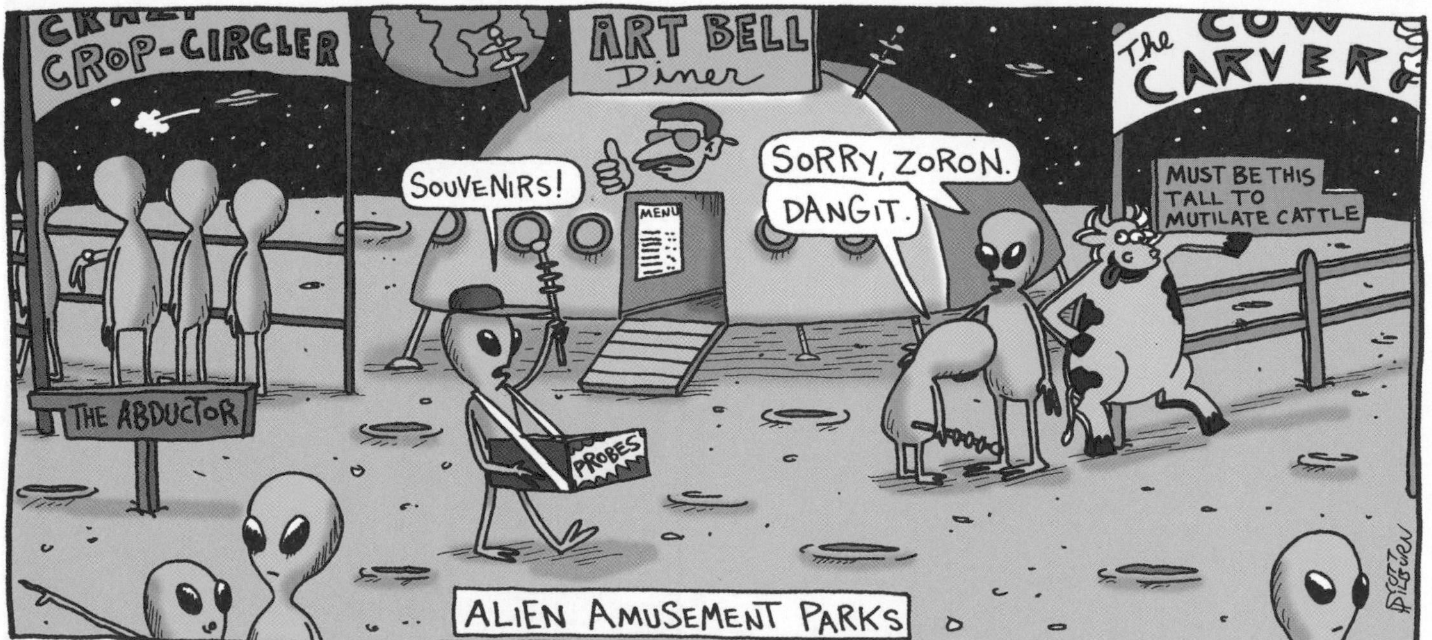
CROP-CIRCLER
ART BELL Diner
The
MENU
SOUVENIRS!
SORRY, ZORON. DANGIT.
MUST BE THIS TALL TO MUTILATE CATTLE
THE ABDUCTOR
PROBES
SCOTT HILBURN

ALIEN AMUSEMENT PARKS

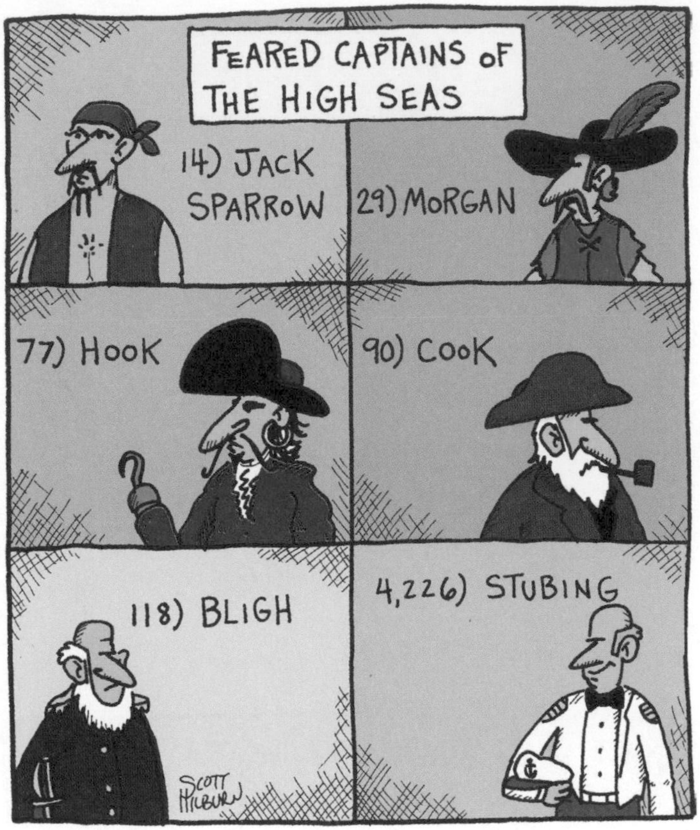
FEARED CAPTAINS OF THE HIGH SEAS
14) JACK SPARROW
29) MORGAN
77) HOOK
90) COOK
118) BLIGH
4,226) STUBING
SCOTT HILBURN

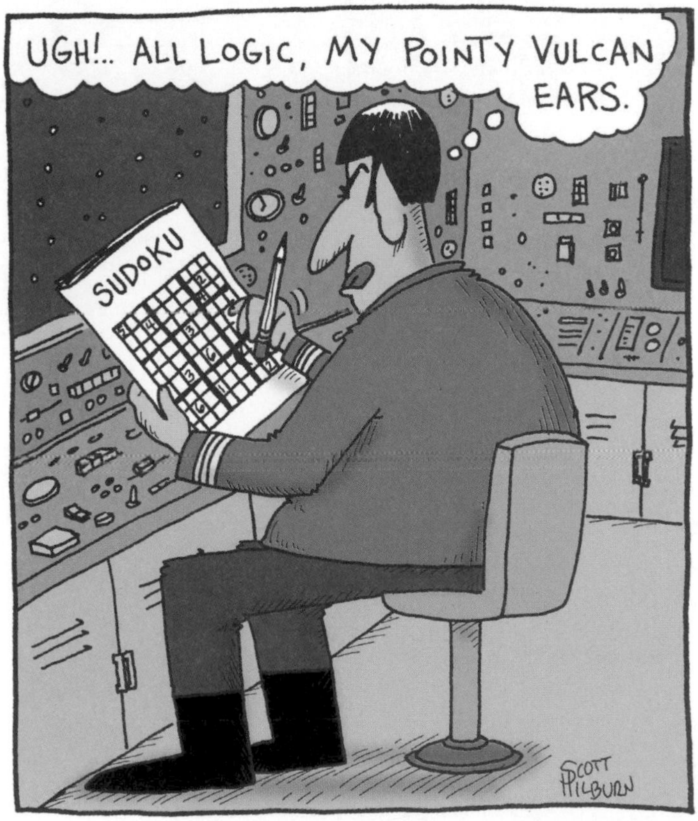
UGH!.. ALL LOGIC, MY POINTY VULCAN EARS.
SUDOKU
SCOTT HILBURN

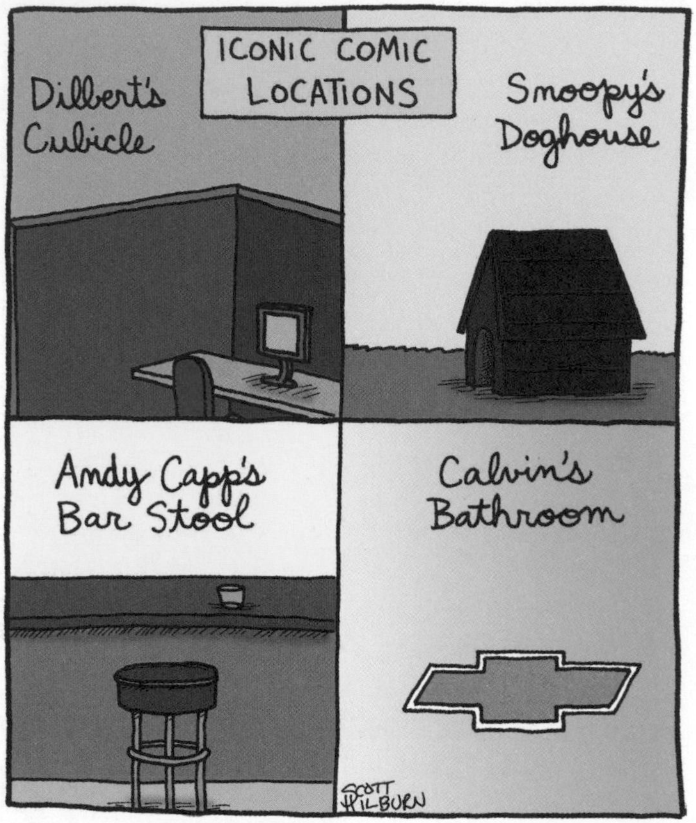
ICONIC COMIC LOCATIONS
Dilbert's Cubicle
Snoopy's Doghouse
Andy Capp's Bar Stool
Calvin's Bathroom
SCOTT HILBURN

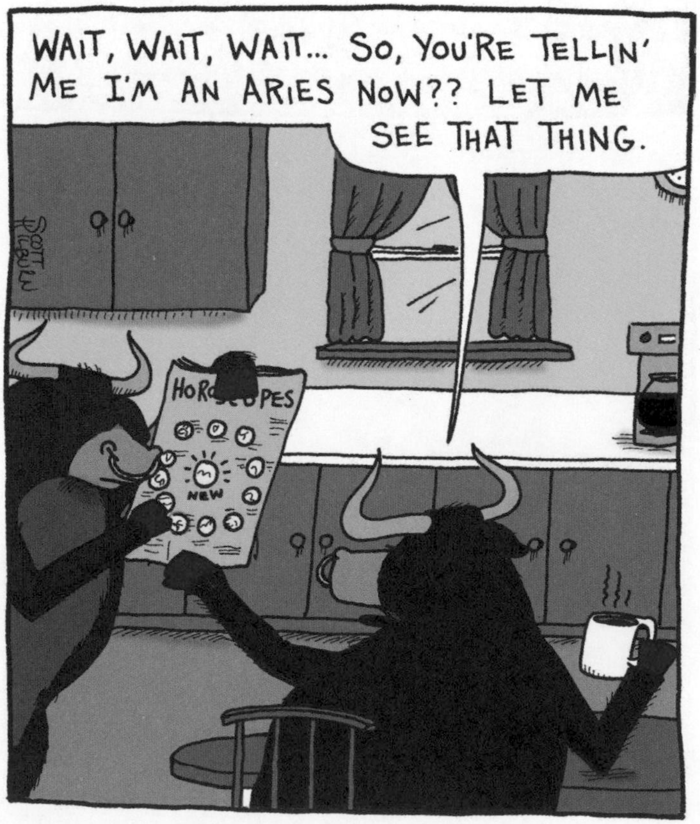
WAIT, WAIT, WAIT... SO, YOU'RE TELLIN' ME I'M AN ARIES NOW?? LET ME SEE THAT THING.
SCOTT HILBURN
NEW

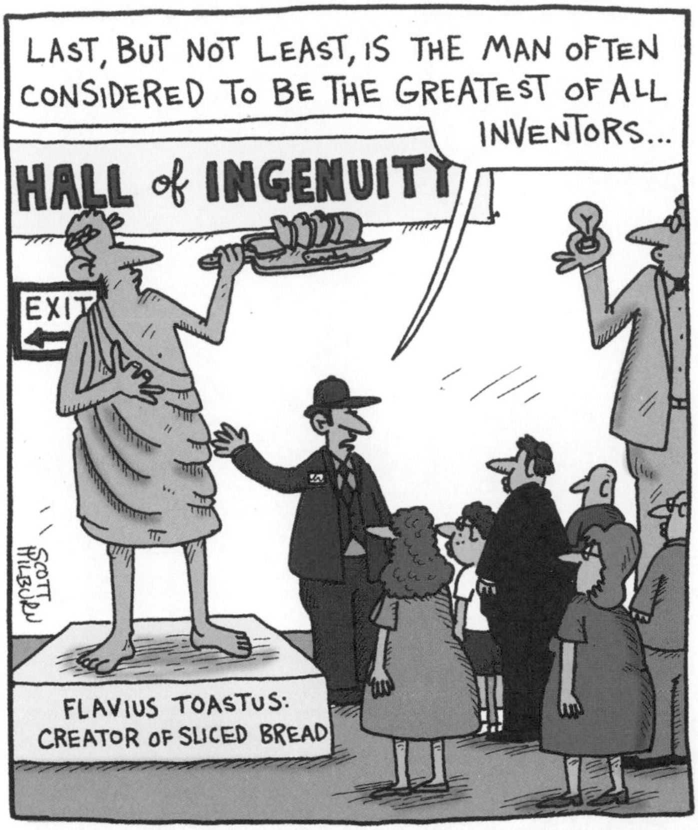
LAST, BUT NOT LEAST, IS THE MAN OFTEN CONSIDERED TO BE THE GREATEST OF ALL INVENTORS...
HALL of INGENUITY
EXIT
FLAVIUS TOASTUS:
CREATOR OF SLICED BREAD
SCOTT HILBURN

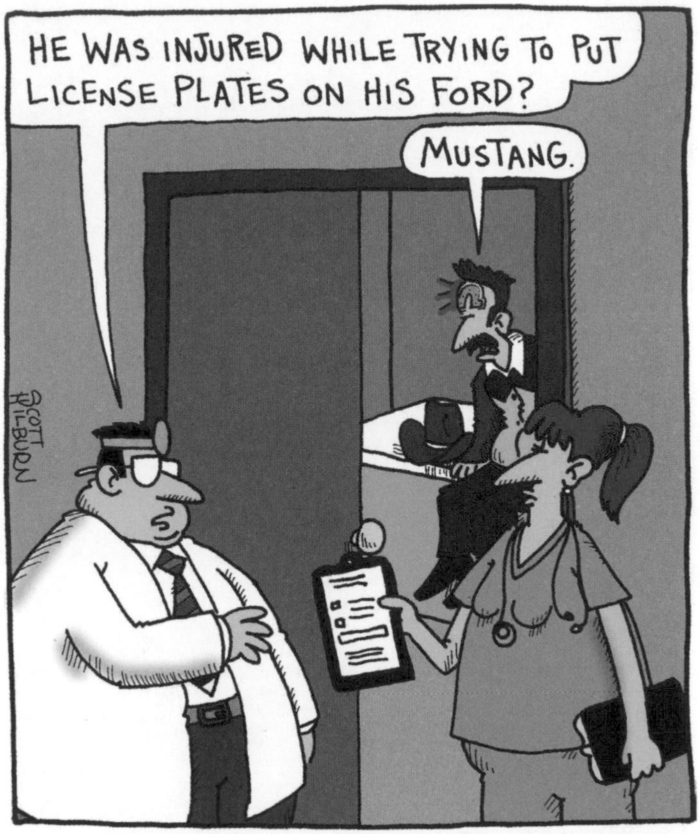
HE WAS INJURED WHILE TRYING TO PUT LICENSE PLATES ON HIS FORD?
MUSTANG.
SCOTT HILBURN

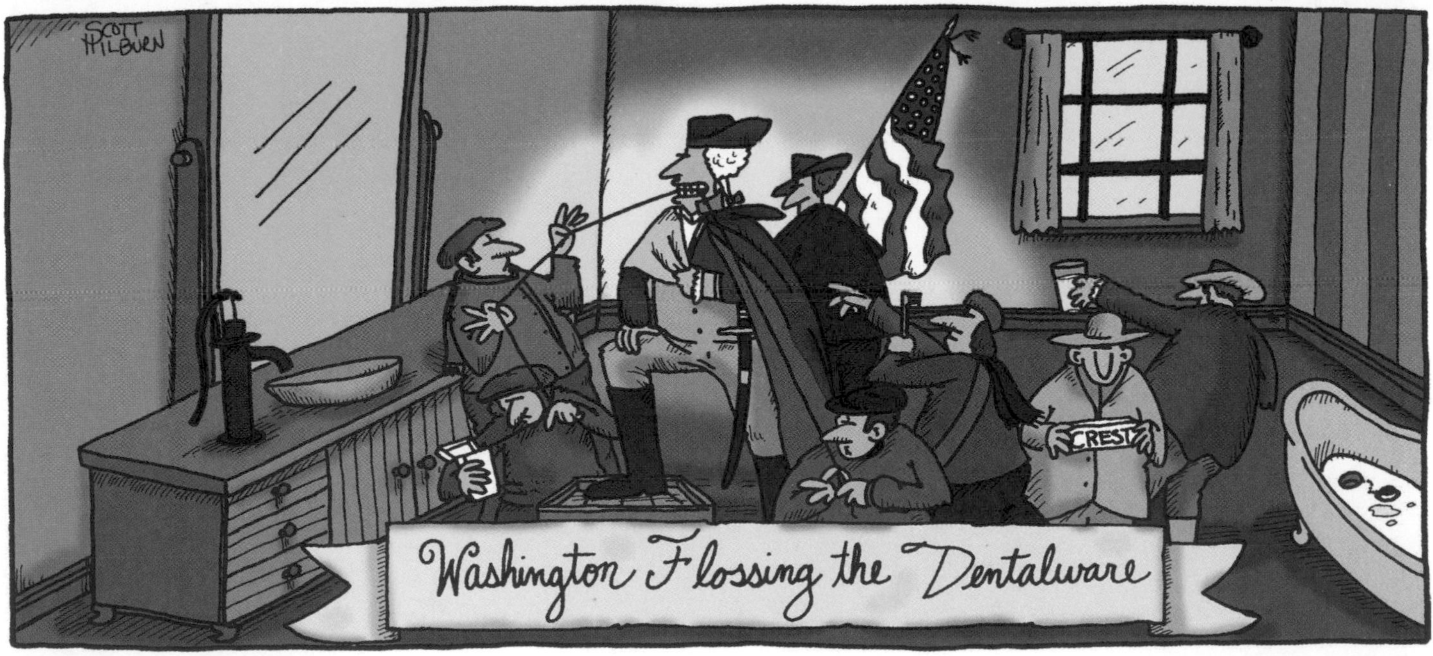
SCOTT HILBURN
CREST
Washington Flossing the Dentalware

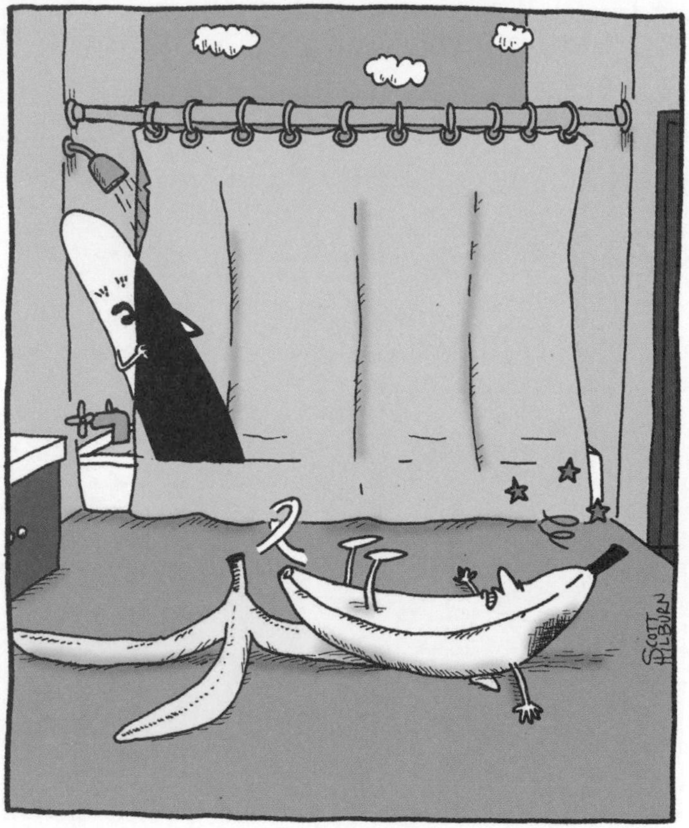
SCOTT HILBURN

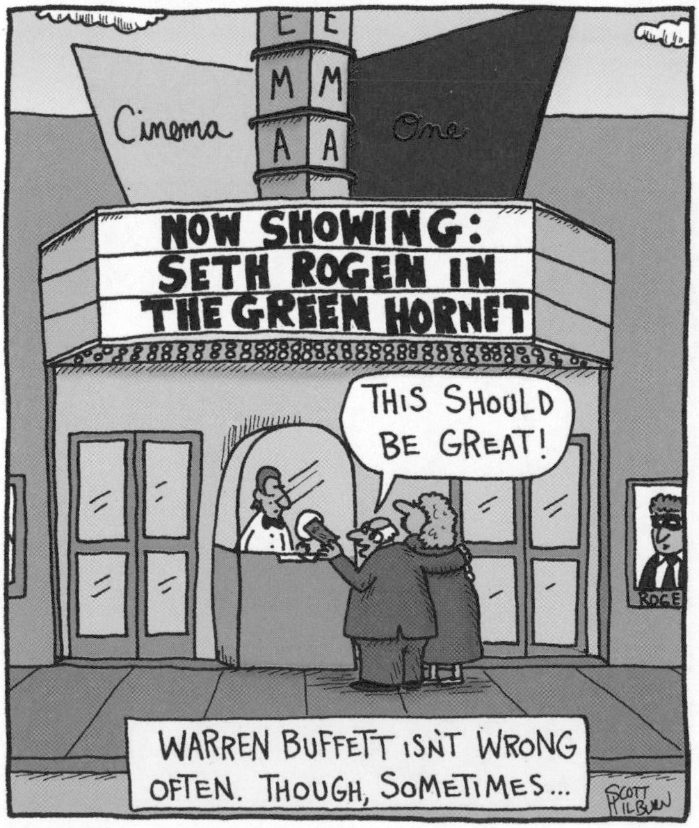
Cinema
One
NOW SHOWING:
SETH ROGEN IN
THE GREEN HORNET
THIS SHOULD BE GREAT!
WARREN BUFFETT ISN'T WRONG OFTEN. THOUGH, SOMETIMES...
SCOTT HILBURN

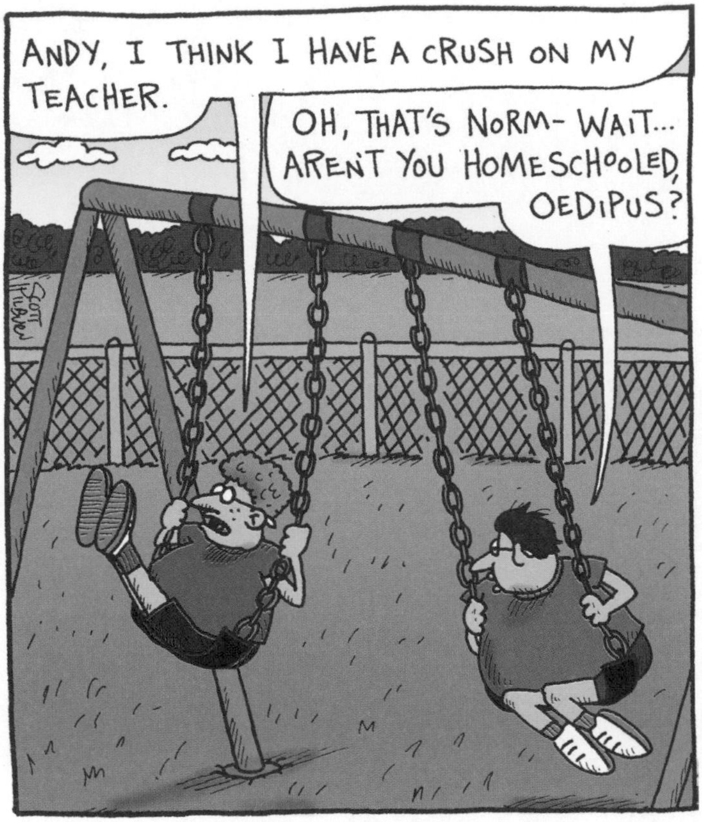
ANDY, I THINK I HAVE A CRUSH ON MY TEACHER.
OH, THAT'S NORM- WAIT... ARENT YOU HOMESCHOOLED, OEDIPUS?
SCOTT HILBURN

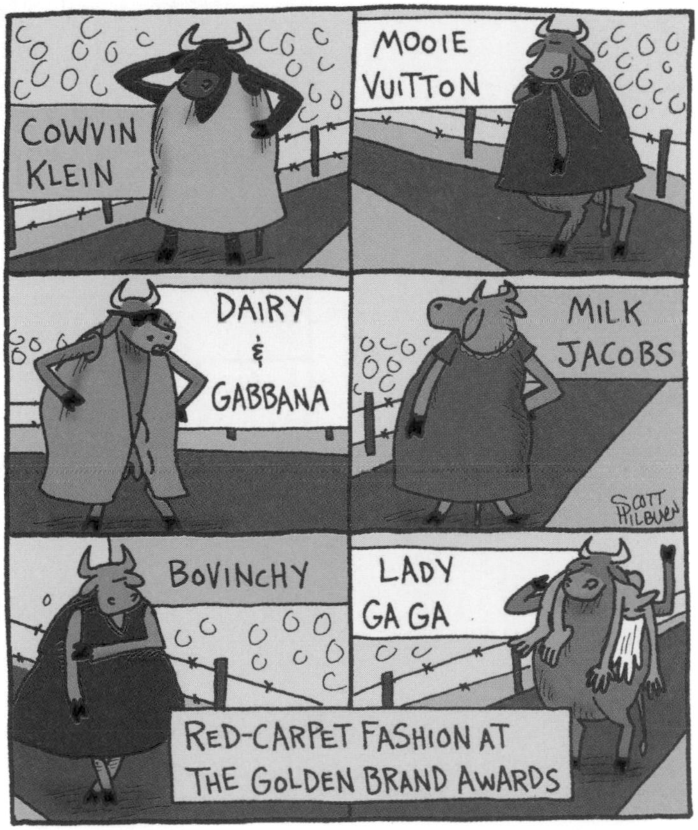
COWVIN KLEIN
MOOIE VUITTON
DAIRY & GABBANA
MILK JACOBS
SCOTT HILBURN
BOVINCHY
LADY GA GA
RED-CARPET FASHION AT THE GOLDEN BRAND AWARDS

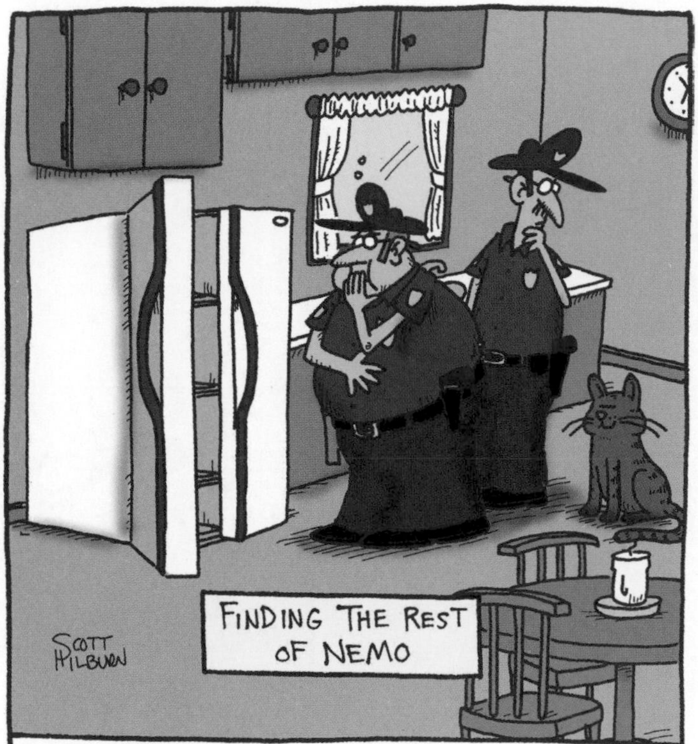
FINDING THE REST OF NEMO
SCOTT HILBURN

CONGRATULATIONS TO JOHN C. OF SELMA, CA
WINNER OF THE ARGYLE SWEATER CAPTION CONTEST